THE RESTORATION OF THE SELF

THE RESTORATION
OF THE SELF

Heinz Kohut

INTERNATIONAL UNIVERSITIES PRESS, INC.
Madison   Connecticut

Seventh Printing, 1988

Library of Congress Cataloging in Publication Data

Kohut, Heinz.
  The restoration of the self.

  Bibliography: p.
  Includes index.
  1. Self. 2. Psychoanalysis. I. Title.
[DNLM: 1. Self concept. BF697 K79r]
BF697.K65   616.8'5   76-45545
ISBN 0-8236-5810-4

To G., and to his generation

CONTENTS

Acknowledgments

The number of colleagues and friends who have generously given me their reactions to the present work in various phases of its growth is so great that I must ask most of them to accept my appreciation without listing their names. But I will mention a few whose help has been especially valuable to me—either because of the emotional support they provided during the unavoidable moments of doubt that every author experiences concerning the worthwhileness of his efforts, or because of the extensive advice they gave with regard to the content and form of my book. And so, even though I mention with particular warmth and appreciation the names of Drs. Michael F. Basch, Arnold Goldberg, Jerome Kavka, George H. Klumpner, J. Gordon Maguire, David Marcus, Paul H. Ornstein, George H. Pollock, Paul H. Tolpin, and Mr. Joseph Palombo, there are a number of others I could have included with almost equal justification. To Dr. Ernest S. Wolf I want to express my special gratitude for undertaking, in a generous act of friendship, the arduous task of preparing the index of this book.

My thanks are also due to a number of colleagues who allowed me to use material from cases they analyzed in consultation with me. An extensive use of cases of my own was unfortunately inadvisable since it would have been very difficult to protect their anonymity. The availability of colleagues' cases was therefore of the greatest value to me. Some of the colleagues whose cases are included asked that their names not be mentioned, as a special safeguard lest, despite careful disguise, their patients' identity might possibly become recognizable. There are three instances, however, where the material could be disguised so securely that I can express my thanks to the analysts. Dr. Anita Eckstaedt allowed me the use of some valuable material, perceptively selected by her, from an expertly conducted analysis; Dr. Anna Ornstein gave me access to clinical data that provided some of my theories with convincing support; and Dr. Marian Tolpin let me use some evocative material from an excellent case study she had prepared for a different purpose.

An author's thanks to his secretary are often routinely enclosed in prefatorial remarks. The warm recognition I want to express to Mrs. Jacqueline Miller is not, however, routine but felt sincerely. Without her unruffled responsiveness to the burdens I put upon her, her devotion to the task, and the intelligence with which she carried it out, this work would have been completed much later.

Financial help supporting all phases of the investigations whose results I am presenting here came to me from the Anne Pollock Lederer Research Fund of the Chicago Institute for Psychoanalysis and from the general Research Fund of the Institute. I acknowledge this support with gratitude.

I add my deeply felt appreciation for the assistance I received from Mrs. Natalie Altman of International Universities Press. For the better part of a year the pages of my manuscript traveled from Chicago to New York and back again to Chicago. They returned studded with perceptive questions and valuable suggestions that urged me to express myself with greater clarity, to provide my assertions with sufficient evidence, and to relinquish excess material. I thank her warmly for her interest, which was truly beyond the call of duty, and I hope that she enjoyed our encounter as much as I did. I know that my book has benefited immeasurably from our cooperation.

Preface

The present volume transcends my previous writings on narcissism in several directions. In the earlier contributions I presented my findings concerning the psychology of the self mainly in the language of classical drive theory. The crucial theoretical concept introduced within this framework was that of the *self-object;* correlated to the concept of the self-object, the most important empirical finding in the therapeutic field was the phenomenon to which I now refer as *transference to self-objects.* Finally, bridging theory and clinical observation, reconstruction of development and theory of therapy, the previous work introduced the concept of *transmuting internalization* and the correlated theory of structure formation in the area of the self.

In comparison with my earlier contributions, the present work expresses more explicitly my reliance on the empathic-introspective stance, which has been defining my conceptual-theoretical outlook ever since 1959. This step — the full acceptance of the consequences of the fact that the psychological field is defined by the observer's commitment to the introspective-empathic approach —

led to a number of conceptual refinements, indicated by terminological changes, as exemplified by my use of the term "self-object transference" instead of the formerly used termed "narcissistic transference." I do not regard these changes in terminology as lying in the forefront of the contributions offered by the present work; still, they are the expression of a move toward a clearly defined psychology of the self—or rather, as I shall state more explicitly shortly, of a move toward two self psychologies that complement each other.

Another feature of the present work is, as it was of all my previous contributions, the intertwining of empathic data-gathering and theorizing. The work begins, therefore, with the presentation of a set of empirical clinical data and a correlated experience-near theoretical proposition. The data concern a particular moment in the course of a specific clinical analysis—the moment when a valid termination phase may be said to have begun; the proposition concerns the advisability of distinguishing between defensive and compensatory structures—a conceptual refinement that allows us to take a fresh look at the definition of what constitutes a psychological cure and, correlated to this definition, to reassess the function and significance of the termination phase in psychoanalysis.

Having come to the end of the chapter that deals extensively with a single crucial moment in the course of an analysis, the reader might well assume that he holds in his hands a technical monograph and a dissertation on clinical theory, outlining the factors that determine an analysand's readiness to end the analysis, and presenting arguments in support of a new psychoanalytic definition of mental health and of the process of achieving a psycho-

analytic cure—particularly as concerns the disorders of
the self. To a certain extent these are indeed the aims of
this presentation, aims that are discussed on a variety of
levels and within a number of frameworks throughout the
book. But in order to define what it is that leads to the
cure of self pathology, a wide range of established theoretical concepts had to be re-examined. In order to describe the restoration of the self, the outlines of a psychology of the self had to be drawn.

How can the theoretical framework of psychoanalysis be reshaped so that it will accommodate the multiplicity and diversity of the phenomena that we are
observing with regard to the self? The answer to this
question which, surprisingly, suggested itself—although
viewed in retrospect it should not have been surprising—
was that we must learn to think alternatingly, or even
simultaneously, in terms of two theoretical frameworks;
that we must, in accordance with a psychological principle of complementarity, recognize that a grasp of the
phenomena encountered in our clinical work—and
beyond—requires two approaches: a psychology in which
the self is seen as the center of the psychological universe,
and a psychology in which the self is seen as a content of a
mental apparatus.

The emphasis of the present contribution is on the
first of these two approaches, i.e., on the psychology of
the self in the broader sense—on a psychology, in other
words, that puts the self at the center, examines its
genesis and development and its constituents, in health
and in disease. But the second approach—an approach
that constitutes no more than a slight extension of traditional metapsychology—the psychology of the self in the
narrower sense, in which the self is seen as a content of a

mental apparatus, is not neglected whenever the explanatory power of its application is adequate. If the present work focuses more frequently on the psychology of the self in the broader sense than on the psychology of the self in the narrower sense of the term, it does so not only for the obvious reason that the contributions that can be made with regard to the former are new and need, therefore, to be spelled out in greater detail, but also, and par excellence, because it is my major objective in this book to demonstrate that there are extensive psychological areas where the significance of the empirical phenomena confronting us lend themselves to a fuller explanation when illuminated by the psychology of the self in the broad sense of the term.

In order to come nearer to the goal of giving the outlines of a psychology of the self[1] and to set up the theoretical basis on which the psychology of the self could be placed, I have had to re-examine a number of established psychoanalytic concepts: How is the psychoanalytic drive-concept affected by our emphasis on the self, and what is the relation of drive theory to the psychology of the self? How is the concept of the libidinal drives, in their oedipal and preoedipal manifestations, affected when we re-evaluate it within the context of a self psychology? How is the concept of aggression as a drive affected by the introduction of a psychology of the self, and what is the position of aggression within the framework of the psychology of the self? And, finally, shifting from the examination of dynamic concepts to the examination of structural theory, we will ask whether it is conceptually proper,

[1] When I speak of the psychology of the self without qualifying the term, I am, unless I specify otherwise, referring to the psychology of the self in the broad sense.

within the framework of the psychology of the self, to speak of constituents of the self rather than of agencies of a mental apparatus which, to the cursory glance, might simply appear to be their counterparts.

Although I admire the elegance of flawless logic and neat consistency in terminology, concept formation, and theoretical formulation, it is not the primary aim of the present contribution to achieve these qualities. The changes in theoretical outlook suggested in the present work are not to be justified on purely theoretical grounds—the essential justification for them is derived from the applicability of the new viewpoint to the empirical data. I do not claim, in other words, that the new theories are more elegant, that the new definitions are more polished, or that the new formulations are more perfectly economical and consistent than the old ones. I do claim, however, that, with all their roughness and flaws, they broaden and deepen our understanding of the psychological field—inside and outside the clinical situation. It is not conceptual and terminological refinement but the expansion of our grasp of the psychological essence of man, the increase of our ability to explain man's motivations and behavior, that will sustain our resolve to shoulder the emotional hardship of dispensing with the reassuring aid of the familiar conceptual framework and to look at certain sets of empirical data—or at certain aspects of these empirical data—from the point of view of the psychology of the self.

The investigations of the past decade have not led me to results that force me to advocate the relinquishment of the classical theories and of the clinical psychoanalytic conception of man, and I remain in favor of their continued employment within a certain clearly defined area. Still, I have come to recognize the limits of the applicability of some of the basic analytic formulations. And with regard to the classical psychoanalytic conceptualization of the nature of man, too—however powerful and beautiful it might be—I have become convinced that it does not do justice to a broad band in the spectrum of human psychopathology and to a great number of other psychological phenomena we encounter outside the clinical situation.

I am fully aware of the strength of the hold that the classical psychoanalytic conception of man has come to exert on our imagination; I know how powerful a tool it has become in modern man's attempt to understand himself. And I know, therefore, that the suggestion that it is inadequate, or even that in certain respects it leads to an erroneous outlook on man, is bound to arouse opposition. Is it really necessary for us, some of my psychoanalytic colleagues will ask, to move beyond the essential framework of drive theory? It has already moved, under the influence of Freud and the next generation of his pupils, from id psychology to ego psychology. Is it necessary now to add a psychology of the self to the psychology of the drives and the psychology of the ego? Is it not, to anticipate an argument on the cognitive side, unnecessary to introduce a psychology of the self in view of the essential correctness and the comprehensive explanatory power of ego psychology? And is it not, to anticipate an argument on the moral side, an escapist move, a cowardly attempt to clean up analysis, to deny man's drive-nature, to deny that man is a badly and incompletely civilized animal? It is in the face of arguments such as these that I assert the necessity for an expansion of the psychoanalytic outlook, for a complementary theory of the self which both enriches our conception of the neuroses and is indispensable for an explanation of the disorders of the self—with the hope that the empirical evidence I shall be adducing and the rationality of the arguments I shall be advancing will prove persuasive.

I now turn to a second group of possible objectors to my work, namely, those who might reproach me for going it alone, for trying to find new solutions without leaning on the work of others who have also recognized the limitations of the classical position and have already suggested emendations, corrections, and improvements.

Among the various commentators on my work on narcissism there have been some who expressed the feeling that there were similarities between the results of my investigations of the area of narcissism and the results of the investigations of others. One critic (Apfelbaum, 1972) saw my contribution as essentially Hartmannian; another (James, 1973) saw it as essentially similar to that of Winnicott; still another (Eissler, 1975) thought I was following in the footsteps of Aichhorn; a fourth (Heinz, 1976) detected in it the philosophy of Sartre; a fifth (Kepecs, 1975) outlined analogies with the work of Alfred Adler; a sixth (Stolorow, 1976) did the same with regard to the client-centered therapy of Rogers; a team of two others (Hanly and Masson, 1976) saw it as an offshoot of Indian philosophy; and, finally, two others (Stolorow and Atwood, 1976) demonstrated connections with the writings of Otto Rank.

I know this list is incomplete, and, what is even more important, I know that there is yet another group of investigators whose names should be added to those already given. I am thinking here of those—such as Balint (1968),

Erikson (1956), Jacobson (1964), Kernberg (1975), Lacan (1953), Lampl-de Groot (1965), Lichtenstein (1961), Mahler (1968), Sandler et al. (1963), Schafer (1968), and others—whose areas of investigation, even if not their methods of approach or their conclusions, overlap the subject matter of my own investigations to varying degrees.

With regard to the members of this group (and the same can be said with certain variations concerning several of those mentioned in the first group, specifically concerning Aichhorn [1936], Hartmann [1950], and Winnicott [1960a]), let me emphasize initially that my continuing lack of integration of their contributions with mine is not due to any disrespect—on the contrary, I have great admiration for most of them—but to the nature of the task that I have set for myself. The present book is not a technical or theoretical monograph written detachedly by an author who has achieved mastery in a stable and established field of knowledge. This book is a report of an analyst's attempt to struggle toward greater clarity in an area that, despite years of conscientious effort, he was unable to understand within the available psychoanalytic framework—even as emended by the work of modern contributors. To the best of my knowledge I am giving full credit to those whose work has in fact influenced my methods and opinions. But my focus is not on scholarly completeness—it is directed elsewhere.

At first I tried to orient myself in the area of my interest with the aid of the existing psychoanalytic literature. But, finding myself floundering in a morass of conflicting, poorly based, and often vague theoretical speculation, I decided that there was only one way that would lead to progress: the way back to the direct observation of clinical phenomena and the construction of new formulations that would accommodate my observations. As I saw it, in other words, it was my task to outline a psychology of the self against the background of a clear and consistent definition of a psychology of complex mental states in general and of psychoanalytic depth psychology in particular.

I did not set myself the task of integrating the results of my work with the results of the work of others — results that had been obtained by approaches that are consistent with viewpoints that are different from mine, or that had been formulated within a vague, ambiguous, or shifting theoretical framework. I felt that to undertake such a task at this point was not only inadvisable but that it would indeed pose an insurmountable obstacle on the way toward my objectives. The attempt, in particular, to intersperse the exposition of my concepts and formulations with those of others who have made contributions to the psychology of the self from different viewpoints and within different frames of reference, would have entangled me in a thicket of similar, overlapping, or identical terms and concepts which, however, did not carry the same meaning and were not employed as a part of the same conceptual context.

Having thus shed the ballast of taking into consideration the various concepts and theories used by other researchers, I trust that my own basic viewpoint will emerge clearly in the present work. Because I have defined it extensively in the past, I here mention only briefly that it is characterized by the commitment to three tenets: the commitment to the definition of the psychological field as the aspect of reality that is accessible via introspection and empathy; the commitment to a methodology of the

observer's long-term empathic immersion in the psychological field — in particular, with regard to clinical phenomena, of his long-term, empathic immersion in the
transference — ; and the commitment to the formulation
of constructions in terms that are in harmony with the
introspective-empathic approach. Stated in everyday language: I am trying to observe and explain inner experience — including the experience of objects, of the self,
and of their various relationships. I am not, methodologi-
cally and in terms of my formulations, a behaviorist, a
social psychologist, or a psychobiologist — much as I acknowledge the value of these approaches.

A final word. The fact that I could not undertake
the attempt to compare my methods, findings, and formulations with those of other investigators who have
studied the self from different points of view and with the
aid of different methodologies — and who have therefore
also formulated their findings in the terms of different
theoretical systems — does not imply that I think such
comparisons should not be undertaken. In order to carry
out such scholarly studies successfully, however, some
time must first have passed. A certain distance, a certain
degree of detachment, is needed, in other words, before a
scholarly reviewer of the various approaches to the self
will be able to evaluate their relative merits and to corre-
late them to each other.

CHAPTER ONE

The Termination of the Analysis of Narcissistic Personality Disorders

The question whether at the point of terminating an analysis the analytic task has been completed, or termination has been premature, confronts the analyst in a variety of circumstances. There are, in addition, a number of specific problems surrounding the termination of the analysis of narcissistic personality disorders. The complexity of the subject matter of termination is increased by the fact that the views an analyst holds concerning many areas of theory and practice will influence his judgments concerning the questions how he should define an ideally completed analysis and how close to the ideal he should expect to come in reality. The topic of termination is therefore a vast one. In the present study, I shall disregard many aspects of the problem and restrict myself to an attempt to illuminate certain theoretical issues. I am undertaking this task because I believe that a change of our traditional theoretical stance will enable us to recognize the genuineness of certain terminations, will enable us to recognize that further analysis was not indicated, that the patient had not taken a flight into health—whereas an assessment of the patient's personality carried out on the basis of the traditional theories might lead us to the opposite view.

The pivotal problem concerns the area of the nucleus of the psychopathology. Insofar as the structural neuroses are concerned, we have learned to formulate our expectations in terms of the completion of the task of analyzing the patient's Oedipus complex, that is, we expect that the patient should have recognized his persisting hopeless (and disturbing) sexual love and his persisting hopeless (and disturbing) rivalrous hate for the great imagoes of his childhood and that, on the strength of this recognition, he should have become able to free himself from the emotional entanglements of his childhood and to turn in affection or in anger to the objects of present-day reality. We know, of course, to use Freud's metaphor (1917b, p. 456), that the decisive battles of the analysis of oedipal psychopathology are not necessarily fought out in the very center of the Oedipus complex itself; but whatever the content and psychic location of the tactical engagements might have been, in the end it is the relative freedom from the object-instinctual involvements of the oedipal period that constitutes the measure of the success or failure of the analysis.

When we turn to the narcissistic personality disorders, however, we are no longer dealing with the pathological results of unsatisfactory solutions of conflicts between structures that are in essence intact, but with forms of psychological malfunctioning arising in consequence of the fact that the central structures of the personality—the structures of the self—are defective. And so, in the narcissistic personality disorders, our description of the process and goals of psychoanalysis and of the conditions that characterize a genuine termination (under what circumstances we can say that the analytic task has been completed) must therefore be based on a definition of the nature and location of the essential psychological defects and on a definition of their cure.

The nuclear psychopathology of the narcissistic personality disorders (corresponding to the repressed unresolved conflicts of the Oedipus complex of the structural neuroses) consists of (1) defects, acquired in childhood, in the psychological structure of the self and (2) secondary structure-formations, also built up in early childhood, which are related to the primary defect in one of two similar, but, in certain crucial respects, different ways. I shall call these two types of secondary structures—distinguishing them on the basis of their relation to the primary structural defect of the self—*defensive* and *compensatory structures*.

Although a definition of defensive and compensatory structures that transcends being merely descriptive and metaphorical cannot be fully understood until the reader has become familiar with the concept of the bipolar nature of the self and with the child's twofold chance to build up a functioning self—topics discussed extensively later on—I shall nevertheless provide one at this point. I call a structure defensive when its sole or predominant function is the covering over of the primary defect in the self. I call a structure compensatory when, rather than merely covering a defect in the self, it compensates for this defect. Undergoing a development of its own, it brings about a functional rehabilitation of the self by making up for the weakness in one pole of the

self through the strengthening of the other pole. Most frequently a weakness in the area of exhibitionism and ambitions is compensated for by the self-esteem provided by
the pursuit of ideals; but the reverse may also occur.

The terms defensive structure and compensatory
structure refer to the beginning and end of a spectrum
which has a broad central area that contains a great variety of intermediate forms. But more or less pure forms
are encountered, and the transitional ones can usually be
assigned to one or the other of the two classes.

Basing myself on this differentiation, I postulate that
the phase of termination of the analysis of a narcissistic
personality disorder has been reached when we have completed one or the other of two specific tasks: (1) When,
after the analytic penetration of the defensive structures,
the *primary defect* in the self has been exposed and,
via working through and transmuting internalization,
sufficiently filled out so that the formerly defective structures of the self have now become functionally reliable.
(2) We have also reached the termination phase in the
analysis of a narcissistic personality disorder when—after
the patient has achieved cognitive and affective mastery
with regard to the defenses surrounding the primary
defect in the self, with regard to the compensatory structures, and with regard to the relationship between
these—the *compensatory structures* have now become
functionally reliable, independent of the area in which
this success was achieved. This functional rehabilitation
might have been achieved predominantly through improvements in the area of the primary defect, or through
the analysis of the vicissitudes of the compensatory structures (including the healing of their structural deficien-
cies through transmuting internalizations), or through

the patient's increased mastery resulting from his comprehension of the interrelation of primary defect and
compensatory structures, or through success in some or
all of these areas.

It is hardly necessary to give an illustration of the
term defensive structure because it refers to a concept not
only well known to every analyst but indeed indispensable
to him when he orders his clinical impressions in accordance with the dynamic point of view. Every analyst knows
those patients, who, for example, often to the embarrass-
ment of those around them, tend to be overly enthusiastic, dramatic, and excessively intense in their responses to
everyday events and who, analogously, romanticize and
sexualize their relation to the analyst, giving at times the
impression of an overtly reinstated display of oedipal pas-
sions (cf. Kohut, 1972, pp. 369-372). In cases of narcissistic personality disorder, it is not difficult to discern the
defensive nature—a pseudovitality—of the overt excitement. Behind it lie low self-esteem and depression—a
deep sense of uncared-for worthlessness and rejection, an
incessant hunger for response, a yearning for reassurance. All in all, the excited hypervitality of the patient
must be understood as an attempt to counteract through
self-stimulation a feeling of inner deadness and
depression. As children, these patients had felt emotionally unresponded to and had tried to overcome their loneliness and depression through erotic and grandiose fantasies. The grown-up behavior and grown-up fantasy life
of these patients is usually not the exact replica of the
original childhood defense because, during an excited,
overly enthusiastic, hyperidealistic adolescence devoid of
meaningful interpersonal attachments, the childhood
fantasies often become transformed by an intense de-

votion to romanticized cultural — esthetic, religious, political, etc. — aims. The romantic ideals, however, do not
recede into the background when the individual reaches
adulthood as would be the normal, expectable course; no
comfortable integration with the goals of the adult personality takes place: the dramatic, intensely, exhibitionistic aspects of the personality do not become securely alloyed with mature productivity; and the erotized, ex-
citedly pursued activities of adult life continue to be but
one step removed from the underlying depression.

Having briefly illustrated the familiar and simple
area of the role played by the *defensive* structures in the
narcissistic personality disorders, I shall now present
clinical material to illuminate the less familiar and also
more complex role played by the *compensatory* psychic
structures in these disturbances.

The Terminal Phase of the Analysis of Mr. M.

Mr. M., who worked as a writer in what he described
as a dependable but limiting job, sought analysis when he
was in his early thirties, when his wife of six years left
him.[1] Ostensibly he wanted to undertake analysis in order
to find out how he might have contributed to the failure
of his marriage. But there was no doubt about the fact
that his motivation for therapy was not primarily a wish
for intellectual knowledge: he sought help because he
suffered from a serious disturbance of his self-esteem and
a deep sense of inner emptiness, a manifestation of his
primary structural defect — chronic enfeeblement of his

---

[1] Mr. M. was in analysis with a student, a woman, under supervision
with the author (cf. Kohut, 1971, pp. 128-129).

self with some tendency toward the temporary fragmentation of this structure. His apathy and lack of initiative made him feel only "half alive," and he attempted to overcome this sense of inner emptiness with the aid of emotionally highly charged fantasies, in particular, sexual fantasies having a strong sadistic cast. These fantasies of sadistic control over women (of tying them up) he also occasionally acted out. He had done this with his wife, who considered his behavior "sick." (In theoretical terms, these fantasies and enactments were attempts to cover a primary defect with the aid of defensive structures.) Of crucial significance in his personality organization, and of pivotal importance in the process of his analysis, were vaguely expressed complaints about a writing block. His work as a writer, which should have made a substantial contribution to the enhancement of his self-esteem, was hampered by a nexus of interrelated disturbances. I shall focus on two of them here. The first one was indeed a manifestation of Mr. M.'s primary structural defect; it was genetically related to the failure of his mother's self-object function as a mirror for the child's healthy exhibitionism. The second one was a manifestation of a defect in the patient's compensatory structures; it was genetically related to the failure of the father's self-object function as an idealized image.

The genetic matrix of the primary defect—stunted development of the grandiose-exhibitionistic aspects of the self—was insufficient mirroring from the side of the mother. If the mother of patients with such a disturbance is still living, it is often possible to ascertain her lack of empathy or her faulty empathic responses first-hand during the analysis, since the patient, having become alerted, through the dynamics of the interplay of reactions in a mirror transference, to the fact that his self is vulnerable to faulty or disrupted empathy, and having begun to reconstruct the genetically decisive circumstances of his early life, will not only remember pathogenic moments from his childhood, but will also observe his mother's flawed empathy vis-à-vis himself or others, especially vis-à-vis children — her grandchildren, for example. In Mr. M.'s case, this direct source of information was not available because the patient's mother had died when he was twelve. Certain transference phenomena, however, as well as childhood memories, indicated that he had experienced his mother's responsiveness to him as insufficient and faulty. He recalled how, on many occasions during his childhood, he tried to look at her suddenly so that she could not have time to cover over by a falsely friendly and interested facial expression the fact that she really felt indifferent about him. And he remembered a specific occasion when he had injured himself and some of his blood had stained his brother's clothes. His mother thereupon, without discerning that it was he and not the brother who was frightened and in pain, had rushed the brother to the hospital and left him behind.

With regard to the first memory a general question of great complexity awaits answering with certainty — namely, why the child repeatedly and actively tried to bring about the very recognition he dreaded (somewhat similar, perhaps, to our repeatedly touching a sore tooth in order to test whether it still hurts — only to find out that of course it does). The psychological flavor of these memories (an anxious yet hopeful eagerness of the child's emotional state) seems to rule out the explanation that he wished to expose himself to his mother's rejection of him in order to gratify a masochistic desire. Nor do I believe

that he looked at his mother's face—transforming passive
into active—primarily in order to retain some control
over a potentially traumatic situation (by actively ascer-
taining the mother's indifference he prevents the traumatic effect of being passively and unexpectedly overwhelmed by her indifference at a time when he is at a
peak of vulnerability, e.g., when he is expecting positive
mirroring from her). The most significant conclusion one
should probably draw from his behavior is that it indicates he had not given up all hope for the mother's in-
tuneness with him—a conclusion in harmony with the
diagnostic category of the patient's psychopathology (that
of narcissistic personality disturbance, not of a borderline
organization). The mother's empathy, one might assume,
was not lacking altogether—it was faulty rather than flat;
when he injured himself, she had, after all, responded—
and it did *occasionally* confirm the child's sense of his
worthwhileness, and thus of the reality of his self.

One result of the mother's incapacity to tune in on
the child and to respond with adequate empathic resonance was a specific maldevelopment in the exhibitionistic
sector of his personality: he did not build up sufficient
sublimatory structures in the sector of his exhibitionism
because, due to the insufficiency of the mother's primary
mirroring responses, no adequate basis had been set up
from which her structure-building, increasingly selective
secondary responses (her optimally increasing frustration
of his needs) could proceed; he therefore remained
fixated on archaic forms of exhibitionism; and inasmuch
as archaic exhibitionism cannot find appropriate gratifications in adult life, he developed brittle defensive structures of the all-or-nothing type—he either suppressed his
exhibitionism to the detriment of healthy forms of self-
esteem and pleasure in himself and his performance, or

his exhibitionism broke through in frantic activity and wild sexualized fantasies (occasionally carried over into actual behavior) in which the mirroring self-object (always a woman) was under his absolute, sadistically enforced control, a slave who had to comply with his every wish and whim.

With regard to his work as a writer—and it must again be stressed that his work should have made the greatest contribution to the enhancement of his adult self-esteem and should have provided the most important outlet for transformed grandiose-exhibitionistic narcissistic tensions through creativity—the structural defect caused by the failure of the maternal mirroring functions led to experiences of frightening and paralyzing overstimulation. He did not possess sufficient structures to curb and neutralize the grandiosity and exhibitionism that became activated when his imagination was mobilized. He therefore often became tense and excited when he was writing and then either had to suppress his imagination—to the detriment of the originality and vitality of the product—or cease working altogether.

The obstacles standing in the way of his creative work can not, however, be explained primarily by a scrutiny of his relation to the mirroring maternal self-object and of the resulting primary structural defect in his psychic equipment, because the abilities he employed in his professional activities were in the main not based on primary structures, i.e., on congenital capacities nurtured in the matrix of his relation to the mirroring self-object, but on compensatory structures, i.e., on talents acquired or at least decisively reinforced later in his childhood in the matrix of the relation to the idealized self-object, the father.

Before dealing with these compensatory structures and their specific defects, it will be helpful to present a reconstruction of the sequence of genetically important psychological events in Mr. M.'s childhood. As I have said, Mr. M.'s central self structures had doubtless been decisively injured by the lack of maternal responsiveness. It is equally certain that he then turned toward the idealized father—this is a very typical psychological move— in order to make up in the relation to the idealized self-object for the harm he had suffered in relation to the mirroring one.[2] Mr. M. must have tried, during his childhood, first to idealize and then to acquire (i.e., to integrate into his own self) certain of his father's abilities— abilities which seem to have played an important role in the father's personality and which the father seemed to have valued highly—especially his father's skill in the use of language, of words. At any rate, it was by means of words that the patient, throughout his adolescence and as an adult, tried to find, in an aim-inhibited, socially acceptable way, fulfillment for the derivatives of his grandiose and exhibitionistic strivings. The sectors of his self, however, from which these strivings originated, had remained unmodified (archaic) because their further development—more exactly: the development of modulating, substitution-offering psychic structures surrounding them —had not been maintained by the pressure of reliable re-

[2] It may be mentioned here that, in retrospect, the explanation given with regard to the move of patient A. toward his father (see Kohut, 1971, p. 67) was inexact. On the basis of my experience with several similar cases seen subsequent to the termination of Mr. A.'s analysis, I would now assume that the intensity of Mr. A.'s idealization of his father (and thus the traumatic intensity of his disappointment in him) was due to his earlier disappointment in the mirroring self-object, not to his disappointment in a more archaic idealized one.

sponses—first joyously accepting responses, later increas
ingly selective ones—from his mother.

It was very instructive for the analyst to witness how
the patient attempted to find his way out of the emotional
cul-de-sac in which the development in the narcissistic
sector of his personality had become blocked. The professional activity he had chosen (it related to art criticism)
put at his disposal some highly specific means that
allowed him to express his particular narcissistic needs. In
his writings, describing and criticizing various artistic
productions, he could now, by using the father's idealized
power, translate his yearning for an empathic mother's
response into appropriate words and sentences; even his
unrelieved primary desires for the texture of the responsive body of his mother could find symbolic expression in
certain verbal descriptions he had to compose in the pursuit of his professional activities.

His tragedy was—and here lay one of the strongest
motivations for his seeking treatment—that he did not
succeed in building up appropriately functioning compensatory structures derived from his dictionary-collect-
ing, word-loving, language-wise father because the father
failed him as had the mother before. (We can conclude,
however, in view of the fact that he was already engaged
in his writing career when he entered analysis, that his
father's failure as a self-object was less severe than the
failure of his mother.) The father, in other words, could
not allow himself to enjoy being idealized by his son, and
he did not foster, by empathic participating responses,
that optimal development of an idealizing relation with
him for which his son yearned and which he required.
The boy was thus again frustrated in the attempt to
strengthen the structure of his self, frustrated in the at-

tempt to build up an apparatus of functions that would allow the socially acceptable display and expression of the self through reliably available creative pursuits.

A successful, phase-appropriate, chip-off-the-old-block-type merger with (or twinship relation to) the idealized father, and the subsequent gradual or phase-appropriate disappointment in him, might yet have enhanced Mr. M.'s self-esteem via the temporary participation in the omnipotence of the idealized self-object, and might yet have provided him ultimately with appropriate buffering structures and discharge patterns in the sector of his greatness-fantasies and of his exhibitionism, undoing the damage that had resulted from the earlier psychological interplay with the insufficiently mirroring mother. True, his compensatory activities in the area of language and creative writing were not altogether unsuccessful, and he derived a modicum of gratification from them. Still, there is no doubt that neither his identification with the quasi-artistic works he produced nor the gratifications obtained from them—directly by way of pleasure in his work, indirectly by way of the public response to it— were sufficient to maintain his narcissistic equilibrium. And the progress in his analysis could indeed to some extent be gauged by taking measure of the improvement that gradually occurred in this realm.

What was the nature of the disease of the compensatory structures Mr. M. had built up in the realm of language and creative writing? And how was it to be cured? Let me put the answers to these two interrelated questions in a nutshell. (1) With regard to the disturbance of the functions of the compensatory structures, it can be said that, from way back, Mr. M. had had a disturbance of his ability to translate the fantasies that welled up in him in the form of visual imagery into appropriate language (a college professor had somewhat cryptically said that he suffered from a defect in "logic"—probably a layman's diagnosis of a mild and circumscribed thought disorder). (2) With regard to the nature of the cure of the disturbed compensatory structures, it can be said that improvement during psychoanalysis ensued via two routes: The first was via working-through processes in the area concerned with the insufficient mirroring responses of maternal self-objects, i.e., by gradual integration into his personality of his grandiose-exhibitionistic urges. Violin playing provided an important transitional safety valve for the tensions stirred up while this sector was worked through (cf. Kohut, 1971, p. 287, concerning the similar function dancing provided during the analysis of Miss F.). The second route was via working-through processes in the area concerned with the father's withdrawal when the patient wanted to attach himself to him (particularly in order to share the father's power in the realm of language) after he had come to the conclusion that it was hopeless to expect the mother's mirroring responses. It is an example of the "telescoping" of genetically analogous experiences (see Kohut, 1971, pp. 53-54) that some of the crucial analytic work done in this sector of the patient's personality did not focus on the genetic pattern of early life, as it must have been outlined for the first time as a result of the father's earliest rebuffs, but on the analogous dynamic pattern of his late preadolescence, which appears to have been decisive from the psychoeconomic point of view in determining the characteristic features of the disturbance of Mr. M.'s adult personality. Specifically, he remembered that after his mother's death, he had tried to lay claim to his idealized father's attention but was disappointed by the father's lack of interest in him, especially by the father's remarriage, which the patient had experienced as a narcissistic injury and a personal rejection.

Contemplating Termination— The Analysand's Remaining Tasks

In the analysis of the transference neuroses, the terminal phase is frequently characterized by a return to structural conflicts that had been the major content of the working through carried out during the main part (the "middle phase") of the analysis. Once more, it seems, as the necessity for the ultimate severance of oedipal ties is now at hand—as the imminent final parting from the analyst confronts the patient with the ultimate relinquishment of the objects of his childhood love and hate—once more does the child in him try to assert the old demands before it finally decides to set them aside for good or succeeds indeed in dismissing them.

In the analysis of those narcissistic personality disorders where working through had on the whole concerned a primary defect in the structure of the patient's self, resulting in a gradual healing of the defect via the acquisition of new structures through transmuting internalization, the terminal phase can be seen to parallel that of the usual transference neuroses. The analysand is exposed to the impact of the realization that he has to face the ultimate separation from the analyst as a self-object. As a result of the pressure of this difficult emotional task, a temporary regression takes place in the analysand, creating a situation in which the healing of the structural defect seems to be again undone. A condition supervenes, in other words, in which it appears that the healing was only sham, that the patient's improved functioning was not a consequence of newly acquired psychic structure but depended on the actual presence of the self-object. Or, to describe the situation in still different terms, it suddenly seems as if the processes of working through had not brought about those optimal frustrations which, through minute internalizations, lay down psychic structure and make the patient independent of the analyst, but that the patient had improved by leaning on the external self-object or, at best, by having borrowed the self-object's (the analyst's) functions through gross, unstable identifications with him. Among the manifestations of the terminal phase in the analysis of these cases, signs indicating the *temporary reconcretization* of the relation to the self-object are therefore often in evidence. Once more the patient feels that the analyst is substituting for his psychic structure—once more he sees him as the supplier of his self-esteem, as the integrator of his ambitions, as the concretely present idealized power that dispenses approval and other forms of narcissistic sustenance.

Certain details of the terminal phase of the analysis of Mr. I., for example (see Kohut, 1971, pp. 167-168), furnish a striking illustration of the reconcretization of the analyst's self-object functions. In a series of dreams of almost humorous openness Mr. I. incorporates the self-object analyst or his attributes of power through various orifices of his body. But then, as the terminal phase comes to an end, he shifts from these symbolic gross identifications back to the result of the transmuting internalizations achieved by means of the working-through processes earlier in analysis—he is able to look forward with enjoyment to his future autonomous functioning.

The situation is different, however, in the termination phase of narcissistic personality disorders, in which, as with Mr. M., the spontaneously activated transference and the working-through processes concern not only the primary defect and the defensive structures surrounding it, but also, and especially, the compensatory structures.

Mr. M. expressed his wish to terminate his analysis approximately seven months before it actually ended. Asking the reader's forbearance, I shall present my theoretical views concerning the emotional state of the analysand at that time in the form of the following imaginary communication from the patient.

"Analyst," he says, "I think our work is more or less done. We have been able to strengthen my compensatory psychological structures sufficiently so that I can now be active and creative; and I am now able to work toward meaningful goals. The devotion to meaningful goals and the very act of creating solidify my self, give me a feeling of being alive, real, and worthwhile. And these attitudes and activities give me a sufficient amount of joy to make life worth living; they prevent the feeling of emptiness and depression. I have acquired the psychological substance that allows me to pursue self-distant goals and yet to be aware of my active creative self in the act of creation. I have, in other words, found a psychological equilibrium between *the product* (an extension of myself)— my absorbing devotion to it, my joy in perfecting it—and *the self* (a center of productive initiative)—the exhilarating experience that I am producing the work, that I have produced it. Although I am thus joyfully aware of myself, I no longer become hypomanically overstimulated while creating, nor do I fear, as I used to, that my self will be drained away into the product of my creative-

ness. The self as a joyfully experienced center of initiative
and the product of which I am proud are in an unbroken
psychological connection now.

"I am, of course, pleased with these new achievements; still, I know the weak spots and the danger points
of my psychological organization. And I also understand
that, in essence, I was able to reach the decisive improvement in this sector of my personality by the increased integration of idealized goals that stand for my father
whom I had wanted to idealize as a child and as a young
adolescent. My father, however, rejected my idealizing
approach to him — a rebuff that deprived me of the experience of the full developmental cycle of idealization
followed by de-idealization and thus of the opportunity
for laying down reliable psychological structures (guiding
ideals) in this area. The transference reactivation of the
old yearning to idealize my father set in motion specific
working-through processes (the repeated experience of
the sequence of idealization, de-idealization, and internalization) which strengthened my leading ideals. And,
as I have now come to recognize, the possession of strong
ideals is of the greatest importance for maintaining my
emotional health. I believe that this process, while of
course not finished, has progressed sufficiently by now to
allow me to be henceforth on my own with it.

"But I also know that I could not have made this decisive progress in the realm of male ideals, work, and
creativity entirely on the basis of dealing with the disappointment vis-à-vis my father. Some fundamental
firming of the self first had to be achieved in the analysis
before I was capable of tackling my father's rejection of
my idealization of him. And no doubt this prior solidifi-
cation of the self related to more basic weaknesses in its

structure than those involved in working through of my guiding ideals. This prior task, in other words, focused on earlier stages of development, and it concerned traumata suffered with regard to my mother's response to me as a very small child—her acceptance of me and her approval. Here, too, the work is incomplete. But its incompleteness differs from the incompleteness of the working-through processes vis-à-vis the idealized father imago. As far as the latter is concerned, all relevant aspects entered into the analysis, and what is lacking is, one might say, further exercise in order to solidify the gains made. So far as the filling in of the centrally located weak spot in my personality is concerned, however—the result of traumata I suffered in consequence of the faulty responsiveness of my mother's flawed empathic capacity—there are indeed certain layers in my personality which we have hardly reached at all: layers I feel we cannot deal with because a healthy instinct in me would prevent a regression to archaic experiences that might bring about a perhaps irremedial disintegration of the self. And we need not deal with them even if we could because, in view of the now solidly functioning sectors of my personality, the maintenance of my self is now secured."

The analyst, reacting to Mr. M.'s speech, will of course ask himself whether, contrary to the patient's wishes, he should insist that further work be done in order to buttress the gains already made. In response to this problem, I advance the tenet that the analysand's capacity to assess his own psychological state is in certain situations potentially vastly more accurate than the analyst's. It must be added, however, that this assertion does not invalidate the equally cogent one that the analyst must carefully scrutinize whether the patient might not, under the influence of specific fears, wish to avoid undertaking psychological tasks that, if indeed performed, would lead to long-term beneficial results. Still, as my experience as an analyst has increased over the years, I have learned to trust a patient's wish to terminate his analysis, especially when it comes about after long years of solid work, when it arises without immediate urgency, and when, in addition, I am able to formulate for myself (and, in appropriate terms, for my patient) the dynamic-structural situation constituting the matrix of the patient's wish.

If we accept the patient's wish to terminate the analysis at this point as a valid one, i.e., as being based on the correct assessment that he had acquired the psychological structures making further analysis unnecessary, we must now inquire into the nature of the structures whose strengthening had such a decisive effect on his well-being. One may assume that they had come into existence in early childhood in reaction to a serious primary structural defect. Stated more precisely: the structures themselves were maturational givens—it was their functional importance that had been heightened in reaction to the primary defect, and the extent of the development was therefore increased beyond the average to be expected for a young child. If we translate the statement that the patient has formed these compensatory structures into metapsychological terms (cf. Freud, 1915, pp. 203-204), we can say that the ascendancy of the child's secondary processes had been prematurely emphasized, that he had developed an excessive interest in words in order to make up for the primary defect, i.e., for a hollowness and insecurity of the preverbal primary-process experiences of his body-self and of his emotions. Although this assumption was not confirmed by direct memories from *early* childhood, it is supported by two sets of data: indirectly obtained evidence appears to support the assertion that he indeed manifested an unusual interest in words in early childhood; and there is no doubt that he turned to his father (and to a preoccupation with language) in early adolescence, under psychological circumstances (his mother's death) similar to those (his mother's emotional distance) which had prevailed in his early childhood.[3]

Whatever the truth about the earliest psychological antecedents of the factors determining the course of Mr. M.'s personality development, the final outcome was a personality organization that strove to achieve narcissistic fulfillment through the use of language. Before the analysis, Mr. M. was unable to reach this goal; analysis, however, succeeded in curing the specific structural defects responsible for his failure in these endeavors.

The two psychological defects that prevented the pa-

---

[3] At this point I cannot resist the temptation to share with the reader a passage from a letter of a colleague who some years ago, grateful for certain insights into his own personality provided him by the study of my work, confided to me that his personality development had been decisively influenced by the fact that he had been traumatized in early childhood by the sudden loss of his idealized self-object, his father. In consequence of this loss, he wrote, he had turned to himself and—as he had done again in the transference he had developed toward me via the study of my writings—to the written word. "It does seem that (for me) a large part of the self-object is the written word... [that] I have developed a certain skill in finding something in literature that will say something to me in time of need.... I have been able in this way to get some access to the guiding hand of a great number of the world's better fathers, by way of their written word...." And then follows a statement describing a developmental step analogous to the one taken by Mr. M.: "An old aunt of mine," he writes, "claimed that I was reading before Kindergarten.... I know they used to cover up the labels on the sauce bottles because I would read them at the table, and apparently the doctors had ordered that my precocious reading be stopped. The books were removed, so I read the labels."

tient from obtaining fulfillment of narcissistic gratifications through the use of his talents in the realm of language and through the mobilization of his interest in
writing were both sufficiently worked through and thus
ameliorated to allow the patient to terminate the analysis.
I shall first describe these defects in terms of the theoretical framework generally referred to as the structural
model of the mind and as ego psychology. Even though I
am employing here a modification of the structural
model, in accordance with a suggestion (Kohut, 1961;
Kohut and Seitz, 1963) that the psyche should be conceived of as being subdivided into (a) an area of progressive neutralization and (b) an area of transferences, a
modification specifically applicable to the task at hand,
the ensuing detailed examination of Mr. M.'s psychopathology will make us realize that the explanatory formulations we can obtain in this way are not fully satisfactory. The framework of the structural model of the
mind, even when employed in conjunction with the most
sophisticated ego-psychological elaborations of drive psychology, is not sufficiently pertinent to the essential
nature of the psychological disturbance we are examining
at this point. In order to comprehend the significant
features of Mr. M.'s problems, we must introduce a new
framework: the psychology of the self—a psychology that
deals with the formation and functions of the self, and
with its break-up and reintegration.

Here, then, are the two disturbances in Mr. M.'s psychological make-up as described within the framework of
a somewhat modified structural model and in the terms
of a somewhat modified ego psychology. Before the analysis there was a structural defect in the "area of progressive neutralization," i.e., there was no smooth transition

from the primary process (his archaic exhibitionism, his merging with the maternal self-object, and the emotions connected with both of these sets of experiences) to the secondary process (his words, his language, his writings). And there was a structural defect in the area of his goals and ideals, leading secondarily to an insufficient channeling of his exhibitionistic-grandiose-creative strivings toward well-integrated, firmly internalized goals. The absence of a sufficiently organized flow of grandiose-exhibitionistic libido toward a securely internalized set of ideals led, in turn, to an insufficient development of those executive (ego) structures that would have enabled him to devote himself successfully to his professional pursuits and to gain his major sustaining narcissistic gratifications from them.

Because my focus is on termination—specifically on the termination of the analysis of narcissistic personality disorders—I shall not examine the details of the specific working-through processes concerning the two structural defects that accounted for the disturbance in the area of the patient's professional work, but only stress again that the defect manifesting itself in the lack of a smooth transition from primary to secondary processes seemed, from the genetic point of view, predominantly related to the flaws in the mirroring functions of the patient's mother, whereas the defect that manifested itself in the patient's inability to persist in the pursuit of his professional activities was genetically related almost exclusively to the flaws in the father's response in his function as an idealized imago.

At the time when the patient felt that the analysis should move toward termination, working through had indeed achieved some improvement in both of these areas. Yet, as I stated before, there was a defect in his personality that had in essence remained unanalyzed — had not become the focus of systematically pursued working-through processes — even though the patient had not only come to realize that his psychological organization was potentially exposed to the danger of diffuse disintegration, but had also obtained intellectual knowledge concerning the etiology[4] of this potentiality toward regression. The patient's wish to move toward terminating the analysis arose, therefore, despite his (at least preconscious) awareness that a centrally located sector of his grandiose self, which rested on and was in communication with a precariously constituted basic layer of his personality, had not been fully analyzed. He knew, however, that to analyze this sector was not a precondition for his future psychological well-being, and he sensed, furthermore, that it could not be analyzed without grave danger — without the serious risk of doing permanent harm to his psychological equilibrium. I believe he dimly recognized that the activation of certain aspects of the mirror transference would expose him to the danger of permanent psychological disruption through the re-experience of primordial rage and greed, and that he indirectly expressed his awareness of these potential dangers in two ways: by developing a psychosomatic symptom, a rash on his elbow — this interpretation of the rash is almost purely conjectural, although I analyzed another patient, Mr. U. who, when his archaic rage and greed were mobilized, developed a rash over his right elbow — and by say-

---

[4] The reader familiar with my thoughts will recognize that I am here distinguishing between the genetic point of view and etiological considerations (cf. Kohut, 1971, pp. 254-255, footnote. See also Hartmann and Kris, 1945).

ing that remaining in analysis much longer could become "addictive."

Most of what I can say about the still unanalyzed aspects of the archaic layers of the mirror transference is speculative. I would nevertheless point out that the patient had been abandoned by his natural mother and that he had been in an orphanage until he was three months old. Taking this into account, I believe we do not go far astray if we conclude that the disruptive effect of the traumata he suffered because of the faulty empathy of his adoptive mother in his later childhood (traumata which refer to the period after speech had developed and about which verbalized memories do exist) cannot be fully appreciated unless we also consider the vulnerability of the child's psyche due to analogous earlier traumatizations. Not only must he have been traumatized by the repeated failure of his adoptive mother to respond appropriately to his needs during the preverbal period, but behind these layers of frustration there hovered always a nameless preverbal depression, apathy, sense of deadness, and diffuse rage that related to the primordial trauma of his life. Such primal states, however, can neither be recalled through verbalized memories, as can traumata occurring after speech has developed, nor expressed through psychosomatic symptoms, as can the more organized rages of later preverbal experience (in Mr. M.'s case, perhaps through the rash on the elbow). The effect of the primordial trauma on the patient's psychological organization (the existence of a weakness of the basic layers in his personality) is attested to only by his fear that further analysis would become "addictive"—by the vague dread, in other words, of a regressive voyage from which there is no return.

The theoretical question arises here whether, and if so, to what extent, a rudimentary self may already exist in earliest infancy. (See in this context the discussion on pp. 98-101 of the question how the beginnings of the self should be conceived.) Translating this question into practical clinical terms, we would have to ask ourselves whether the patient's fear of an irreversible regression is the fear of the total loss of the self in the form of a permanent profound apathy, or the fear of the reactivation of a rudimentary archaic self in the form of the experience of oscillations between intense greed, diffuse rage, and contentless depression.

A further set of related questions concerns the mother's response to the baby—in this case, the adoptive mother's response. Whatever the endopsychic reality of the baby's experience might be, it can be affirmed that the mother responds to the infant *ab initio,* at least at certain times, as if he had already built up a cohesive self. (For a more detailed discussion of the mother's gradual shift from responding predominantly to the child's parts to responding predominantly to the whole child, see Kohut, 1975b.) If the relation of Mr. M.'s adoptive mother to her baby is examined against the background of the foregoing considerations, the question arises whether (and if so, how) the baby's stay in the orphanage might have indirectly disturbed his adoptive mother's later responses to him.

Two possibilities must be contemplated. The fact that the adoptive mother did not establish a relation to the baby during the first three months of his life deprived her of participating in one basic step in the developmental sequence of maternal experiences vis-à-vis a new child. Under normal circumstances, maternal responses anticipate the consolidation of the baby's self—the mother imagines it to be more consolidated than it actually is; or, in different terms, the mother, by being ahead of the child's actual development, does indeed experience the joy of furthering this development by her own expectations. That Mr. M.'s adoptive mother was not allowed to participate in these first steps toward the consolidation of the baby's basic self might have had several consequences: it might have deprived her later responses to him of the reverberations of the memories of this earliest merger with him; in consequence of this deprivation, it might have produced a certain emotional flatness in her attitudes toward him and prevented the development of that total intimacy which normally establishes itself between a mother and her baby; and in consequence of both of these restrictions of the mother's capacity to respond to the child, it might have brought about the development of a vicious cycle in the relation between mother and child because the mother's limited ability for phase-appropriate mirroring responses would, in turn, call forth an emotional withdrawal from the side of the baby.

The baby's stay in the orphanage might be held responsible for another possible disturbance in the mother's responsiveness toward her child. In view of the fact that as a baby he had been severely traumatized during the first three months of his life, it is likely that he reacted to self-objects of the later preverbal and early verbal stages of development (in particular to his adoptive mother) with a variety of abnormal responses. One would expect that a child who had suffered severe traumatizations in early infancy will, as an older baby and as a young child, develop a propensity toward unusually great demanding-

ness vis-à-vis the mother (a result of the continuing reverberations of the intensified oral greed of the earliest
stage), followed by manifestations of a tendency toward
violent temper tantrums and/or immediate emotional retreat upon minor delays of gratification (a continuation
of the rages and contentless depressions of the earliest
stage). Or there might be a general lessening of the child's
responsiveness to the maternal self-object in the later
stages, as a residual of the apathy of the earliest stage.
Such a disturbance from the side of the baby may well
overstrain the mother's ability to persevere in her attempt
to perceive the baby's needs accurately and to respond to
them appropriately. Overtaxed by the baby's intense
voracity, and frustrated by his quick retreat, ragefulness,
and/or apathy, she will shrink from a relationship that
exposes her to a sense of failure instead of providing her
with the glow of narcissistic fulfillment she had expected.

Replicas of the baby's various reactions in such a
situation can of course also be observed during the analysis of patients suffering from narcissistic personality disorders. And, repeating the baby's effect on his mother,
these self-object transferences may overtax the analyst's
empathy and lead to his emotional retreat from the patient or to the tendency to attack him by a display of open
annoyance or, more frequently, with the aid of moraliz-
ing exhortations and pseudointerpretations.

The practical importance of the analyst's narcissistic
frustrations with certain types of analysands should not
be underestimated. I know, from self-observation and
from scrutinizing the behavior of students I have super-
vised and of colleagues to whom I have served as a consultant, that even the analyst's best intentions, based on a
broad understanding of the psychology of analysands

with narcissistic disorders, do not reliably protect him against reactively withdrawing from the patient, and, what is worse, from rationalizing his withdrawal by the seemingly objective judgment that the patient is not analyzable. I believe, however, that no great harm—and perhaps even some good—can result from the analyst's feeling temporarily emotionally distant from the patient, so long as he is aware of his conflict and does not permanently turn away.

In Mr. M.'s case, I would be inclined to extrapolate a specific reconstruction from the analyst's description of the transference—namely, that the primordial experience in the orphanage had left him with an increased rage-potential and with a readiness toward quick emotional retreat in response to maternal frustrations, rather than with a tendency toward pervasive apathy. But whatever specific deviations from the norm might have been manifested by the baby's personality, there can be no doubt about this conclusion: a mother's faulty empathy can rarely be judged in isolation; as in the case of Mr. M.'s adoptive mother, in most instances it has to be evaluated as a failure vis-à-vis an unusually difficult task.

It should be stressed that so far as the analyst's work is concerned these considerations are of only limited importance. The analyst is interested in his analysand's childhood not primarily because he wants to unearth the *etiological* factors responsible for the analysand's disorder but because he wants to determine its decisive *genetic* roots (see p. 24, fn. 4). His attention is focused predominantly on the analysand's subjective transference experiences, and, on the basis of his understanding of their form and content, he reconstructs the experiential world of the patient's childhood during the genetically decisive

junctures. The analyst does not — at least not in the performance of his essential task — focus predominantly on
the data of objective reality, not even on the objectively
ascertainable subjective psychological state of parental
figures in the child's environment (although this latter
may at times be "tactically useful" [see Kohut, 1971, p.
254]). In Mr. M.'s case, the essential psychological fact
(the reactivation of the decisive genetic determinant of an
important aspect of his psychological disturbance) was
that he experienced his mother, and in the transference
the analyst, as traumatically unempathic vis-à-vis his
emotional demands and as unresponsive to them. True
enough, the analyst might occasionally wish to point out
(in order to retain a realistic framework — if, for example,
because of the intensity of the frustrations he experiences
in the transference, the patient might seriously consider
quitting the analysis) that the patient's expectations and
demands belong to his childhood and are unrealistic in
the present. And he might at the appropriate moment
also wish to explain to the patient that the intensity of his
childhood needs may have led to a distortion of his perceptions of the past (in Mr. M.'s case, to a falsification of
his perception of his adoptive mother's personality). The
essential structural transformations produced by working
through do not take place, however, in consequence of
such supportive intellectual insights, but in consequence
of the gradual internalizations that are brought about by
the fact that the old experiences are repeatedly relived by
the more mature psyche.

I will here, in addition, give voice to the opinion that
the tenet just stated — namely, that the beneficial structural transformations occurring in a successful analysis do
not take place as the result of insights — holds true, not

only for the analysis of patients with narcissistic personality disorders, but also for the analysis of patients suffering from structural neuroses. It is not the interpretation that cures the patient. And while it is correct to say that the work of analysis consists in making conscious what had been unconscious, this statement is only an appropriate metaphor about one aspect of the gross psychological transformations that do indeed occur during the analytic process.

I believe we are describing the curative process more accurately and cogently if we focus on the changes in the psychological "microstructures." (I am borrowing this term from Dr. Douglas C. Levin, who compares the development of depth psychology—from the stage when the investigator's attention was focused on psychological "macrostructures" to that when it became centered upon psychological "microstructures"[5]—with the analogous de-

---

[5] For a description of the laying down of neutralizing microstructure via experiences of optimal frustration, see Kohut and Seitz (1963, p. 137). The terms macrostructure and microstructure have also been used in a related context for the agencies of the mind and for the engrams of memory traces and ideas by Gill (1963, pp. 8n, 51, and 135-136).

I will add here that the parallelisms between the development of physics from Newtonian theory to quantum theory (Bohr, Heisenberg) and the development of psychoanalysis from Freudian metapsychology to the psychology of the self goes beyond the facts that the physicist's attention shifted from the investigation of large masses and their interactions to the investigation of minute units of matter and that the psychoanalyst's attention shifted from the investigation of macrostructures (the agencies of the mind) and macrorelationships with objects (the Oedipus complex) to the investigation of molecular units of psychic structure. Leaning again on a line of thought formulated by Dr. D. C. Levin, I would also point out that the emphasis that modern physics places on the essential identity of matter and energy finds its parallel in the emphasis that the psychology of the self places on structure formation via microrelationships with self-objects. And there is finally the fundamental claim of modern physics that the means of observation and the target of observation constitute a unit that, in certain respects, is in principle indivisible. This claim finds it counterpart in the equally fun-

velopment in physics—from the physics of the mechanics of large masses to the physics of the subparticle.) To put the description of these microstructural changes in the classical transference neuroses into a nutshell: (1) interpretations remove defenses; (2) archaic wishes intrude into the ego; (3) under the repeated impact of the archaic strivings, new structures are formed in the ego which are able to modulate and transform the archaic strivings (discharge delay, neutralization, aim inhibition, substitute gratification, absorption through fantasy formation, etc.). The analysand, in order to keep open the access of the archaic strivings to his ego, despite his anxiety (in the classical transference neuroses: castration anxiety in the face of incestuous libidinal and aggressive strivings), uses the analyst as a self-object—even in the analysis of structural neuroses!—, i.e., as a precursory substitute for the not-yet-existing psychological structures. (See in this context the remarks on p. 187n. below concerning the use of self-object relationships on all developmental levels and in psychological health as well as in psychological disease.) Little by little, as a result of innumerable processes of microinternalization, the anxiety-assuaging, delay-tolerating, and other realistic aspects of the analyst's image become part of the analysand's psychological equipment, *pari passu* with the "micro"-frustration of the analysand's need for the analyst's permanent presence and perfect functioning in this respect. In brief: through the process of transmuting internalization, new psychological structure is built. It must be added that the opti-

---

damental claim of the psychology of the self that the presence of an empathic or introspective observer defines, in principle, the psychological field (cf. Kohut, 1959; Habermas, 1971).

mal result of an analysis not only rests on the acquisition of new structures directly related to the previously repressed and now liberated archaic drive-wishes, but that, secondarily, the heretofore isolated pathological sector of the personality establishes broad contact with the surrounding mature sectors, so that the preanalytic assets of the personality are strengthened and enriched.

To return to the topic of termination: I have already (see pp. 15-20) mentioned two varieties of the termination syndrome—the well-investigated psychological events that tend to take place in the terminal phase of the analysis of the classical transference neuroses, and the so far comparatively uninvestigated psychological events that tend to occur in the terminal phase of the analysis of narcissistic personality disorders. The latter merit further description at this point. They occur in two forms: one in cases where the principal focus of the analytic work had concerned a primary structural defect; the other where it had concerned the rehabilitation of compensatory structures. In the first of these two subgroups we see, as I pointed out before, a reconcretization of the narcissistic transference—a return to the unmitigated insistence that an external self-object should maintain the patient's narcissistic equilibrium—as if all the progress that had been made in transmuting the self-object into psychological structure had been sham. In the second of these two subgroups, i.e., in the instances with which I am dealing at present, where the main focus of the work had concerned the functional rehabilitation of compensatory structures, we encounter, as I shall demonstrate in the case of Mr. M., a re-externalization of the compensatory structures and a concretization of the work of structure-building in this area in the form of gross "acting out." In

these cases, too, analogous to the terminal phase of analyses in which the major focus had been on the primary
structural defect, it looks for a while as if all the results
that had been obtained via the working-through processes had been sham — as if the compensatory structures
had not really become stronger. In short, one might gain
the impression that only the crudest precursors of the processes of working through and of internalization were now
just barely beginning to be mobilized. To put it somewhat schematically: Mr. M.'s analysis had succeeded first
in activating certain layers of the (maternal) mirror transference which related to pathogenic experiences of the
later part of early childhood, i.e., to experiences at an
age when speech had already been acquired. On the basis
of the progress made in this sector, the analysis was able
to activate certain crucial aspects of the (paternal) idealizing transference and, as the result of working through
in this sector, to achieve the strengthening of certain
specific structures whose rehabilitation contributed decisively to the establishment of Mr. M.'s psychological
well-being. The examination of three seemingly unrelated acts carried out by the patient at different times late
in the analysis will illuminate the significance of the terminal phase of Mr. M.'s analysis — in my opinion, largely
a *genuine* termination phase.

Here are the three acts that related to the beginning
of the termination phase of Mr. M.'s analysis, in the sequence in which I discuss them: (1) the patient bought an
expensive new violin; yet, almost simultaneously, he decided to devote himself less to the playing of this instrument; (2) he turned toward a relationship with an adolescent boy whom he allowed to idealize him; and (3) he
founded a "writing school" in which people from all walks

of life would learn "how to break down their ideas into manageable portions" and how to transform them into written language through an "increase of their receptivity to word imagery."

The order in which these three activities made their first appearance in the analysis is the reverse of the order in which I shall discuss them: Mr. M. began to consider the founding of the writing school in the late fall of the year that preceded the termination of his analysis; his relationship with the boy began in December of that year, culminating in March of the following year (the year of termination) in a specific, poignant experience during a baseball game; and he bought the violin shortly afterward, early in April of the year of termination. The order of the ending of these three events is, however, more significant than the order of their beginning. Mr. M.'s interest in the expensive violin was very short-lived; his involvement with the boy went on beyond it; and his preoccupation with the writing school persisted even longer, leading to the intensification of his own activities as a writer and to the deepening of the significance these activities had for him. The importance of the chronological order of the *end* of the three termination activities derives from the fact that it indicates the unrolling of a specific epigenetic sequence: the buying and selling of the violin was the manifestation of the emotional shift that was the precondition for Mr. M.'s readiness for his experiences with the adolescent boy; and the violin transactions and the experiences with the boy were the manifestations of the even greater internal shift that enabled him to make the last and most decisive step toward the establishment of a functioning self, the step that was achieved through the medium of his activities in the writing school.

I would emphasize my view that such activities—I will call them *action-thought*—do not constitute "acting out" in the usual sense. They should not, in other words, be looked upon as resistances, as defensive replacements of remembering or of insight by action.[6] They are the last

---

[6] I am reminded, in this context of the view held by some investigators of scientific methodology that certain pioneering experiments in science are not repeatable, that they constitute illustrations of a thesis or newly discovered principle and that, contrary to the experimenter's own belief, they do not provide sets of controlled empirical data upon which the theories could have been built by inductive reasoning. Such experiments, in my view, are also *action-thought*, i.e., a form of acted-out thought. If this view is correct, then these experiments would be analogous to those acts of analysands —such as those of Mr. M.—which are illustrations of the insights they are currently acquiring. These experiments, in other words, are enactments— concretizations of thought processes of a pioneering mind. They are not primarily arrangements designed to facilitate discovery or to test hypotheses. I might add that it would be interesting to examine not only certain key experiments in the physical sciences in this light—as has been done with regard to Newton's experiments and observations (cf. Koyré, 1968)—but also certain basic observations in the behavioral sciences. Some aspects of Freud's early clinical observations, for example, especially the cures he achieved on the basis of the theory that he had made the unconscious conscious, might be fruitfully examined within this context. In light of today's knowledge, the working-through processes mobilized and maintained in these early analyses were inadequate, and no analyst could nowadays repeat such cures with the means that Freud, according to his description, employed at that time. The actual cause for the disappearance of the patient's symptoms was probably that Freud, having discovered an important aspect of the principle underlying the achievement of a psychoanalytic cure, impressed his patients with his deep conviction concerning his newly found insight. It was the pressure of his personality, his charismatic certainty that, via suggestion, brought about a behavioral alteration which he took to be a manifestation of a structural change achieved via interpretation. The early cures were thus perfectly enacted illustrations of a correct principle. The real cures, however (the attainment of behavioral changes that were the manifestations of structural changes), began to be achieved only much later when, in addition to having understood the basic structural principle of the cure, Freud had also grasped the importance of the economic principle (repetition, working through). The derivation of the correct theory of the psychoanalytic cure of structural neuroses (making the unconscious conscious) from observations of situations that did not include working-through processes corresponds to some extent to the derivation of the correct mathematical formula about the acceleration

steps made on the path to the psychological equilibrium the analysand is at the point of establishing. True, action-thought is the nonverbal carrier of messages whose meaning should ultimately be interpreted to the patient. But in the main it consists of action patterns, creatively initiated by the patient on the basis of his actual talents, ambitions, and ideals, not meant to be given up, but to be further modified and perfected in order to provide him in the end with the reliable means of establishing the post-analytic maintenance of a stable psychoeconomic equilibrium in the narcissistic sector of his personality. Although, as I said, the meaning of such activities should be interpreted to an analysand, and their functions should be explained to him, the analysts must not expect them to be given up in response to insight. To speak in terms of the "appropriate metaphor" referred to earlier (p. 31), the analyst must not expect them to dissolve, in consequence of a correct interpretation, as if they were the symptoms of a psychoneurosis. They are not regressive steps, but constitute a not-quite-but-almost completed forward movement; they are partial achievements which neither will nor should be given up, except insofar as they are replaced by other activities the patient might recognize as more genuine realizations of his self when he reaches the permanent deployment of the narcissistic forces in the pursuit of his long-term goals.[7]

---

of freely falling bodies (cf. Koyré, 1968) from observations that do not take into account such factors as the shape of the falling body and air-resistance, and the influence of sea level and geographic latitude.

[7] For a specific example of creative activities undertaken by an analysand under the impact of the dissolution of a largely narcissistic transference focused upon the analysand's "compensatory structures," see Moser (1974). Moser wrote this moving presentation of the experience of an analysand before and after the termination of his analysis. I must stress that I

Let us now take up each of the three activities to which Mr. M. turned before the session in which he for the first time expressed his conviction that he was nearing the end of the therapeutic work.

Mr. M.'s buying an expensive violin while simultaneously abandoning his dominant interest in playing this instrument was an enactment of an important step away from preverbal emotionality (music), an enactment of his relinquishment of the attempt to gratify his exhibitionism through direct sensual appeal. As we will learn from the scrutiny of his other enactments, he was moving from music toward verbal thought, from (for him) cruder forms of exhibitionism to the (for him) more aim-inhibited attempt to bind his exhibitionistic excitement through writing. In interpersonal terms, the patient was turning from the mirroring mother to the idealized father.

Playing the violin, which Mr. M. had taken up during the analysis, was part of working through the maternal mirror transference of later childhood. As I mentioned earlier, like Miss F.'s dancing lessons (Kohut, 1971, p. 287), his violin playing was a form of psychoanalytic homework through which he tried to learn to ex-

---

cannot, on the basis of this nonscientific, belletristic autobiographical literary document, evaluate the analytic appropriateness (i.e., the nondefensive nature) of this particular attempt to channel newly liberated narcissistic energies into a specific creative pursuit. But I have observed a number of patients who began to devote themselves during the terminal phase to some deeply absorbing creative endeavor. The evaluation of the analysands' total behavior pattern—especially an attitude of quiet certitude—led me to the conclusion that the creative activity of such patients—and Mr. M. appears to belong to this group—is not a manifestation of a defensive maneuver meant to prevent the completion of the analytic process, but rather an indication that these analysands have at least preliminarily determined the mode by which the self will from now on attempt to ensure its cohesion, to maintain its balance, and to achieve its fulfillment.

press his exhibitionistic strivings in realistic yet gratifying ways. The patient's newly acquired structures, however, enabled him to enjoy the expression of his exhibitionistic strivings: in the fantasies that accompanied his playing he offered his grandiose self to the admiring view of multitudes which he experienced as "maternal," without being inhibited by the fear that he would suffer the crushing frustration of maternal disinterest, and without the even greater fear that he would become hypomanically overstimulated and thus experience the dissolution of his exhibiting self. The violin playing and the accompanying fantasies of admiring listening crowds were able to deal with the excess of his exhibitionistic needs that had become activated in the transference yet could not be fully absorbed within the psychoanalytic situation. The violin playing enabled the patient to persevere in the analytic work by lessening the psychic tensions to which the transference exposed him, and it made its own positive contribution to the goal of working through by creating provisional, temporarily useful structures in the sector of the creative employment of his narcissistic strivings.

His decision not to devote himself to the new, expensive violin after buying it was, however, the enactment of another important message concerning the stage of the psychological development he had reached. He was not unusually gifted in the musical sphere; the use of music as the vehicle for the transformation and expression of his grandiosity and exhibitionism was, in other words, not predominantly determined by innately present or early acquired specific abilities. It is explained by these facts: (a) the step from his unformed archaic exhibitionism to display via musical expression was smaller than the step from his unformed archaic exhibitionism to display via verbal expression would have been;[8] and (b) the step toward committing the major part of his grandiose-exhibitionistic strivings to creative aims in the sphere of verbal expression through writing—a step that would indeed ultimately engage his innate abilities and thus provide him with a secure balance in the narcissistic realm—required the prior firming of his ideals as a professional writer, or perhaps even as an artist in the sphere of words. This step, in other words, could be made only after the patient had successfully worked through the traumata he had suffered from the side of his idealized father, inasmuch as it was the father imago that functioned as the organizing ideal of the patient's creative activities in the sphere of words. Stated in still different terms, it was the ultimate achievement of Mr. M.'s analysis that it enabled him to bring about, in his creative work, the cooperation of the three major constituents of the narcissistic sector of his personality and thus the synthesis of his self. The analysis opened the road to an activity that permitted him joyful self-realization. His work as a writer enabled him to gratify his grandiose-exhibitionistic strivings to display himself to his mother, satisfy his need to merge with his idealized father, and enjoy the employment of the genuine talents he possessed.

[8] This statement appears self-evident at first sight, and, indeed, the comparative estimate of the two steps is doubtlessly accurate insofar as the great majority of people is concerned. It is more open to question, however, whether the same can also be said with regard to people who are musically very gifted and who, in addition, are trained in the subtleties and varieties of musical expression. There can be no doubt about the presence of highly developed nonverbal musical processes in the truly musical person, and about the decisive contribution musical activity can make to the maintenance of the narcissistic equilibrium of such a person. (For a detailed examination of these problems see Kohut and Levarie, 1950, pp. 73-74 and Kohut, 1957, pp. 395-397 and pp. 399-403.)

It might appear possible to formulate the result of Mr. M.'s analysis in dynamic-structural terms and in harmony with the principle of multiple functions (Waelder, 1936) as the smooth cooperation of the id (sexual love for the mother) and superego (identification with the rival-father) brought about by the ego (talent for the execution of certain ego functions). Object-instinctual strivings however, played, at best a subordinate role in Mr. M.'s psychological disturbance and in the process of its cure. It was a functioning self that had to be reassembled and strengthened through the analysis of its two major constituents. There is little question that this achievement led, secondarily, to an improved balance in the object-instinctual sector of Mr. M.'s personality, which, having previously been forced to work in the service of narcissistic goals, had not been free to pursue its own aims. But the improvement in this area was not the direct result of the analysis, must not be conceived as the result of the transformation of narcissistic into object-instinctual drives, i.e., as the shifting of drive aims from the self upon objects. The improvement in the object-instinctual realm must rather be regarded as a welcome bonus, obtained secondarily in consequence of the rehabilitation of the self. It was the more firmly and more satisfactorily cathected self, able to attain the joys of narcissistic fulfillment, that now, in addition to its commitment to these primary narcissistic aims, could also calmly and relaxedly become the center and coordinator of object-directed pursuits—freeing the latter from the burden of having to be undertaken in the service of defensively sought-after needs for the enhancement of self-esteem.

The second activity that ushered in Mr. M.'s decision to terminate constituted another way station in the curative process. During the third year of his analysis Mr. M. became intensely devoted to an adolescent boy whom he allowed to idealize him. Although this friendship began to develop before Mr. M. actually began to ponder whether he should terminate the analysis, it arose in a psychological setting and it accompanied working-through processes (related to the area of the idealized father imago) that were directly related to the fact that he subsequently began to consider termination. I am deriving my view that Mr. M.'s great interest in the fourteen-year-old boy should be seen in the context of the dynamics of termination predominantly from the scrutiny of the intrinsic psychological content re-enacted in the relationship. That, in addition, the most striking re-enactment with the boy—an episode I shall shortly describe and discuss—took place almost immediately preceding Mr. M.'s first saying he felt the analysis was nearing its end, supports the hypothesis of a causal relationship between the two events. Stated in different terms, the relation to the boy was the external enactment of the pivotal internal move (the separation from the father as an external self-object, the internalization of the idealized parent imago) that enabled the patient to announce his wish to leave the analysis and be on his own.

Mr. M. had befriended a family, which he visited often, mainly because he had developed a strong interest in the youngest son. He was fascinated both by the father's attitude toward the boy and by the boy's personality, which he saw as an outgrowth of the boy's relation to his father. According to the account Mr. M. gave to the analyst, the father respected his son, interacting with him on a mature level, seeing the son as independent from him, on the one hand, yet feeling close to him, not withdrawing from him, on the other. And the boy, at least in the patient's eyes, was proud, independent, self-assured — yet warmly respectful to his father.[9]

Mr. M.'s usual contact with the boy occurred within the setting of the boy's whole family, but he also took him out several times — to ball games and rock concerts, playing the role of older friend, older brother, or father. Although the boy was open in his admiration for the patient, and although Mr. M. was conscious of his own fascination with his relation to the boy, no gross homosexual feelings were aroused in Mr. M. There was one episode, however, while attending a ball game, in which Mr. M.'s feelings for the boy might easily be misinterpreted — especially by a psychoanalytically tutored mind. On the face of it, one might easily deduce from Mr. M.'s report of what he felt and how he behaved, that he thought — on the basis of projecting his own feelings, as the traditional analytic mode of thought would suggest — that the boy was in love with him. Here are the details. The patient had noticed a former girl friend in the crowd of spectators at the ball park, but he avoided her at first because he was worried lest his adolescent companion feel hurt if, by turning to the young woman, he ceased to give him his complete attention. After some hesitation, however, he greeted her after all, watching closely, and apparently anxiously, to see how the boy would react. (It will be recalled how Mr. M., as a child, had anxiously observed his mother's facial expression — see pp. 8-9.) When he realized that the boy was not in the least disturbed, the patient felt

[9] Within the framework of our inquiry it is, I believe, of no great importance to ascertain whether Mr. M.'s evaluation of this father-son couple was indeed correct or whether he emended it in accordance with the needs of the working-through processes in which he was engaged at that time.

unaccountably joyful. He knew that something important had happened in *him,* something he could not understand but wanted to figure out.

Analytic scrutiny did indeed lead to a satisfactory explanation of the significance the event had for him. What he experienced with regard to the boy was not the repetition of a passive erotic relation to his father, was not the re-enactment of an old jealousy vis-à-vis his father's new wife (in a reactivated negative Oedipus complex). It was a portrayal of the manifestations of a mature developmental level, with the boy as principal actor, and with himself playing both the supporting role and the audience. It was the portrayal of a psychological level the patient had not reached before, one he was in the process of reaching, one he wanted first to observe in a (discardable) self-object (a kind of twin—perhaps a figure derived from his relation with his brother) before he could allow himself to acknowledge that it was he and not the boy who was in fact now making this step. (Cf. the description of the working-through processes that take place on the basis of a twinship transference [Kohut, 1971, pp. 193-196].) In this episode with the boy he had indeed enacted a maturational step, one he had been unable to complete in his own adolescence. His participating experience did therefore not concern a triangular situation. The mise-en-scène he had arranged concerned the attainment of independence from the idealized father, the attainment of psychological self-sufficiency through transmuting internalization of the functions of the idealized father. And he experienced a deep sense of joy—not sensual pleasure!—as the accompaniment of his awareness that he had achieved a decisive firming of his self.

I will add here that I do not use the terms joy and pleasure at random. Joy is experienced as referring to a more encompassing emotion such as, for example, the emotion evoked by success, whereas pleasure, however intense it may be, refers to a delimited experience such as, for example, sensual satisfaction. From the point of view of depth psychology, we can say, moreover, that the experience of joy has a genetic root different from that of the experience of pleasure; that each of these modes of affect has its own developmental line and that joy is not sublimated pleasure. Joy relates to experiences of the total self whereas pleasure (despite the frequently occurring participation of the total self, which then provides an admixture of joy) relates to experiences of parts and constituents of the self. There are, in other words, archaic forms of joy relating to archaic developmental stages of the whole self just as there are archaic stages in the development of the experience of parts and constituents of the self. And one may speak of sublimated joy, just as one speaks of sublimated pleasure.

The third activity Mr. M. undertook was his founding of a writing school. The idea of such an enterprise did not come to him for the first time at this point; he had spoken of it early in the analysis. But that it now reoccurred with increased vigor was a manifestation of his determination to undertake in earnest the last of the steps that led to the restoration of his self. The inner conviction that he would soon complete this task was therefore the logical precursor to his subsequent feeling that he was ready for termination. That the idea came to him with the sense of being an inspiration, i.e., that he woke up from his sleep one night with this idea reborn as an effec-

tive motivating force impelling him toward action, can, I
believe, be taken as a sign that he was mobilizing all his
forces in order to pursue a difficult psychological task.[10]

Before examining the nature of the task to which
Mr. M. responded by reviving his plan to found a writing
school, let us look at the details of his reactions to the
enterprise he wanted to undertake. When he first began
to focus on the idea, he worried that his plan would
come to naught, that it would turn out to have been no
more than a content of his mind, a thought; that he
would lose interest in it and would not put it into action.
This worry is significant. It expressed his dimly recognized fear that something in his psychological make-up
was still missing, that insight alone would not cure this
defect, that a void would still have to be filled—in psychoanalytic terms, that new structure would yet have
to be formed. When patients express the fear that the
analytic work will result in failure, when, in particular,
despite fully worked-through insight into all causes of
some inhibition (i.e., despite full understanding of possibly relevant structural conflicts) they feel unable to
change their behavior, unable to become constructively
active, the analyst should consider not only the effect of
unconscious guilt feelings (a negative therapeutic reaction), but also, and foremost, the presence of a persistent

[10] In the course of an investigation (not yet published) of certain heroic
figures—lone resisters to the Nazi regime—and of others who are facing extremely difficult and/or dangerous tasks, I found that prophetic dreams and
even hallucinatory experiences during waking hours could occur in individuals who are clearly not psychotic. I concluded that the ability to create, in ex-
treme situations, the fantasy of being supported by a godlike omnipotent
figure should be evaluated as belonging to the assets of a healthy psychological organization. (Cf. the remarks about "transference of creativity" in
Kohut, 1971, pp. 316-317; see also Miller, 1962.)

structural defect—often within the realm of an unrecognized disturbance of the self.

Mr. M., as he had done through his enactment with his adolescent alter ego in the ball park, was once again demonstrating that the healing of the structural defect would take place—actually it had already taken place, but had yet to be consolidated—within the framework of a relation between a father and his son. And again he took the role of the father. But it was not the idealized aspect of the father figure that he offered to the son. This time he was a teacher and, as such, he was part of an institution (a school), i.e., of an external structure designed to be internalized by the son (the students, the pupils). And it was, of course, also of specific significance that the subject matter to be taught (the specific structure whose internalization Mr. M. promoted by undertaking the project) concerned the use of language, of words. The psychological structure that the students had to acquire was designed to enable them to transmute formless imagery into well-defined words. Accurately used language became the structure that performed the psychoeconomic function of breaking down the students' "ideas into manageable portions" as a way station to the attainment of the school's ultimate goal: to enable the students to become creative writers. Expressed in metapsychological terms, the structure Mr. M. offered to his alter egos (taught his students) were the aim-inhibiting, discharge-delaying, substitution-providing verbal patterns that transform primary-process imagery into secondary-process verbal ideation. But he gave them even more. What Mr. M. did not tell the analyst, when he first sketched out his teaching plans and later described his actual teaching, but what the analyst could clearly infer by reading between the lines of Mr. M.'s excited reports about his school, was the inspiration his enthusiasm for the work provided for his students. In founding the school and in being its inspiring teacher, he demonstrated that he realized not only that a defect existed in an important sector of his own psyche — by proxy, that the students had to acquire a new skill — but also that the filling in of this void by new structure (and the functional maintenance of this new structure) depended on the presence of an inspiring paternal ideal. The pupils thus stood not only for M. the child who despite his talents had remained clumsy with words (Mr. M.'s mild thought disorder), they also stood for M. the adolescent whose goal-setting ideals had not yet been laid down fully into the structure of the self and who still needed to internalize an idealized father-teacher. It was only the organizing effect of his goal-setting ideals that, in combination with his specific talents and skills, could provide Mr. M. with what he himself described as a "constant flow of energy" instead of the former "bursts which were always disorganizing," of which he had been complaining to the analyst.

Outline of the Functional Rehabilitation of the Self through Psychoanalysis

I presented the foregoing clinical data in order to support my claim that an analysis can be considered as having in essence been completed even though not all structural defects have been mobilized, worked through, and filled in through transmuting internalization. A genuine termination, it may be added here, is not brought about by external manipulation. Like the transference, it is predetermined; correct psychoanalytic technique can do no more than allow it to evolve.

Mr. M.'s preanalytic personality was characterized by these important features: (1) he was suffering from defects in various areas of his nuclear self; (2) he had developed defensive structures designed to cover over the defects in his grandiose self; and (3) he had developed compensatory structures designed to increase the activity of the healthy parts of the nuclear self and to isolate and bypass the defective ones.

The damage to his nuclear self was widespread. It affected all three of the major constituents of this structure, namely, the two polar areas—the grandiose-exhibitionistic self and the idealized parent imago—and the intermediate area—the executive functions (talents, skills) needed for the realization of the patterns of the basic ambitions and basic ideals that were laid down in the two polar areas. Damage was, however, neither equally severe nor similarly distributed in each of these three constituents of the self. In the area of the grandiose-exhibitionistic self the defect was most severe and involved the deepest layers; in the area of the idealized parent imago the damage was only moderately severe and involved only the more superficial layers; and in the area of the talents and skills that the self needed in order to express its patterns, the damage seemed to be slight and circumscribed. Stated more loosely, we might say that Mr. M.'s preanalytic personality showed a serious disturbance of his self-esteem, a moderate disturbance of his guiding ideals, and a mild, circumscribed flaw in his ideational processes.

Mr. M.'s defensive structures, having undoubtedly arisen early in life, seemed to constitute a firmly entrenched part of his personality. These structures (and

the ideational and behavioral manifestations that emanated from them) were not discussed extensively; they did
not warrant our primary attention because they were not
involved to any appreciable extent in the nexus of psychological events relating to the patient's wish to terminate the analysis and, what on the whole may be taken
as a good prognostic sign, they did not become significantly intensified during the termination period. True,
they were clearly in evidence at the beginning of the treatment; and they were reactivated repeatedly in the working-through process while certain aspects of the primary
defect of the self became involved in the transference.
They receded into the background, however, and finally
almost disappeared from sight when the transference
shifted from the mirroring mother to the idealized father
—when the emphasis of working through no longer concerned exhibitionistic needs and their frustration but the
internalization of ideals and the concomitant rehabilitation of the compensatory structures.

A genetic-dynamic relation existed between the layer
of Mr. M.'s low self-esteem that was the result of his
mother's defective empathy for him and the emergence of
sadistic fantasies about women. Although these fantasies
occasionally entered directly into the transference, they
soon receded into the background as the focus of the
analysis shifted to the paternal ideal, and they were not
significantly reactivated during the termination phase.

Why did the defensive structures play a comparatively minor role in Mr. M.'s personality and why were they
therefore dealt with comparatively easily as the initial
mirror transference was worked through? And why did
the most clearly defined defensive configurations, Mr.
M.'s sadism toward women, express themselves mainly

through fantasies rather than being lived out? A reply to these specific questions requires an examination of the related general problem why some people act out while others create endopsychic changes. In the area of our main interest, it requires a discussion of the difference between *narcissistic personality disorders* and *narcissistic behavior disorders*. This task—including the confrontation of the specific question why Mr. M.'s disturbance belonged more into the former than into the latter category—will be undertaken later (see pp. 193-198). Here I shall only say that, despite its shortcomings, Mr. M.'s relation with his father (and thus the compensatory structures of his personality that had arisen from the matrix of this relation) had been at least partially successful in providing him with narcissistic sustenance. The least one can say is that the relation to the idealized father must have provided him with the hope that he might yet be able to find reliable ways of gaining narcissistic satisfactions even though the mother imago could not be relied upon to respond with self-confirming joy to his narcissistic display.

Although the cure of Mr. M.'s narcissistic personality disturbance was not brought about exclusively, or even predominantly, through the healing of the primary structural defect in his self (after the analysis of the defensive structures), during the early part of the analysis the analytic work had focused intensively on this sector of the patient's personality. And during this phase Mr. M. came to understand increasingly, for example, that his sadistic fantasies served defensive purposes. He came to recognize that these were not the expressions of autonomous instinctual strivings, but were mobilized in reaction to narcissistic injuries he felt he had suffered—that they appeared in the transference in response to some activity of the analyst (ill-timed or inaccurate interpretations, for example) that he experienced as unempathic. The sadistic fantasies were, on the one hand, an expression of his narcissistic rage, and, on the other, they protected him against the painful awareness of depression and low self-esteem. Some analytic gains in the area of Mr. M.'s primary defect were therefore made: the working-through processes of this phase of the analysis (a primary mirror transference) led to internalizations, i.e., to the acquisition of a modicum of solid, self-generated self-acceptance and self-esteem. Still, the investigation of this sector of Mr. M.'s personality was far from complete — the deeper layers of his defective (depressive, lethargic, "dead") self (the self of his stay in the orphanage) were never exposed to full view in the transference. And I believe it is proper to draw the conclusion that the analytic work done in this sector could not account for the vastly improved state of psychological well-being Mr. M. finally reached through the analysis, would not justify the acceptance by the analyst that his wish to terminate the treatment was legitimate. The results achieved in the area of Mr. M.'s defensive structures and of the primary defect of his self could not, in other words, have led to his recognition that a state of more or less reliable inner balance was in the offing — a recognition on which in actuality his wish to terminate was based. And the spuriousness of a decision to terminate treatment under these conditions would have become evident because the defensive activities — sadistic fantasies about women — would have returned with full force as soon as the patient realized that the end of the analysis was in sight and that the transference relation (a mirror transference) was to be relinquished.

The fact, it may be added, that in Mr. M.'s case the decisive improvement took place in the compensatory structures, and not in the area of the grandiose-exhibitionistic self, establishes the principle that the valid termination of an analysis *may* be reached in this way. It surely goes without saying that in many other instances the decisive improvement concerns the defects in the fountainhead of self-expression — the nuclear grandiose-exhibitionistic self.

In Mr. M.'s case, however, the analysis led to the exclusion of the defective deepest layers of the personality from the organization of the grandiose-exhibitionistic self, while it enabled the strivings of the now strengthened and broadened healthy layers of the grandiose-exhibitionistic self to express themselves through creatively elaborated activities. These activities could now be carried out effectively because the analysis had established a more firmly functioning structure of idealized goals, which served as organizers for the archaic ambitions of the revitalized grandiose self. And the analysis had also led to the strengthening and refinement of the already existing executive apparatus. The pressure of exhibitionism and ambitions, on the one hand, and guidance of ideals of perfection, on the other, would now, it may be hoped, harness pre-existing talents, and his correlated partially developed skills, in the service of long-term realistic goals and thus set into motion and maintain an ongoing process of functional improvement in skill and in performance.

Translating this summary into a general statement, we can say, then, that the psychoanalytic treatment of a case of narcissistic personality disorder has progressed to the point of its intrinsically determined termination (has brought about the cure of the disorder) when it has been

able to establish one sector within the realm of the self
through which an uninterrupted flow of the narcissistic
strivings can proceed toward creative expression — however limited the social impact of the achievements of the
personality might be and however insignificant the individual's creative activity might appear to others. Such a
sector includes always a central pattern of exhibitionism
and grandiose ambitions, a set of firmly internalized
ideals of perfection, and a correlated system of talents
and skills, which mediate between exhibitionism, ambitions, and grandiosity, on the one hand, and ideals of
perfection, on the other. Returning to our clinical example, and stating the formulation of psychological
health in the realm of narcissism in the simplest terms, we
might say that a genuine termination stage was reached
when Mr. M. abandoned the fruitless attempt to
strengthen his rejected and enfeebled self with the aid of
fantasies of sadistically enforced acclaim and turned to
the successful attempt to provide the healthy sector of his
self with patterns for creative expression.

Further Clinical Illustrations

With the end of my discussion of the genetic-dynamic constellations that emerged in Mr. M.'s analysis in relation to his decision to terminate the treatment, I am ap-
proaching the end of the first part of this presentation, in
which it was my aim to demonstrate the special position
of the compensatory structures in the personality and
thus to furnish a concrete clinical basis for the more abstract general considerations in some of the ensuing chap-
ters. Let me round out this part of my work by describing

briefly two other patients whose psychodynamics resemble those of Mr. M.

The first concerns the analysis of Mr. U., a single man in his early fifties, a potentially brilliant but in fact comparatively unsuccessful associate professor of mathematics at a small college. The patient's chief symptom, a fetishistic perversion, had not yielded to the protracted efforts of two previous analysts who, according to the analysand, appeared to have focused their attention on his oedipal anxieties and, following the classical formulation, seemed to have interpreted the significance of the fetish on the basis of a (split in the ego) denial (Freud, 1940, p. 277), motivated by castration anxiety, that the woman (the mother) was not equipped with a penis (Freud, 1927a, pp. 156-157). In his analysis with me, however, the associative material concerning the fetish and its significance ordered itself in a different fashion. The patient's fetishistic preoccupations had arisen in reaction to a primary structural defect in his grandiose self due to faulty mirroring by his oddly unempathic, unpredictable, emotionally shallow mother. As could be reconstructed in the transference, and from the scrutiny of her later behavior (toward her grandchildren, the children of the patient's younger brother), the mother had exposed the patient to intolerably intense and sudden swings in his nuclear self-esteem. On innumerable occasions she appeared to have been totally absorbed in the child—overcaressing him, completely in tune with every nuance of his needs and wishes—only to withdraw from him suddenly, either by turning her attention totally to other interests or by grossly and grotesquely misunderstanding his needs and wishes.

From the traumatic unpredictability of his mother

he had retreated early to the soothing touch of certain tissues (such as nylon stockings, nylon underwear) which were readily available in his childhood home. They were reliable, and they constituted a distillate of maternal goodness and response. The transference material also alluded to the existence of earlier (prefetishistic) substitutes for the unreliable self-object: he used to simultaneously touch certain soft self-object surrogates (the silky rim of a blanket) and stroke his own skin (the lobe of his ear) and hair, thus creating a psychological situation of merger with a *nonhuman* self-object that he totally controlled, and thereby depriving himself of the opportunity to experience the structure-building optimal failures of a *human* self-object.

The crucial work in the analysis was not done with regard to the substitute for the maternal self-object, the fetish, however—it concerned the idealized imago, the father. Already in early childhood the patient had tried to secure his narcissistic balance by turning from the attempt to obtain confirmation of his self with the aid of his mother's unreliable empathy to the attempt to merge with his idealized father who (similar to Mr. M.'s father) was excellent with numbers (he was also a fine chess player) and was interested in abstract logic. But Mr. U.'s father, like Mr. M.'s, could not respond appropriately to his son's needs. He was a self-absorbed, vain man, and he rebuffed his son's attempt to be close to him, depriving him of the needed merger with the idealized self-object and, hence, of the opportunity for gradually recognizing the self-object's shortcomings. The patient had therefore remained fixated on two sets of opposite responses to ideals—responses he repeated again and again as a part of the secondary idealizing transference which was in effect during the main part of the analysis. He either felt depressed and hopeless vis-à-vis an unreachable ideal, or he felt that the ideal was worthless and that he, in grandiose arrogance, was vastly superior to it. These swings in Mr. U.'s self-esteem were an outgrowth of his not having achieved the gradual and thus secure internalization of the idealized parent imago. The child's failure to form reliable ideals, which would have regulated his self-esteem, had this further result: because of his need to raise his self-esteem, his fixation on the mother-fetish became intensified. The transference itself, however, never reinstated the earliest preoccupations with soothing self-objects for sufficiently long periods; a thorough working through of the structural defects in the self resulting from the deprivations from the mother's side was therefore not achieved. But despite this, the patient made a satisfactory recovery: he lost interest in the fetish, and, after the disappointments with regard to the idealized father's responses to him had been worked through for a number of years, he was able to devote himself intensely (and more successfully than before) to his professional activities, which now provided him with a reliably organized framework for the experience of the joys of self-expression. I should add here that Mr. U.'s interest in the fetish was not dissolved by insight—the fetish became less important. This shift occurred not only in consequence of his improved ability to obtain a sense of heightened self-esteem from the responses of empathic women, but also and primarily because his internalized ideals were strengthened and he could thus obtain greater joy in creative self-expression via his professional work.

In behavioral terms, Mr. U.'s fetishistic preoccupation had receded at the time of termination to the point of playing a much less significant role in his life—the fetish had lost its magic, as the patient expressed it—but it had not disappeared completely. I cannot prove it, of course, but I surmise that the success of the analysis would have been much greater had the patient not already been in his fifties when I began to treat him.[11]

The second clinical illustration demonstrating the importance of the rehabilitation of the compensatory structures in the course of therapy concerns the analysis of Miss V., a forty-two-year-old single woman, a talented but unproductive artist, who had sought analysis because of recurrent episodes of fairly severe but nonpsychotic, empty depression. Miss V.'s treatment was terminated more than ten years ago when I had barely begun to recognize that patients with narcissistic personality disorders developed a number of distinct, characteristic transferences and were thus analyzable. I have in recent years, after gathering a considerable amount of clinical experience in this area, analyzed two other patients suffering from recurrent episodes of nonpsychotic, empty depression—i.e., depressive episodes in which guilt feelings and/or self-accusations played no significant role— suffered by women whose personality make-up was not unlike Miss V.'s. The genesis of the disturbance of these two patients also appeared to be more or less similar. I cannot speak with absolute certainty, however, with regard to the genetic factors because the treatment did not penetrate deeply enough to allow the reliable reconstruction of the relevant constellations in childhood.

---

[11] Addendum: While preparing the final version of this manuscript, I accidentally received some indirect information that leads me to believe—although I cannot be certain—that even my guardedly hopeful feelings concerning the outcome of Mr. U.'s analysis may have been too optimistic.

The primary defect in Miss V.'s personality structure — dynamically related to the periods of protracted enfeeblement of her self when she was lethargic, unproductive, indeed felt lifeless — referred genetically to the interplay with her mother in childhood. Her mother who, like the patient, was subject to periodic depressions, was emotionally shallow and unpredictable; in addition to the periodic affective disorder from which she suffered increasingly throughout her life, schizoid features — already present during the patient's childhood — were unmistakeable. To the amusement, and sometimes the annoyance, of those around her, she was prone to malapropisms; these were undoubtedly manifestations of a mild "disorder of thinking and feeling in a setting of clear consciousness" (Bleuler, 1911). The patient's mother was still living during Miss V.'s analysis; there was a good deal of interaction between the two (see pp. 7-8 above), and an assessment of the mother's personality, suggesting borderline schizophrenia, could therefore be made.[12]

[12] The recognition of serious (but latent and denied) parental psychopathology requires the analyst's alertness to small clues. The presence of a crucially important severe disturbance of the mother of one of the other patients, for example, whose psychological make-up was similar to Miss V.'s, was ascertained in consequence of the analyst's alertness to a seemingly unimportant feature of the mother's behavior, a peculiar kind of kiss, which the patient mentioned only in passing. The patient's reaction to these kisses, however — "creepy kisses" as she called them — was the first indication of her (denied) awareness of her mother's pervasive emotional shallowness. These kisses were manifestations of the mother's pseudoemotionality, i.e., in structural terms, they were not the expression of deeply anchored emotions, but were initiated by a psychic surface that was not in contact with an active nuclear self. (Cf. Freud's theory of schizophrenic neologisms, 1915.) The scrutiny of inappropriate behavior and, especially of malapropisms such as those of Miss V.'s mother, may at times provide the first clue that a patient's seemingly psychologically healthy parent is in fact seriously disturbed. In the case of Mr. D., for example (see Kohut, 1971, p. 149, p. 257), the first clues to the mother's serious personality disturbance came through the examina-

Whatever the exact diagnostic category may have been into which her mother's disturbance fell, it is clear that as a small child the patient had been exposed to traumatic disappointments from the side of her mother, whose mirroring responses had not only been deficient much of the time (either altogether absent or flat), but also frequently defective (bizarre and capricious) because they were motivated by the mother's misperception of the child's needs or by the mother's own requirements, which were unintelligible to the child.

In truth, the term "unintelligible" covers only part of the pathogenic influence of the maternal demands. Although when Miss V. was depressed she was not oppressed by guilt feelings that had a specific, verbalizable content, the depressions triggered in the transference allowed the reconstruction that as a very small child she must have experienced her total world as making demands on her which she could not fulfill. Were I formulating my interpretation to her today, I would say that positive mirroring responses from the environment would be forthcoming only if she could first relieve her mother's

---

tion of two of the patient's memories about her concerning items which at first appeared to be quite innocuous. He talked about the fact that his mother played a good deal of bridge and made remarks that made everyone laugh. The investigation of the bridge-playing led to the recognition that the mother was totally walled-off emotionally from her family, including the patient. The cards were indeed a wall behind which she was retreating. And the investigation of her so-called "cute" remarks led to the recognition that the mother must have suffered from a thought disorder. Mr. D. mentioned one day, seemingly in passing, that during a high school game in which the patient participated his mother had expressed her delighted amazement at the "coincidence" that the players of each of the teams happened to be dressed alike. It was through the pursuit of the implications of this story — against Mr. D.'s strong resistance, it may be added — that the presence of the patient's mother's serious chronic personality disturbance was first suspected in the analysis.

depression. Her depressions were therefore partly the re-enactment of her deep sense of failure vis-à-vis this de-mand from her depressed mother. Or, seen from a slight-ly different viewpoint, she was convinced that the mater-nal self-object would not provide her with self-esteem-enhancing acceptance and approval unless she, the small child, could first fulfill the mother's similar needs.

The propensity toward the periodic enfeeblement of Miss V.'s self was thus established in early childhood in the pathogenic matrix of her relation to the mirroring mother. Miss V. had, however, been a vigorous and well-endowed child who did not give up the struggle for emo-tional survival. Trying to extricate herself from the pathogenic relation with her mother, she had attached herself with great intensity to her father, a successful manufacturer with frustrated artistic talents and am-bitions who, on the whole, responded to his daughter's needs. Her relation with the father thus became the matrix from which she developed those interests and talents — in the terms of clinical theory: those compensa-tory structures — which ultimately led to her career. And from it also grew the idealized aims that stimulated the creative potential of her self. The relation to her idealized father, in other words, provided her with the outlines of an internalized structure — a paternal ideal — which was a potential source of sustenance for her self. In creating works of art she was not trying to live out an oedipal fantasy (giving babies to her father) as I had thought at first. And her lack of productivity was not due to guilt (about an incestuous wish) as I had originally assumed. Her artistic activities were an attempt to live up to a pa-ternal ideal of perfection; and her preanalytic failure in this endeavor was not owing to any paralyzing structural

conflicts; it occurred because her ideals had been insufficiently internalized and consolidated. The transference
reactivated, therefore, not oedipal psychopathology but
a disturbance of the self. And, furthermore, during the
most important phases of the analysis the focus of working through was not directed, as one might expect, at the
primary structural defect of her self (psychopathology
correlated to the mother's flawed responsiveness to the
child), but, during a secondary idealizing transference, at
the insufficiently established compensatory structures
(psychopathology correlated to the father's failures). And
the partial success of the analysis—her depressive
reactions did not disappear altogether, but they became
less severe and were of much shorter duration—was
therefore due not to a healing of the primary defect in the
self but, as I now understand in retrospect, to the
rehabilitation of the compensatory structures. Specifically, the crucial transference revivals concerned events in
childhood when the father himself appeared to be so
severely disappointed by his wife's frustrating emotional
flatness and lack of empathy that he, too, seems to have
become temporarily depressed and thus emotionally
unavailable to his daughter. I am not certain whether he
was occasionally depressed during the patient's childhood; from the patient's transference reactions, however,
we could reconstruct that he retreated, principally by
staying away from home (fleeing from the mother to his
work or to playing golf with his friends), at the very time
his daughter needed him most, when the mother was
depressed and the daughter expected her idealized and
admired father to be a bulwark against the pull of lethargy that emanated from the mother and threatened to en-
gulf the child's personality.

CHAPTER TWO
Does Psychoanalysis Need a Psychology of the Self?

On Scientific Objectivity

In the preceding chapter I presented clinical material in support of the thesis that we may consider an analysis completed when by achieving success in the area of compensatory structures it has established a functioning self—a psychological sector in which ambitions, skills, and ideals form an unbroken continuum that permits joyful creative activity. The definition of psychoanalytic cure implied by the foregoing statement must now be evaluated against the background of the definitions that have been traditionally accepted by psychoanalysts.

Before going into details, let me emphasize that I am focusing here on a principle: I am *not* concerned with issues evoked by such terms as analytic wisdom, reasoned expediency, and the like, even though I fully recognize their clinical relevance and that I would probably avoid a number of difficulties if I addressed myself primarily to them, inasmuch as no analyst will make the unrealistic claim that he has ever analyzed a person completely in all sectors of his personality or that he should even attempt to achieve such perfection. I *am* concerned here with the problem raised by the fact that I am speaking of a valid termination of an analysis that has—in terms of structures—*not* dealt with all the layers of the essential pathology of the analysand, that has—in terms of cognition—*not* led to the undoing of all infantile amnesias, to the expansion of knowledge concerning all those events of childhood that are genetically and dynamically related to the psychopathology from which the patient suffers.

Freud was, of course, convinced of the fact that psychoanalysis had a wholesome effect on the analysand, that it constituted a process whose momentum should be maintained, and that it should be carried forward as far as possible. But while he provided us with the outline of the essentials of this process, which, put briefly, can be defined either, in terms of cognition, as making the unconscious conscious, or, in terms of structures, as extending the domain of the ego, he never elaborated—at least not in scientific seriousness, i.e., in theoretical terms—his conviction of the wholesome effect of analysis in the form of the claim that psychoanalysis cures psychological illnesses, that it establishes mental health. Freud's values were not primarily health values. He believed in the intrinsic desirability of knowing as much as possible: he was—through the convergence and mutual reinforcement of the dominant world view of his time and some personal preferences (no doubt determined by experiences in early life) which transformed that scientific world view into his personal categorical imperative, his personal religion—intransigently committed to the task of knowing the truth, facing the truth, seeing reality clearly.

One of the most moving anecdotes about Freud's life concerns this deeply anchored aspect of his personality. When he learned that there had been some doubt whether he should be told he was suffering from a malignancy, he responded with the expression of profoundly felt anger. What right does anyone have to keep this knowledge from me? he asked, discounting the possibility that kindness and concern and not patronizing arrogance might have been responsible for the brief moment of doubt whether he should be told the ominous truth (cf. Jones, 1957, p. 93).

Freud's writings offer a plethora of evidence (1927b; 1933, Chapter 25) to demonstrate that his supreme value was the value of courageous realism, of bravely facing the truth. His anger at the mere fact that to keep an important truth from him had even been considered could of course be interpreted in a variety of ways. Many analytically trained observers would, I believe, be inclined to suspect that the anger he expressed was only a substitute for the anger he felt about the fact that he was afflicted with a malignancy and was facing death—that he could now express this anger because he could justify it as a reaction to the possibility that the truth might have been withheld from him. I am strongly inclined to offer a different explanation. I believe the core of Freud's self was related more to the function of perceiving and thinking and knowing than to physical survival and that his nuclear self was threatened more by the danger that knowledge was withheld from him than by the danger of physical destruction.

Freud's commitment to truth is admirable and, viewed in isolation, beyond debate. In addition, it has become, via our identification with him, the leading value of analysts. The influence exerted by the primacy of knowledge-expansion values on the theories and the therapeutic outlook of psychoanalysis forces us, however, despite our reluctance to do so, to re-examine it, to question its formidable position of power over our thinking, because it has come to be a limiting factor as we are trying to grasp forms of psychopathology and modes of cure that are not encompassed when seen from the classical point of view.

Fascinating though the task might be—and potentially valuable if properly handled, *sine ira et studio*—I am setting aside the investigation of the personal factor, particularly the search for any genetic data that would explain why Freud's intense commitment to the confrontation of the unmitigated truth, however painful it might be, became such a powerful attribute of his personality. Instead, I shall focus on the examination of Freud's position as a representative of nineteenth-century science—specifically with regard to the influence his "Scientific World View" (1933) exerted on the form, content, and scope of his theories.

Freud gave this significant response to Ludwig Binswanger's observation that his (Freud's) personality was characterized by an enormous will to power: "I do not trust myself to contradict you in regard to the will to power—but I am not aware of it. I have long surmised that not only the repressed content of the psyche, but also the innermost core of our ego is unconscious, though not incapable of consciousness. I infer this from the fact that consciousness is after all only a sensory organ, directed toward the outside world, so that it is always attached to a part of the ego [in modern terminology: the self] which is itself unperceived" (Binswanger, 1957 p. 44).

I consider this statement—the statement of a man who had investigated his own inner life, including the countertransferences that can becloud or distort the vision of the psychological observer, more broadly and profoundly than any man had ever done before—the perfect expression of the basic attitude of the scientist of his day. It is the statement of the man of the Renaissance, of the era of Enlightenment, of nineteenth-century science. It is the statement of the man who has become all vision and vision-explaining thought. It is the statement of the man of clear-eyed empirical observation whose mental processes are engaged in the service of his proud realism. It is a statement that is in fully harmony with the fact that one aspect of the basic stance of the classical nineteenth-century scientist was the clear distinction between observer and observed, or, to put my meaning more tersely, it is the expression in theoretical terms of the ideal of scientific objectivity.

Evaluated from this point of view, Freud took the ultimate step that could still be taken by "objective" science: he investigated the inner life of man, including—and especially—his own. But—and here lies the crucial issue—he gazed at man's inner life with the objectivity of an external observer, i.e., from the viewpoint that the scientist of his day had perfected vis-à-vis man's external surroundings, in the biological sciences and, above all, in physics.

The adoption of this basic stance had a profound influence on the formation of the theoretical framework of psychoanalysis. Just as the great physicists and biologists of his day observed the physical and biological field, abstracted and generalized their observations, and formulated the nexus of their data in terms of the interaction of mechanical and chemical forces, so did Freud, by devising the conceptual framework of a mental apparatus fueled by drives—i.e., by forces striving for expression, hampered by counterforces, and in conflict with each other—create the magnificent explanatory edifice of psychoanalytic metapsychology. It was, *and is,* an explanatory framework that allows for expansion and change (from topographic to structural theory; from libido theory to ego psychology). And it is a framework particularly attuned to the explanation of certain phenomena that presented themselves with great frequency to the observer at the turn of the century: the structural neuroses—par excellence, hysteria.

But, however pertinent Freud's theoretical conceptualizations remain with regard to the structural neuroses and to other similarly constructed psychological phenomena, they are not, as the present work will attempt to demonstrate, sufficiently relevant with regard to the disorders of the self and other psychological phenomena that lie within the domain of self psychology—phenomena that require for their observation and explanation a more broadly based scientific objectivity than that of the nineteenth-century scientist—an objectivity that includes the introspective-empathic observation and theoretical conceptualization of the participating self.

Although I am fascinated to see that modern physics, too, has moved from the observation of the world in terms of large masses and their interaction to the observation of particles, and from a sharp separation between the observer and the observed to a stance that considers the observer and the observed as a unit which is, in principle, in certain respects not divisible (cf. p. 31n. of the present work), I know too little about modern physics to allow myself to be supported by this analogy. But I believe I can supply sufficient evidence within the psychological field — I will begin my task by turning to a re-evaluation of drive concept and drive theory — to affirm the relevance of the psychology of the self.

Drive Theory and the Psychology of the Self

I shall begin by comparing my outlook with that of Franz Alexander who more clearly and unambiguously perhaps than any other analyst in recent times subscribed to the classical drive theory. He saw the human mind as a field in which large-scale forces strove in various specific directions (cf., for example, his vector theory [1935]), and he explained psychopathology as the result of conflict between drives and of conflicts concerning drives and drive demands. In all these contexts he was especially interested in the vicissitudes of the oral drive and (cf. his paper of 1956) stressed the point that dyadic-preoedipal transference attitudes, especially the analysand's oral clinging to the analyst, were in many instances regressive evasions designed by the patient to avoid facing the emotional hardships and anxieties of the central transference, which was triadic-oedipal. Taken as a theoretical proposition, the positive aspect of Alexander's assertion is unassailable — his formulation claims with regard to the significance of regressive orality what the classical formulation (cf. Freud, 1909, p. 155; 1913a, p. 317; 1917b, pp. 343-344; 1926, pp. 113-116) stated with regard to the significance of regressive anality in obsessive-compulsive neurosis. Alexander's clinical emphasis, however, was in error because his understanding of a large number of the phenomena he attempted to explain within the confines of the conceptual framework of drive psychology and the

structural model of the mind was insufficient. Most instances of the oral-clinging behavior that Alexander rejected as infantile attitudes preconsciously or consciously
assumed by the patient in order to escape confrontation
with the oedipal rival and fear of his revenge cannot in
fact be adequately described within the conceptual
framework of the structural model of the mind and in the
terminology of drive psychology. In most instances—cer-
tainly in the cases I refer to as narcissistic personality disorders—this behavior is not a manifestation of an attitude of pretended infantilism but the expression of the
needs of an archaic state; it becomes comprehensible
when seen, within the conceptual framework of a psychology of the self, as a manifestation of archaic narcissism—
in particular, as the expression of narcissistic transference
needs. Even where Alexander concedes that a patient's
intense attachment to the analyst may not be primarily
defensive, he explains it as a drive fixation on oral aims
and a developmental arrest of the ego, with the implicit
and explicit demand upon the patient that these drive-
aims be suppressed and relinquished as quickly and completely as possible, and with the exhortation that the patient grow up.

The attempt to explain the transference manifestations activated in the analysis of narcissistic personality
disorders with the aid of drive psychology and of the conceptual framework of the structural model of the mind—
defenses vs. drives, ego vs. id; drive maturation vs. drive
regression (or drive fixation); ego development vs. ego regression (or developmental arrest)—can be compared to
the attempt to explain, within the framework of aes-
thetics, the beauty or ugliness of a painting by examining
the types and distribution of the pigments used by the

painter; or, within the framework of literary criticism, to the attempt to explain the success or failure of a novel by determining the vocabulary or sentence structure employed by the author. To be sure, there are instances in which such examinations will lead us to important discoveries; but the focus of the sophisticated art critic will generally be directed upon more complex aspects of the work of art than on the simple units I mentioned. To approach the disorders of the self via classical metapsychology can, for the medically trained reader, be most tellingly compared to the attempt to explain the complexities of human physiology in health and disease within the framework of inorganic chemistry. To be sure, a few rare instances exist (hypothyroidism due to iodine deficiency, for example) whose etiology and treatment can be formulated in terms of inorganic chemistry — but even in these conditions such an approach does not do justice to the complexity of the biochemical disturbance. And the same considerations may also apply in exceptional instances of disturbances of the self. Even though I believe that the psychopathology of diffusely disturbed "oral-dependent" personalities is, in the great majority of cases, not encompassed by Alexander's formulation of a sequence of oedipal fears and defensive orality — not even when we refine this formulation with the conceptual armamentarium of the most advanced insights of modern ego psychology — but that only the application of the psychology of the self will give us a satisfactory conceptual framework, exceptional cases of this type may well exist that can be adequately conceptualized in these classical terms. There are instances, in other words, where the therapeutic leverage is indeed appropriately and successfully applied at the point of the Oedipus complex and where the remainder of the psychopathology, however widespread it may be, will yield in consequence of the solution of the centrally treated nuclear conflict. There may, in addition, exist still other instances in which a primary disorder of the self will become ameliorated in the course of an analysis, even though the analyst's conceptual framework was inadequate—even though, in other words, the self and its pathology were disregarded and the relevant structure-building working-through processes had not become knowingly engaged. The improvement of the patient's disturbance in such instances is, I believe, brought about by the responses from the side of the analyst that he considers to be peripheral and which he thinks of as perhaps only tactically important but theoretically not significant accompaniments to the essential interpretative activities to which he attributes the success of the therapy. In other words, I believe that appropriate responses to primary self pathology have in the past been given, at times reluctantly and even guiltily, by a number of intuitive analysts—and with good results. The analyst saw these analytic activities, however, as an expression of analytic "tact" or justified them as serving to maintain a therapeutic working alliance—the reconstitution of the self, however, he explained as having taken place in consequence of interpretations that dealt with the analysand's structural conflicts.

But to return to Alexander's interpretation of the oral-dependent personality in accordance with Freud's theory of the complementary relationship between regression and fixation of drives (1917b, pp. 340-341), we must now consider those instances where, according to Alexander's view, it is drive fixation and not primarily a retreat from the anxieties of the Oedipus complex that is to be considered an adequate explanation of the patient's serious disturbance. On purely theoretical grounds the possibility cannot be dismissed that such cases may actually exist — that there are, in other words, exceptional cases in which a disorder of the self may yield to an analytic approach that assumes that the psychopathology is the manifestation (1) of a drive fixation on oral fixation points, and (2) of a corresponding developmental arrest of the ego, in consequence of infantile gratifications to which the analysand's pleasure-oriented immature ego had become addicted. But while I believe that there are rare instances in which a cure of primary self pathology can be achieved by an empathic analyst in the course of an analysis that is transacted in terms of ego infantilism in consequence of a retreat motivated by castration anxiety, I cannot imagine that an analytically valid cure of a primary self disturbance could be achieved, even fortuitously, by an analyst who deals with the patient on the basis of his conviction that the patient had remained fixated on the oral drive. Such cases, I am convinced, are not encountered in our offices[1] and an analyst who formulates his patient's self pathology in these terms will be experienced as grossly unempathic by the analysand, and he will at best achieve an educational result, i.e., the formation of mature psychological layers (defensive structures) on the basis of the analysand's gross identification with the therapist. If such cases existed, their eti-

---

[1] Advanced stages of chronic addiction may give the impression of pure drive fixation and of total infantilism of the ego, but the disorganization of the personality and the organic changes that have by then taken place make it impossible to arrive at a reliable assessment of the genesis of the disorder, particularly of the nature of the psychological needs the patient originally attempted to satisfy.

ology would have to be sought in parental attitudes which, on the one hand, indulged the child's pregenital drives and, on the other, blocked the demands of the child's phallic-genital needs. I do not believe that such a decisive blocking of a child's maturing drive-apparatus could be carried out by parents who are in even minimal empathic contact with the maturational aspirations of their child. My clinical experience with patients whose severe personality distortions I would formerly have attributed to a fixation of the drive organization at an early level of development (orality), and to the concomitant chronic infantilism of their ego, has increasingly taught me that the drive fixation and the widespread ego defects are neither genetically the primary nor dynamic-structurally the most centrally located focus of the psychopathology. It is the self of the child that, in consequence of the severely disturbed empathic responses of the parents, has not been securely established, and it is the enfeebled and fragmentation-prone self that (in the attempt to reassure itself that it is alive, even that it exists at all) turns defensively toward pleasure aims through the stimulation of erogenic zones, and then, secondarily, brings about the oral (and anal) drive orientation and the ego's enslavement to the drive aims correlated to the stimulated body zones.

It is not easy to describe the quasi-addictive use made of his body's erogenic zones—with or without the aid of accompanying fantasies which become the crystallization points for later psychopathology, for example, adult perversions—by the depressed child who attempts to counteract the experience of the fragmentation or enfeeblement of the self. The explanations of drive psychology, of the structural model of the mind, and of ego psychology are satisfactory only insofar as the circum-scribed area of the psychology (and especially of the psy-chopathology) of conflict is concerned. They deal with conceptual units too elemental to encompass the more complex psychic configurations we can recognize in health and disease, as soon as our focus begins to encom-pass the participating self, especially, of course, when the self and its diseases have become the very center of our at-tention. The breakthrough, for example, that Freud (1908) and Abraham (1921) achieved in correlating cer-tain characterological features with the persisting fixa-tion on certain pregenital drives—for example, in the conceptualization of "anal" penuriousness—gave us a brilliant explanation of a complex set of psychological phenomena. Yet, the very brilliance of this intellectual achievement has prevented us from recognizing the limi-tations of the insight provided, has even skewed our at-titude toward certain psychological states. The tradition-al emphasis on the drive-psychological elements of the interplay of mother and child—in the present example: during the anal period—is not a satisfactory explanation for the fact that the child had become anally fixated and that the subsequent establishment of defenses against the expression of undisguised anality had become the starting point of the development of psychological structures which then manifested themselves as the characterologi-cal attitude of penuriousness. We do indeed, I believe, reach a more satisfactory explanation if, in addition to the drives, we consider the self of the anal period, a self during an early stage of its consolidation. If a mother accepts the fecal gift proudly—or if she rejects it or is un-interested in it—she is not only responding to a drive. She is also responding to the child's forming self. Her attitude, in other words, influences a set of inner experiences that play a crucial role in the child's further development. She responds — accepting, rejecting, disregarding — to a self that, in giving and offering, seeks confirmation by the mirroring self-object. The child therefore experiences the joyful, prideful parental attitude or the parent's lack of interest, not only as the acceptance or rejection of a drive, but also — this aspect of the interaction of parent and child is often the decisive one — as the acceptance or rejection of his tentatively established, yet still vulnerable creative-productive-active self. If the mother rejects this self just as it begins to assert itself as a center of creative-productive initiative (especially, of course, if her rejection or lack of interest is only one link in a long chain of rebuffs and disappointments emanating from her pathogenically unempathic personality) or if her inability to respond to the child's total self leads her to a fragmentation-producing preoccupation with his feces — to the detriment of the cohesion-establishing involvement with her feces-producing, learning, controlling, maturing, total child — then the child's self will be depleted and he will abandon the attempt to obtain the joys of self-assertion and will, for reassurance, turn to the pleasures he can derive from the fragments of his body-self. The adult's "anal character" — his penuriousness, for example — cannot therefore be adequately explained by references to his anal fixation or to his anal-retentive inclinations. The anal fixation is present, of course, but it becomes fully meaningful only on the basis of the genetic reconstruction that, as a child, feeling that his self was crumbling and/or empty, he had tried to obtain reassuring pleasure from the stimulation of a fragment of his body-self.

With regard to the foregoing example we can now state that the application of the theoretical framework of a psychology of the self is a necessity if in our descriptions and explanations we want to comprehend the full range of the content of the experiences of the child during the "anal" phase of development and if we want to give credit to the full significance of this stage to the child's psychological development. If, however, the broader experiential configurations have been shattered, i.e., if the child's self has been seriously fragmented and weakened by the lack of empathic responses from the self-object, then the formulations of drive psychology, while not adequately encompassing the crucial psychological oscillations between the cohesive and the fragmented self, may be well suited to explain the new state in experience-distant terms.[2]

It is in this context that we can justify such drive-psychological formulations of phenomena that belong, above all, within the explanatory framework of a psychology of the self as, for example, my explanatory description of shame and of narcissistic rage in the terms of classical metapsychology (1972, pp. 394-396). Healthy pride and healthy assertiveness, I might add, are less easily formulated in drive-psychological terms than are the disintegration products of these wholesome basic experiences—shame and rage—that appear after the break-up of the primary psychological constellation. What I am suggesting is that one might employ here and elsewhere two different theoretical frameworks—that, in analogy to the principle of complementarity of modern physics, we

[2] For some general remarks about theory—in particular with regard to the acknowledgment of the relativity of all theoretical statements and the admissibility of complementary approaches—see pp. 206-207.

might indeed speak of a psychological principle of complementarity and say that the depth-psychological explanation of psychological phenomena in health and disease requires two complementary approaches: that of a conflict psychology and that of a psychology of the self.

We can also, from the vantage point of these considerations, fruitfully address ourselves to a question that might be raised by those who are skeptical of the validity of the genetic explanations of a psychopathology provided by psychoanalysis. The question refers to the fact that some people with serious forms of adult psychopathology appear to have had extremely devoted mothers in their early life who, in addition, appeared to have been empathically in tune with the wishes of their children and to have responded by lovingly providing them with the gratification of their wishes. Basing ourselves on the important metapsychological "principle of optimal frustration," we will, of course, immediately be inclined to argue, in the terms of instinct theory, that full gratification — "spoiling" — deprives the child of the opportunity for building psychic structure — i.e., that in consequence of the nonfrustration of drives the ego remains immature (does not sufficiently develop its drive-controlling, drive-modulating, and drive-sublimating functions)—, that maternal empathy can be excessive and that "mothering" must have its limits if it is not to be harmful to the child. But while I believe that the principle of optimal frustration is a very valuable one, I do not believe that many cases of harmful maternal spoiling through overempathy and an excess of "mothering" do in fact exist. Such instances as I have been able to study retrospectively in the analysis of disturbed adults revealed themselves as having been determined in a more complex way. I believe we can make immediate progress toward greater clarity if we re-evaluate the question of the harmfulness of over-mothering or spoiling against the background of not only the psychology of the drives but also, and predominantly, of the psychology of the self. Certain aspects of the severe psychopathology of Mr. U., for example (see pp. 55-58 above), particularly those concerning his fixation on the fetish, appeared at first to be due to his having been, as a child, overly gratified by his doting mother and grand-mother, who fulfilled his every wish and who by thus spoiling him contributed to his later unwillingness to make realistic compromises. It was this insistence on per-fect mothering, we thought at first, that had set up the formation of a psychological enclave—the fetish, its gratifying perfection—in which perfect maternal func-tioning continued to hold sway to the detriment of more realistic and mature modes of pleasure gain. As the anal-ysis progressed, however, and especially as the reactiva-tion of his needs and wishes in the transference was worked through systematically, a different aspect of the maternal gratifications in early life emerged with great clarity. Mr. U.'s mother and grandmother had formed a team in their shared attitude to the boy and apparently acted out an unconscious fantasy of their own, gratifying the child's drive-wishes for their own purposes. Fully in tune with his every drive demand, they simultaneously disregarded the boy's maturing, changing self, which cried out for maternal (and later also paternal) confirm-ing-admiring responses and approval. The fixation on the fetish was therefore essentially not the result of over-gratification, but of a specific traumatic absence of maternal empathy for the healthy grandiosity and the healthy exhibitionism of his forming independent self.

The result, in brief, was the formation of a depleted, depressed sector of his self and a depressively undertaken return to drive gratification, i.e., to the use of archaic pleasure-gains (the drive-satisfying mother, the fetish) because the expansive display of the gifted child—of his self as an independent center of initiative—remained unresponded to by the mother and was not sufficently responded to by the father.

The application of the principle that it is not a libidinal drive that, psychologically speaking, attains its momentum in the child, but that, from the beginning, the drive experience is subordinated to the child's experience of the relation between the self and the self-objects, is of crucial importance on two counts. It changes our evaluation of the significance of the libido theory on all levels of psychological development in childhood; and, consequently, it changes our evaluation of some forms of psychopathology which classical theory viewed as being caused by the personality's fixation on or regression to this or that stage of instinct development.

Let me, in this context, add one more illustration to those already presented: the triad of oral fixation, pathological overeating, and obesity. This syndrome could be scrutinized against the background of the assumption that we are dealing with a regressive and/or primary drive-fixation on the oral level (flight from castration fears and/or oral indulgence), and the goal of psychoanalytic therapy as defined from this point of view would ultimately—except for the theoretically imaginable but in practice hardly encountered cases of *pure* regression—include the achievement of deepened drive-awareness with the collaterally achieved increased ability to control the drive (via its suppression, sublimation, inhibition of its aims, displacement, or neutralization). I submit again, however, that this theoretical stance is unsatisfactory. By contrast, it is my claim that we are coming nearer to the truth and will provide a more accurately reasoned explanation of a successfully unrolling psychoanalytic process in the majority of these cases if we apply the following formulation: It is not, we will say, the child's wish for food that is the primal psychological configuration. Seen from the point of view of the psychology of the self, we will affirm instead that, from the beginning, the child asserts his need for a food-giving self-object—however dimly recognized the self-object might be. (In more behavioristic terms we might say that the child needs empathically modulated food-giving, not food.) If this need remains unfulfilled (to a traumatic degree) then the broader psychological configuration— the joyful experience of being a whole, appropriately responded-to self—disintegrates and the child retreats to a fragment of the larger experiential unit, i.e., to pleasure-seeking oral stimulation (to the erogenic zone) or, expressed clinically, to depressive eating. It is this fragment of psychological experience that becomes the crystallization point for the later addiction to food. And it is the increasing awareness of the depressive-disintegrative reaction to the unempathic self-object milieu—not an increasing awareness of the drive (and an, in essence, educational emphasis on the mastery of the drive)—that becomes the basis from which a renewed movement toward psychological health can proceed.

To summarize in more general terms, the establishment of drive fixations and of the correlated activities of the ego occurs in consequence of the feebleness of the self. The unresponded-to self has not been able to transform

its archaic grandiosity and its archaic wish to merge with
an omnipotent self-object into reliable self-esteem, realistic ambitions, attainable ideals. The abnormalities of the
drives and of the ego are the symptomatic consequences
of this central defect in the self.

Analogous considerations also apply to the general
question of the conceptual framework within which the
compensatory structures should be placed. Should we
think of them in ego-psychological terms—as defenses
that have achieved "secondary autonomy" from the drive
that had originally stimulated their growth? Or should we
view them in terms of a psychology of the self—as a constituent of a self that has become reconsolidated under
the influence of specific relations between the self and the
self-object? I maintain that it is inappropriate to use the
concepts of primary or secondary autonomy in our theoretical formulations when we are dealing with disorders
of the self. These concepts belong essentially within the
framework of a psychology of structural conflict, i.e., one
that conceptualizes psychological illness as the result of
the conflict between sets of forces (drives and defenses) in
opposition to each other. I would therefore think that it is
indeed useful to apply the concept of secondary autonomy to defensive structures that have in the course of
development become independent in their functions from
the drive demands they originally opposed. Despite the
fact that compensatory structures may become autonomous—those, for example, that have been rehabilitated
as the result of the analysis of narcissistic personality disorders—the terms primary and secondary autonomy, in
the ego-psychological sense, are irrelevant with regard to
them. True, the choice of the specific compensatory
functions that become important to the child in order to

substitute for others which are stunted (in the area of the primary defect) may well be partly influenced by innate factors (talents), and we might therefore speak of their "primary autonomy." But the child's selection of certain functions out of the number of those at his disposal (and his developing them into efficacious talents and skills) and the direction of his major pursuits as ultimately laid down permanently in the psyche as the content of his ambitions and ideals—i.e., the child's acquisition of compensatory structures—are best explained in the context of his having been able to shift from a frustrating self-object to a nonfrustrating or less frustrating one. The decisive issue, in other words, is not that the functions expressing the pattern of the self are autonomous, but that a self that had been threatened in its cohesion and functioning in *one* sector has managed to survive by shifting its psychological point of gravity toward *another* one.

Interpretations and Resistances

The explanatory power of the postulates of drive psychology that, in normal development, narcissism is transformed into object love and that drives are gradually "tamed," and the explanatory power of the postulates of the psychology of the self that, in normal development, self/self-object relations are the precursors of psychological structures and that transmuting internalization of the self-objects leads gradually to the consolidation of the self, can also be compared by applying these complementary viewpoints to concrete psychological configurations that emerge during the analytic process.

Let us focus, for example, on Hartmann's (1950) subtle and sophisticated discussion of drive-taming via countercathexes, particularly his assertion that the ego uses neutralized aggressive energy to hold drives in check. It might be added here that the countercathexes of which Hartmann speaks were presumably acquired by the mental apparatus as a result of the early interplay with the instinctually cathected parental object. Hartmann suggests that what Freud (1937) called "resistance against the uncovering of resistances" in the psychoanalytic situation is "metapsychologically speaking . . . reaggressivized energy of the countercathexes, mobilized as a consequence of our attack on the patient's resistance" (1950, p. 134). Hartmann's theory—as does all metapsychology when applied to the relations of the child to his parents or of the patient to the analyst—shifts between two essentially incompatible conceptual frameworks, the framework of the mental apparatus and the framework of social psychology. This is a forgivable and, in the present context, inconsequential inaccuracy that I have discussed elsewhere (1959) and shall not pursue here. I am, in other words, not concerned here with any flaws in theory and concept formation, do not aim at proving Hartmann's theory to be in error, but want to demonstrate that the psychology of the self—a psychology that differentiates objects that are experienced as part of the self (self-objects) from those that are experienced as independent from the self, as independent centers of initiative (true objects)—is able to explain the phenomena under scrutiny—the analysand's angry response to the attack on his resistances—altogether more cogently than does the drive-psychological method employed by Hartmann.

To create a basis for my approach, I shall first examine a childhood situation that is in certain decisive respects prototypical for the analytic situation: the child's merger with the empathic omnipotent idealized self-object (see Kohut, 1971, p. 278; cf. Freud, 1921, pp. 111-116).

The child that is to survive psychologically is born into an empathic-responsive human milieu (of self-objects) just as he is born into an atmosphere that contains an optimal amount of oxygen if he is to survive physically. And his nascent self "expects" — to use an inappropriately anthropomorphic but appropriately evocative term[3] — an empathic environment to be in tune with his psychological need-wishes with the same unquestioning certitude as the respiratory apparatus of the newborn infant may be said to "expect" oxygen to be contained in the surrounding atmosphere. When the child's psychological balance is disturbed, the child's tensions are, under normal circumstances, empathically perceived and responded to by the self-object. The self-object, equipped with a mature psychological organization that can realistically assess the child's need and what is to be done about it, will include the child into its own psychological organization and will remedy the child's homeostatic imbalance through actions. The *first* of these two steps, it must be emphasized, is of far greater psychological significance for the child than is the second, especially with regard to

[3] Schafer, among modern analysts, has been the most outspoken objector to the reification of theory (see his discussion of psychoanalytic concept formation, 1973b). His argument is in general well taken, and his valuable contribution should exert a wholesome influence by alerting analysts not to blur the distinction between clinical-observational fact and the abstractions of theory. I maintain, nevertheless, that we should not therefore become pallid in our communications. There is a decisive difference between the use of colorful, evocative language and concretizing (e.g., anthropomorphic) thought. I also believe that, however logical Schafer's line of thought may be, he does not take into account the need for gradualness in theory change if the psychoanalytic "group self" is to be preserved.

the child's ability to build psychological structures (to consolidate his nuclear self) via transmuting internalization. The formulation that the mother tames the child's aggressive drive by neutralizing it with her love or by opposing it via her neutralized aggression (firmness) rests on an attractively simple analogy with the gross mechanics of events in the physical world. It does not, however, do justice to the events in the psychological field. I believe we come closer to the truth when we say that the child's anxiety, his drive needs, and his rage (i.e., his experience of the disintegration of the preceding broader and more complex psychological unit of unquestioning assertiveness) have brought about empathic resonances within the maternal self-object. The self-object then establishes tactile and/or vocal contact with the child (the mother picks up the child, talks to it while holding and carrying it) and thus creates conditions that the child phase-appropriately experiences as a merger with the omnipotent self-object. The child's rudimentary psyche participates in the self-object's highly developed psychic organization; the child experiences the feeling states of the self-object — they are transmitted to the child via touch and tone of voice and perhaps by still other means — as if they were his own. The relevant feeling states — either the child's own or those of the self-object in which he participates —, in the order in which they are experienced by the self/self-object unit, are: mounting anxiety (self); followed by stabilized mild anxiety — a "signal" not panic — (self-object); followed by calmness, absence of anxiety (self-object). Ultimately, the psychological disintegration products that the child had begun to experience disappear (the rudimentary self is re-established), while the mother (as seen in terms of behaviorism and social psychology) readies the food, improves temperature regulation, changes diapers, etc. It is the experience of this sequence of psychological events via the merger with the empathic omnipotent self-object that sets up the base line from which optimum (nontraumatic, phase-appropriate) failures of the self-object lead, under normal circumstances, to structure building via transmuting internalization. These optimal failures may consist in the self-object's briefly delayed empathic response, in mild deviations from the beneficial norm of the self-object's experiences in which the child participates, or in the discrepancy between the experiences provided through the merger with the empathic self-object and the actual satisfaction of needs. It is my impression, I might add, that the last-mentioned instance is of far less importance with regard to psychological structure formation in childhood than are the psychological failures of the self-object. I believe, in other words, that defects in the self occur mainly as the result of empathy failures from the side of the self-objects—due to narcissistic disturbances of the self-object; especially, and I think, more frequently than analysts realize, due to the self-object's latent psychosis—and that even serious realistic deprivations (what one might classify as "drive" [or need] frustrations) are not psychologically harmful if the psychological environment responds to the child with a full range of undistorted empathic responses. Man does not live by bread alone.

The importance of the two-step sequence—step one: empathic merger with the self-object's mature psychic organization and participation in the self-object's experience of an affect signal instead of affect spread; step two: need-satisfying actions performed by the self-object—cannot be overestimated; if optimally experienced during childhood, it remains one of the pillars of mental health throughout life and, in the reverse, if the self-objects of childhood fail, then the resulting psychological deficits or distortions will remain a burden that will have to be carried throughout life. The fact that psychoanalysis is a psychology that explains what it has first understood is intimately connected with the two-step principle that defines human psychological functions *ab initio*. And it must also be stressed that the same principle underlies the analyst's attitude toward his analysands. Every interpretation, in other words, and every reconstruction, consists of two phases; first the analysand must realize that he has been understood; only then, as a second step, will the analyst demonstrate to the analysand the specific dynamic and genetic factors that explain the psychological content he had first empathically grasped. Some of the most persistent resistances encountered in analysis are not interpersonally activated defenses against the danger that some repressed psychological ideation will be made conscious by the analyst's interpretations or reconstructions; they are mobilized in response to the fact that the stage of understanding—the stage of the analyst's empathic echo of or merger with the patient—had been skipped over. In some analyses—though by no means in all—the analyst will even have to realize that a patient whose childhood self-object had failed traumatically in this area will require long periods of "only" understanding before the second step—interpretation, the dynamic-genetic explanations given by the analyst—can be usefully and acceptably taken.

It might be well to add here the complementary lines of thought that will explain the various forms of psychopathology resulting from disturbances in the empathic merger of the self and the self-object at the stage of psychological development preceding firm establishment of the self. If the self-object's empathic resonance to the child is absent or severely dulled, either diffusely or vis-à-vis selected areas of the child's experience, then the child will be deprived of the merger with the omnipotent self-object and will not participate in the aforementioned sequence of experiences (spreading anxiety, anxiety signal, calmness) and will therefore be deprived of the opportunity to build up psychological structures capable of dealing with his anxiety in the same way. And if, to adduce another example, the self-object reacts hypochondriacally to the child's mild anxiety, then the merger with the self-object will not produce the wholesome experience of mild anxiety changing into calmness, but, on the contrary, will produce the noxious experiential sequence of mild anxiety changing into panic. In instances of the first type the child is not given the opportunity to establish a wholesome merger; in instances of the second type the child will either be drawn into a noxious one or will actively try to escape it by walling himself off from the noxious response of the self-object. The end-result in all these instances is either a lack of normal tension-regulating structure (a weakness in the ability to tame affects — to curb anxiety) or the acquisition of faulty structures (the propensity toward active intensifications of affect — toward developing states of panic). I believe that not only the pathogenesis of anxiety-proneness but also the propensity for affective disorders has to be investigated from the point of view of the merger of the nascent self with the self-object's depressive and/or manic responses. I believe, in other words, that the psychological aspects of the affective disorders cannot be adequately formulated in terms of the gross dynamics of drives and structures (depression as unneutralized aggression turned from the object toward the self; or as the sadistic attack of the superego against the ego), but that the investigation of the merger with the omnipotent self-object—a precursor of psychological structure—will lead us to a more adequate understanding.

But to return to Hartmann's hypothesis that the "resistances against the uncovering of resistances" is a manifestation of the "reaggressivized energy of the countercathexes, mobilized as a consequence of our attack on the patient's resistance." On the basis of much careful observation in the clinical situation, both in analyses I have conducted myself and those in which I served as supervisor or consultant, I feel certain that this formulation leads to a misinterpretation of the clinical facts. Despite its elegance, the drive-defense model of mental functioning, to which Hartmann's formulation intrinsically belongs, does not accommodate the empirical facts under scrutiny. When the analysand becomes enraged in consequence of our attack on his resistance, he does so, not because a correct interpretation has loosened defenses and has activated the aggressive energy that was bound up in them, but because a specific genetically important traumatic situation from his early life has been repeated in the analytic situation: the experience of the faulty, nonempathic response of the self-object. The patient's rage is not the manifestation of aggressions directed outward against the analyst who by his correct interpretations seems to be on the side of the dangerous drives and has to be defended against. The patient's rage is "narcissistic rage." And I believe that an interpretation formulated within the conceptual framework of a metapsychology of the self in general, and concerning the relation of the self to the self-object, in particular, therefore accommodates the empirical facts more nearly correctly than explanations referring to a mental-apparatus psychology of drives and defenses—even if they are given with warmth or kindness and couched in behavioral terms. The approximately correct interpretation is this: The precariously established self of the child (as revived in the analytic situation) depends for the maintenance of its cohesion on the near-perfect empathic responses of the self-object. In harmony with the developmental stage of its self (phase-appropriately), the child demands total control over the self-object's responses; it demands perfect empathy, both in the content of the understanding that is offered and with regard to the perfect in-tuneness with the traumatic effect produced by deviations from the optimum which for the early self is the expected norm. Concretely speaking, whenever a patient reacts with rage to the analyst's interpretations, he has experienced him, from the point of view of the archaic self that has been activated in analysis, as a nonempathic attacker of the integrity of his self. The analyst does not witness the emergence of a primary primitive-aggressive drive, he witnesses the disintegration of the preceding primary configuration, the breakup of the primary self-experience in which, in the child's perception, the child and the empathic self-object are one.

These insights, it might be necessary to stress here, must not burden the analyst with the demand on himself that he should be able to perform superhuman feats of never-failing, perfect empathy with his patients. While our analysands have a right to expect above-average empathic responses from us, and while I believe that, *in principle,* the functional basis of the analytic situation is empathic responsiveness, our unavoidable failures should

not produce undue guilt in us. Our grasp of the significance of the patient's anger does, however, decisively influence the direction of our interpretations. When the
patient is enraged after an interpretation, we will not
continue to focus on the underlying psychopathology to
which the interpretation had referred, will not, for example, focus on either the repressed or defensive side of
the structural conflict that had been the target of the interpretation, but will shift our attention to the narcissistic
imbalance to which the patient was exposed. And, in the
case of analysands who suffer from a narcissistic personality or behavior disorder rather than from a structural
neurosis, we will not only focus on the dynamics of the
narcissistic imbalance as it may occur in all types of
psychopathology in response to an interpretation that was
experienced as unempathic, but we will also gradually
shift our attention to the precursors of the patient's transference experiences—tensions that arose between the self
and the self-objects in childhood. To repeat, a specific,
frequently encountered empathy failure from the side of
the analyst does not concern the ideational content of the
analysand's communications, but the analysand's sometimes protracted need to hold fast to the first of the two
phases of interpretations (the understanding phase) before focusing his attention on the second one (the explaining phase). True enough, most analysts have always responded with tact and human warmth to their analysands' narcissistic vulnerability in the face of interpretations—and even if they considered Hartmann's theory essentially correct, they did not necessarily act in accordance with their theoretical conviction, but allowed their
analysands to regain their narcissistic balance when they
reacted with rage to an interpretation. Nevertheless, I be-

lieve that the application of the preceding theoretical considerations to the clinical situation has very wholesome results. Even the slight shift in the analyst's attitude that comes from his now responding to the challenge of an essential task with theory-based conviction, when he formerly, with some theory-based misgivings, bowed to the necessity of a practical expedient, will reduce the unnecessary tenseness at times encountered in the analytic situation and, by removing artifacts, will outline the endogenous psychopathology of the analysand with greater clarity.

Origins of the Self

The theories of an empirical science are derived primarily from generalizations and abstractions that refer to the data of observation. In psychoanalysis they are derived from the data obtained by introspection and empathy. As we address ourselves to the question whether psychoanalysis needs a psychology of the self in addition to ego psychology, the psychology of the structural model of the mind, and the psychology of the drives, we can take our first step toward an affirmative answer by adding a new dimension to the old principle (cf. A. Freud, 1936, Chapter I) that the contents of structures in conflict with each other will impinge on our introspective awareness, while the contents of structures in harmony with each other will not. And if we say, in a variation of Anna Freud's maxim, that a feeble, fragmented self will impinge on our awareness, while an optimally firm, securely coherent self will not, we can immediately add these three further statements: (1) A psychology of the self will be unimportant, unnecessary, irrelevant, or even inapplicable with regard to psychological states in which a self is either not present or present only in a rudimentary or residual form (such as, perhaps, in earliest infancy and in certain states of serious psychological disorganization and regression). (2) A psychology of the self will be relatively unimportant and unnecessary when we are dealing with psychological states in which self-cohesion is firm and self-acceptance is optimally established (such as during the oedipal period of a child whose self had developed healthily, or in the corresponding psychological states of adult life—the classical structural neuroses—where the cohesion of the self is not disturbed and where the swings of self-acceptance and self-esteem are within normal limits). (3) A psychology of the self will be most important and most relevant whenever we scrutinize those states in which experiences of disturbed self-acceptance and/or of the fragmentation of the self occupy the center of the psychological stage (as is the case par excellence with the narcissistic personality disorders).

The first and second of the foregoing statements need amplification.

On the face of it, it seems evident that a psychology of the self will not apply with regard to states in which the self (either because it has not yet been sufficiently established or because it has been seriously damaged or even destroyed) cannot function as an effective independent center of initiative and as a focus of perceptions and experiences—including those of heightened or lowered self-esteem. Since, in the absence of the self, the drives will occupy the center of the psychological stage, we can expect that a drive psychology will serve us well when we are empathically scrutinizing the behavior of the very young infant and the experiential world of the severely regressed psychotic. Even in these two states, however, the self-objects (whose anticipatory image-building with regard to the infant must not be disregarded, as I discuss later on) are filling the place of the self, so that the adequacy of a psychology that focuses on the drives and a rudimentary ego is not beyond question. And whereas in the case of the regressed psychotic, the fragments of the patient's self react in ways that are adequately explained with the aid of conflict theory, the focus of our attention should not center on these conflicts but on the changes in the state of the self—its greater or lesser fragmentation—and on the vicissitudes of the relation between the self and the self-objects of the psychotic that explain these changes. Crude drive-defense conflicts about openly expressed incestuous wishes, for example, emerge as psychological disintegration products whenever the truly causal event has occurred—it lies within the nexus of archaic relations to self-objects—,i.e., whenever the surroundings have been experienced as nonempathic.

With regard to those stages of mental life in which the self is firmly established, independently of whether we are dealing with states of mental health or mental disturbances (specifically, with structural disorders), it is necessary to elaborate the previous statement that here a psychology of the self can also largely be dispensed with. It may be best to confront the problem by posing this concrete question: Why has it in fact been possible up to now for psychoanalysts using a drive-defense model of the mind without a psychology of the self to deal with the psychological processes characteristic of the later stages of childhood and with the analogous processes encountered in those forms of adult psychopathology that constitute a reactivation of the unsolved conflicts of these stages of de-

velopment? Should we not have expected that the complexity of these mature states of psychic development
would especially demand the application of the psychology of the self, that for these stages the drive-and-defense
and the structural models would prove inadequate?
(When comparing the classical psychoanalytic models
with the psychology of the self, the structural model may
be looked upon as an extension of the drive-defense
model of the mind.)

In attempting to reply, I do not claim that the application of a psychology of the self would not enrich our
understanding and give greater depth to our explanations
of the relevant mental processes in health and in disease.
But I do indeed feel that the drive-and-defense and
the structural models of the mind provide an adequate
framework for explaining the essentials of those processes
to which a firm self is exposed, or of processes initiated by
a firm self, or in which a firm self is a participant, e.g.,
processes that concern the gradual acculturation of the
growing child, including those involved in the Oedipus
complex[4] — as they originally occur and as they are reactivated in the classical neuroses of adult life.

It is not difficult to spell out why the classical explanations that disregarded the self and its vicissitudes
had been satisfactory with respect to these conditions.
The classical model was successful because — if I may be
permitted a simple algebraic analogy — an undisturbed
self participates on both the drive and defense sides of
structural psychological conflicts and may thus be left out
of the psychological equation. It is true, of course, as I

---

[4] These considerations do not, however, apply to an Oedipus complex
that was activated as a defense against a primary disturbance of the self. (See
Kohut, 1972, pp. 369-372.)

have pointed out before, that when we are studying mental processes beyond early infancy we are never observing drives or defenses in isolation. Whenever we are observing a person who strives for pleasure or pursues vengeful or destructive purposes (or who is in conflict concerning these aims or opposes them), it is possible to discern a self which, while it includes drives (and/or defenses) in its organization, has become a supraordinated configuration whose significance transcends that of the sum of its parts. Still, if the self is healthy, firmly coherent, and of normal strength, then it will not spontaneously become the focus of our empathic (or introspective) attention; our attention will not be claimed by the encompassing supraordinated configuration that is in balance, but by those of its subordinated contents (narcissistic aims, drive aims, defenses, conflicts) that are not.

The foregoing statement is accurate insofar as the relative adequacy of the drive-defense model of the mind for the interpretative approach to states of psychic conflict is concerned. In a variety of circumstances, however, secondary changes in the state of the self will occur even when the self is sound—and they can and often will impinge on our awareness. The very pursuit of libidinal and aggressive aims, for example, may, if intensely engaged in, lead to alterations in self-esteem which will claim our attention; and the success or failure of our libidinal and aggressive pursuits may result in changes of self-esteem which, manifested as the triumph of victory (heightened self-esteem) or as the dejection of defeat (lowered self-esteem) may in turn become important secondary forces on the psychic stage. If the psychoanalyst focuses his attention upon the self, therefore, his understanding of the states he is investigating will be enriched even when he is dealing with a healthy self. It nevertheless remains indisputable that certain essential dynamic relationships can indeed be formulated without regard to the self— witness the explanatory capacity of classical theory with regard to the structural neuroses and to broad aspects of the growing child's progressive acculturation (conceptualized as neutralization, sublimation, and other vicissitudes of drives).

Having acknowledged the explanatory power of the structural model, I will not hide my belief that in the long run a psychology of the self will prove to be not only valuable but indispensable even with regard to the areas where the psychology of drives and defenses now does the job. I have no doubt, in other words, that with the aid of a psychology of the self—the study of the genesis and of the development of the self, of its constituents, its aims, and its disturbances—we will learn to recognize new aspects of mental life and to penetrate into greater psychological depths, even in the areas of normal acculturation and of the structural conflicts of the classical neuroses.

How could it be otherwise? A complexly organized empathic-responsive human environment reacts to the child *ab initio:* and we may well discover, as we investigate early states of infancy with more and more refined psychological means, that a rudimentary self is already present very early in life. But how could we corroborate this expectation; how could we substantiate a hypothesis of the presence of a rudimentary self in infancy? The psychological penetration into archaic mental states, especially into experiences that mark the very beginnings of a specific developmental line, is always precarious—there can be no doubt that our reconstructions are here es-

pecially exposed to the danger of adultomorphic distortion. These considerations should surely persuade us to
desist from even embarking on such a voyage, were it not
for a set of circumstances that provides us with unexpected assistance.

I suggest that we undertake the examination of the
question of the existence of a rudimentary self in earliest
infancy from a perhaps surprising starting point, namely,
by stressing that the human environment reacts to even
the smallest baby as if it had already formed such a self.
The idea that the affirmation of a specific aspect of the
primary empathic merger between the infant and the
infant's self-object should be taken as evidence in support
of the hypothesis of the existence of a self in infancy
might well be taken on first blush as being no more than
unscientific sophistry. The crucial question concerns, of
course, the point in time when, within the matrix of
mutual empathy between the infant and his self-object,
the baby's innate potentialities and the self-object's
expectations with regard to the baby converge. Is it permissible to consider this juncture the point of origin of the
infant's primal, rudimentary self?

I believe we must not reject this idea out of hand.
True, we must assume — on the basis of information available to us through the work of neurophysiologists — that
the newborn infant cannot have any reflective awareness
of himself, that he is not capable of experiencing himself,
if ever so dimly, as a unit, cohesive in space and enduring
in time, which is a center of initiative and a recipient of
impressions. And yet, he is, from the beginning, fused via
mutual empathy with an environment that does experience him as already possessing a self — an environment

that not only anticipates the later separate self-awareness of the child, but already, by the very form and content of its expectations, begins to channel it into specific directions. At the moment when the mother sees her baby for the first time and is also in contact with him (through tactile, olfactory, and proprioceptive channels as she feeds, carries, bathes him), a process that lays down a person's self has its virtual beginning—it continues throughout childhood and to a lesser extent later in life. I have in mind the specific interactions of the child and his self-objects through which, in countless repetitions, the self-objects empathically respond to certain potentialities of the child (aspects of the grandiose self he exhibits, aspects of the idealized image he admires, different innate talents he employs to mediate creatively between ambitions and ideals), but not to others. This is the most important way by which the child's innate potentialities are selectively nourished or thwarted. The *nuclear* self, in particular, is not formed via conscious encouragement and praise and via conscious discouragement and rebuke, but by the deeply anchored responsiveness of the self-objects, which, in the last analysis, is a function of the self-objects' own nuclear selves.

If these concepts are valid, may we then not speak of a self *in statu nascendi* even at a time when the infant in isolation—a psychological artifact—can be looked upon only as a biological unit? As a unit, in other words, whose behavior must be studied with the methods of the biological investigator because the immaturity of his biological equipment precludes the existence of endopsychic processes in him which we could grasp by extending our empathy to him.

The foregoing conceptualization of a self at the beginning of life, it may be added, is not burdened with the Kleinian fallacy that specific verbalizable fantasies are present in earliest infancy. One might say, in order to further illuminate the difference from Kleinian constructions, that the newborn baby's self (whose existence *ab initio* I am willing to consider) is a *virtual* self, corresponding in reverse to that geometric point in infinity where two parallel lines meet. I hold, indeed, that the states existing before the apparatus of the central nervous system has sufficiently matured and before the secondary processes have yet been established, must be described in terms of tensions—of tension increase, of tension decrease—and not in terms of verbalizable fantasies (cf. Kohut, 1959, pp. 468-469).

The analyst's conception of the conditions that exist in infancy often decisively influences his outlook on the conditions he encounters in adults, particularly in the therapeutic situation. And it is a well-known aspect of the history of psychoanalysis that certain conceptual changes concerning the nature of the infantile mind have led to crucial changes in therapeutic approach. In some instances the shift in outlook concerning the conditions in early life impoverishes the analyst's perception of the varieties of significant human experiences and brings about a narrowing of the focus of his attention upon a single thread in the complex weave of the patient's psychopathology. This error was, for example, committed by Rank whose theory of the "trauma of birth" (1929) led him, according to Freud (1937, pp. 216-217), to a single-minded therapeutic preoccupation with the problems of separation anxiety. The point of view I have presented, however, does not narrow the range of our empathic ability—it broadens it.

Let me support my claim by turning to the analyst's scrutiny of the analysand's anxieties as they arise in the clinical setting. If the analyst examines his patient's anxiety from the vantage point of the psychology of the self, his perception will be significantly enriched because he will be aware that two basically different classes of anxiety experiences exist, rather than only one. The first comprises the anxieties experienced by a person whose self is more or less cohesive—they are fears of specific danger situations (Freud, 1926); the emphasis of the experience lies in essence on the specific danger and not on the state of the self. The second comprises the anxieties experienced by a person who is becoming aware that his self is beginning to disintegrate; whatever the trigger that ushered in or reinforced the progressive dissolution of the self, the emphasis of the experience lies in essence on the precarious state of the self and not on the factors that may have set the process of disintegration into motion.

Although the analyst's acquaintance with the two types of anxiety experiences is the precondition for his accurate assessment of the nature of the analysand's anxiety, he must also become familiar with the fact that the initial manifestations of the two types can lead him astray, that only by virtue of his prolonged empathic immersion into the patient's total psychological state will he be able to arrive at the crucially important distinction between them. The expression of circumscribed fears vis-à-vis the threat of abandonment, or disapproval, or physical attack (fear of loss of the love-object, fear of loss of the love of the love-object, castration fear), whether in the social field (*"Realangst"*) or imposed by the superego (*"Gewissensangst"*), may initially be veiled; the analysand may at first produce associations that refer to a variety of vague tension states, and he will only gradually and against resistances move closer to the central verbalizable content of his actual fears. And the expression of the ill-defined yet intense and pervasive anxiety that accompanies a patient's dawning awareness that his self is disintegrating (severe fragmentation, serious loss of initiative, profound drop in self-esteem, sense of utter meaninglessness) also may initially be veiled; the analysand may attempt to express his awareness of the frightening alterations in the state of his self through the medium of verbalizations about circumscribed fears — and it is only gradually and against resistances that his associations will begin to communicate the central content of his anxiety, which, indeed, he can only describe with the aid of analogies and metaphors.

The first instance — the analysand's attempt to evade the direct confrontation with his specific fears — is well known to all analysts and I will therefore not dwell on it here. Suffice it to mention as an illustration the defensive maneuvers that frequently occur when, in the context of oedipal rivalry fantasies in the transference, a male patient's fears of the revenge of the father figure is mobilized. Instead of confronting his castration fears directly, the analysand may first talk about experiencing some vague dread. Later he may speak of a number of different more or less specific fears whose distance from the central fear, namely castration, will, however, gradually diminish if the analysis is conducted properly.

The second class of anxiety experience encountered in the clinical situation requires broader elaboration because it has not been clearly delineated in our scientific literature. True, Freud (1923b, p. 57) speaks of "libidinal danger" which is experienced as a fear "of being overwhelmed or annihilated"; and later (1926, p. 94) he mentions, in the context of a discussion of primal repressions, "earliest outbreaks of anxiety" that are related to "quantitative factors such as an excessive degree of excitation and the breaking through of the protective shield against stimuli." And Anna Freud, too (1936, pp. 58-59), refers to the "dread of the strength of the instincts," i.e., as one could paraphrase, to an insufficiency of the mental apparatus, conceptualized in quantitative terms. I believe that we have here attempts to deal with disintegration anxiety within the framework of the classical mental-apparatus psychology. But I feel that these anxieties cannot be properly conceptualized outside the framework of a psychology of the self. The nucleus of the patient's anxiety is, in other words, related to the fact that his self is undergoing an ominous change—and the intensity of the drive is not the cause of the central pathology (precariousness of self-cohesion), but its result. The core of disintegration anxiety is the anticipation of the breakup of the self, not the fear of the drive.

How then do we recognize the emergence of disintegration fear? How do we distinguish it from the circumscribed fears of the first group, especially from castration anxiety? If disintegration anxiety arises in the course of a properly conducted analysis of an analyzable disorder of the self, the movement of the patient's associations—including the sequential unrolling of the relevant dream imagery—usually goes in the opposite direction from the sequences described for the first class of anxieties. In other words, the associations usually move from the description of circumscribed fears to the recognition of the presence of diffuse anxiety because of the danger of the dissolution of the self.

Initially the fears of such analysands often have a clearly hypochondriacal and phobic cast. Here are some examples taken at random from my clinical practice: a negligible crack in the plaster in one room might indicate the presence of a serious structural defect of the patient's house; a tiny skin infection of the patient or of someone he experiences as an extension of himself is the first sign of a dangerous septicaemia; or, in dreams, the frightening infestation of the living quarters with spreading vermin; or the ominous discovery of algae in the swimming pool. Much as these fears might occupy the patient's mind, however, leading to states of endless brooding, worry, or panic, these fears do not constitute the core of the disturbance, but have been generated as the result of the patient's attempt to give a circumscribed content to a deeper unnamable dread experienced when a person feels that his self is becoming seriously enfeebled or is disintegrating. The ability of the analyst to conceive of psychic conditions that cannot be described in terms of verbalizable meaning allows him to consider an important band in the spectrum of possibilities as he scrutinizes the analysand's anxiety: the dread of the loss of his self—the fragmentation of and the estrangement from his body and mind in space, the breakup of the sense of his continuity in time.

It must not be overlooked that the problem of differentiating the anxieties that are associated with the anticipation of indescribable states of self-dissolution from those that relate to specific verbalized fears becomes complicated by virtue of the fact that erroneous interpretations may under certain circumstances have beneficial results (cf. Glover, 1931) because they strengthen the defenses. The paradoxically wholesome effect of the wrong interpretation—manifested, for example, by a diminution of anxiety—results, in the first case, from the patient's not needing to face a specific fear (e.g., castration anxiety)—he is confirmed in his evasively laying stress on the experience of vague tension-anxiety. In the second case, too, an erroneous interpretation—the analyst's focusing, in harmony with the patient's insistence, on verbalized fears (e.g., castration anxiety) which, however, cover a deeper, nameless dread (of self-disintegration)—may temporarily be experienced by the patient as a relief. And in crisis situations, e.g., when he is dealing with severe to traumatic states in the course of the analysis of narcissistic personality disorders, the analyst will not infrequently find it advisable not to oppose the patient's erroneous self-interpretations. In these instances, however—and the same holds true for the beneficial effect produced in the opposite case (of an analyst's affirming the presence of nameless tensions when the analysand's anxiety is in fact due to a circumscribed, verbalizable fear)—the beneficial effect is not of long duration; enduring results can be achieved only if the interpretations acknowledge the actual level of the disturbance.

When we are dealing with prepsychotic states, however, or with a precariously maintained postpsychotic equilibrium, or with other borderline states,[5] the fact that the interpretation offered to the patient focuses on a higher level of psychic activity than the level actually involved may indeed have been an important remedial effect. By supplying the patient with verbalizable contents,

---

[5] For a differentiating definition of the diagnostic category of *borderline cases* (*latent psychoses*) see p. 192.

the idealized therapist supports the patient's own attempt to stem the tide of disintegration with the aid of a defensively undertaken shift of attention to verbalizable conflicts and anxieties—i.e., with the aid of rationalizations. In this way the disintegration of the self may occasionally be slowed down or even prevented. It goes without saying that the therapeutic efficacy of supplying secondary processes to a psyche being threatened by disintegration must not be taken as proof that the ideational content of these secondary processes (the information contained in the interpretation) has indeed correctly identified the pathogenic forces. The therapist is here not helping the patient increase his mastery over endopsychic processes by making the unconscious conscious (as is the case in the structural disorders), but is attempting to prevent the disintegration of the self by stimulating and supporting the cohesion-producing activity of the patient's reasoning function.

The preceding considerations may explain why analysts who hold the opinion that the psychopathology of narcissistic personality disorders and borderline cases and psychoses is encompassed by the framework of the structural model of the mind and of the experiential world of the Oedipus complex, and whose interpretations are in harmony with these views, will at times be able to improve such patients' condition. Helpful though these maneuvers might be, however, my clinical experience has taught me that it is vastly better to support a crumbling self by explaining the events that triggered its threatening dissolution than by supplying it with rationalizations. There can, in particular, be no doubt about the fact that the analyst, when he is dealing with a traumatic state in the course of the analysis of narcissistic personality disorders, should not actively supply the patient with rationalizations concerning oedipal psychopathology, but should, in proper time, focus on the trigger event that overburdened the analysand's psyche—the analysand would otherwise soon recognize that he has been exposed to a tactical manipulation. Indeed, he will react to an intentionally provided erroneous interpretation, at worst, as tantamount to lying and, at best, as patronizing hypocrisy from the side of the analyst. I believe the same holds true for a self acutely threatened by psychotic dissolution. With patient's who have reached a stable post-psychotic equilibrium, however, or with those who have never been manifestly psychotic but whose self is in danger of protracted dissolution and who have therefore formed a protective layer of rigidly maintained beliefs and preoccupations which deflect their awareness from the vulnerability of the self, the therapeutic strategy is not as clear-cut. Here it may sometimes be the better part of wisdom not to insist on an approach that would require the patient to withdraw his attention from his intense preoccupation with certain endlessly described conflicts and worries which protects him against the awareness of his potentially crumbling self. And here it is also often better not to try to alter his perception that the world is filled with enemies who are the despicable targets of his righteous hatred. Socially deleterious though these attitudes might be, they protect him by providing a modicum of control over the diffuse and nameless archaic stimuli—by attaching them, secondarily, to ideational contents—that are threatening the cohesion of his self.

As I implied earlier, similar considerations apply to dreams and dream analysis. Basically there exist two types of dreams: those expressing verbalizable latent contents (drive wishes, conflicts, and attempted conflict solutions), and those attempting, with the aid of verbalizable dream-imagery, to bind the nonverbal tensions of traumatic states (the dread of overstimulation, or of the disintegration of the self [psychosis]). Dreams of this second type portray the dreamer's dread vis-à-vis some uncontrollable tension-increase or his dread of the dissolution of the self. The very act of portraying these vicissitudes in the dream constitutes an attempt to deal with the psychological danger by covering frightening nameless processes with namable visual imagery. Analogous to the considerations presented earlier, it is the analyst's task, with regard to the first type of dream, to follow the patient's free associations into the depths of the psyche until the formerly unconscious meaning has been uncovered. In the second type of dream, however, free associations do not lead to unconscious hidden layers of the mind; at best they provide us with further imagery which remains on the same level as the manifest content of the dream. The scrutiny of the manifest content of the dream and of the associative elaborations of the manifest content will then allow us to recognize that the healthy sectors of the patient's psyche are reacting with anxiety to a disturbing change in the condition of the self—manic overstimulation or a serious depressive drop in self-esteem —or to the threat of the dissolution of the self. I call these dreams *"self-state dreams"*; they are in certain respects similar to dreams of children (Freud, 1900), to the dreams of traumatic neuroses (Freud, 1920), and to the hallucinatory dreams occurring with toxic states or high fever. Examples of this second type of dream can be found in prior contributions (e.g., Kohut, 1971, pp. 4-5, 149). Associations to these dreams did not lead to any deeper understanding, did not uncover any deeper hidden meaning, but tended to focus increasingly on the diffuse anxiety that had been part and parcel of the dream in the first place. And the correct interpretation—not a supportive psychotherapeutic maneuver—explains the dream on the basis of the analyst's knowledge of the vulnerabilities of his patient in general, including his knowledge of the particular situation that, by dovetailing with a specific vulnerability, had brought about the intrusion of the hardly disguised archaic material. In the case of Mr. C.'s "God" dream (Kohut, 1971, p. 149), for example, the analyst said, after he had patiently and carefully listened to the associative material for the better part of the analytic session, that recent events—the patient's looking forward to being publicly honored while simultaneously being frightened at the prospect of having to take leave of the analyst—had rekindled his old grandiose delusions, that he was frightened by their emergence, but that even in the dream he seemed to give evidence of the capacity for mastery through humor. The result of this interpretation was a substantial diminution of anxiety and—what is of much greater significance—the emergence of formerly hidden genetic material from childhood which the patient's strengthened ego was now able to confront. I close my brief excursion into dream psychology by stating that the dreams quoted above are comparatively pure examples of that second type of dream in which archaic self-states are presented in an undisguised (or only minimally disguised) form. Transitional and mixed forms also occur—for example, dreams in which certain elements (often the total setting of the dream, its atmosphere) portray aspects of the archaic self that have emerged, while other elements are the result of structural conflict and are resolvable through the analysis of free associations that gradually lead toward formerly hidden wishes and impulses.

The Theory of Aggression and the Analysis of the Self

Apart from the discussion of Hartmann's theory that resistances are energized by aggression (pp. 83-93), the preceding considerations regarding the psychology of the drives and of the drive-defense-structural model of the mind, as contrasted to a psychology of the self and of the model of the relation of the self to the self-object, were focused on the libidinal strivings. I must therefore now, in order to complete my exposition, turn to aggression.

I will affirm initially that, just as in the case of the phenomena within the realm of love, affection, and interest, the phenomena dealing with assertiveness, hate, and destructiveness can be considered within a framework of drives. Man's destructiveness, in other words, can be looked upon as a primary given of his psychological equipment, and his ability to overcome his killing instinct can be seen as secondary, and can be formulated in terms of his having been able to tame a drive. This outlook on man and the theoretical framework correlated to it have been very fruitful in the past and they remain a powerful explanatory tool inside and outside the clinical situation.

Here is an example of an explanatory statement about man's aggressions made within the framework of the classical drive theory. It can be asserted that man, because he uses eating utensils and consumes his food cooked, must relinquish a great deal of oral-sadistic drive-satisfaction — or, stated in the obverse, he has had to have been able to tame his oral-sadistic drives to a considerable extent in order to be able to eat in a civilized fashion, to relinquish the pleasure of tearing apart raw meat with his teeth and fingernails.

I wish to emphasize again that it was possible to make the preceding statement concerning a hypothetical step in the history of civilization in terms of drive psychology and without reference to the self. Certain limitations of the explanatory power of this approach, however, can be recognized as soon as we ask ourselves why the acquisition of civilized habits bestows a feeling of heightened self-esteem. I believe that the answer is not to be found with the aid of a drive-and-defense psychology, not even with the aid of structural psychology (that is, on the basis of the concept of the superego)—it must be approached through a comparative examination of the participating self and its constituents. True, parental approval transmits the cultural value, and the child may be said to exchange direct drive satisfaction for parental approval (and later the approval of the superego). But this formulation remains unsatisfactory to the empathic observer of cultural progress and individual behavior— while accurate, it remains incomplete so long as it restricts its focus to the drives and to the mental apparatus. What, we ask, for example, are the grandiose fantasies of the self when it initiates an act of tearing apart and devouring? And what, in comparison, are the grandiose fantasies of the self when it initiates the skillful use of eating tools and proudly remains erect as the food is lifted upward to the mouth?[6]

___

[6] The prideful or self-assertive behavior of some animals (the dog's exhibiting himself to his master—chest out, tail up—when he has performed well; certain primates' exhibitionistically getting up on their hind legs) expresses itself via antigravity movements. This pattern of affect expression is

The preceding self-psychological emendations, couched as questions, to a statement made in the terms of classical drive theory were small but by no means insignificant. Still, I know that by themselves they would carry little weight and the need for them would hardly justify the claim that a drive theory of aggression is inadequate, that an additional theory that deals with the phenomena of aggression within the framework of the psychology of the self is needed.

The classical psychoanalytic position that aggressive tendencies (including the tendency to kill) are deeply rooted in man's biological make-up, that aggression must be considered as a drive, rests on a firm basis. Man not only possesses a biologically preformed apparatus enabling him to perform destructive acts—he is, for example, equipped with teeth and with nails, with tools, in other words, that are meant to tear apart, to destroy—he also uses his aggressive potentialities. Indeed, the evidence supporting our conceptualization of man as an aggressive animal, unsuccessful in taming his destructive impulses—i.e., the data concerning man's actual destructive behavior both as an individual and as a member of groups—is overwhelming. No wonder, then, that the

---

in harmony with the theory that flying fantasies and dreams of flying are the expression of the aspirations of man's grandiose self, the carrier and instigator of his ambitions. Are psychology and the theory of the evolution of species here related to one another? Is it the "upright posture" (see E. W. Straus, 1952) which, as the newest acquisition in the sequence of developmental steps, lends itself most aptly to become the symbolic act that expresses the feeling of triumphant pride? The flying dream and the fantasy of flying could then, of course, if this speculation has merit, be taken as the individual expression of the delight of the race—re-experienced by each new generation of toddlers—in the fact that the head is now above the ground, that the perceiving eye, a central organ of the self, has moved upward, has overcome the pull of gravity.

depth psychologist who is not satisfied with the adequacy of the classical formulation will be suspected by his colleagues of being an idealistic escapist who tries to cover up an unpleasant piece of reality. That I have come to see the classical formulation as inadequate, that I think, in particular, that the conceptualization of destructiveness as a primary instinct which strives toward its goal and searches for an outlet is not helpful to the analyst who wants to enable his patients by analytic means to master their aggressions, does not mean that I deny man's destructiveness or that I want to make its manifestations appear to be less frequent or its consequences less momentous than they are. The extent and the importance of man's destructiveness are not in question—what *is* in question is its significance, i.e., its dynamic and genetic essence.

As an empirical scientist and psychoanalytic clinician, I have not arrived at my views concerning the nature of human destructiveness via speculation; my theoretical formulations are derived from empirical data, obtained through the study of my analysands' communications concerning their experiences, especially those that refer to the transference. And it is on the basis of studying those aspects of my patients' transferences that relate to the question of the significance of human destructiveness—particularly their "resistances" and their "negative transferences"—that I have come to see their destructiveness in a different light, i.e., not as the manifestation of a primary drive that is gradually unveiled by the analytic process, but as a disintegration product which, while it is primitive, is not psychologically primal. The aggressions we encounter in the transferences are not psychological bedrock—neither when they occur as "resistances" nor when they occur as "negative transferences." In the first case they are most frequently the result of actions from the side of the analyst (especially, of course, interpretations) that the patient experiences as empathy failures (as lack of in-tuneness with him),[7] with the weight of the motivation resting on the analyst's present behavior. In the second case, they are revivals of reactions to empathy failures from the side of the self-objects of childhood (their lack of in-tuneness with the child), and the weight of the motivations resting on the past (frequently related to the psychopathology of the self-objects of childhood).

Are we justified in drawing general conclusions about the psychological essence of one of man's most pervasive attributes from observing him *in vitro*—particularly from observing and interpreting such a seemingly narrow sample of his behavior as an analysand's resistances and negative transferences? I do not believe that the behavioral scientist outside the psychoanalytic field will take kindly to an affirmative reply to this question. Yet I cannot help but maintain that the access to the significance of the experiential world of man, and thus to the signficance of his behavior, that is opened to us by the observation of (dynamically) broadly and (genetically) deeply understood phenomena in the psychoanalytic situation is unequaled and that the conclusions to which we

[7] It may be advisable to stress here that there is no connotation of guilt or blame involved if the analyst acknowledges the limitations of his empathy. Empathy failures are unavoidable—indeed they are a necessity if the empathy-craving analysand is ultimately to form a firm and independent self. It is, nevertheless, of crucial importance to state to the patient that he, too, is not to blame—at least not in the sense of having manifested some nuclear viciousness—but that his rage was a reaction to a move from the side of the analyst that he experienced as a narcissistic trauma.

come on the basis of these observations deserve indeed to be applied broadly.[8]

In essence then, I believe that man's destructiveness as a psychological phenomenon is secondary; that it arises originally as the result of the failure of the self-object environment to meet the child's need for optimal—not maximal, it should be stressed—empathic responses. Aggression, furthermore, as a psychological phenomenon, is not elemental. Like the inorganic building blocks of the organic molecule, it is, from the beginning, a constituent of the child's assertiveness, and under normal circumstances it remains alloyed to the assertiveness of the adult's mature self.

Destructive rage, in particular, is always motivated by an injury to the self. The deepest level to which psychoanalysis can penetrate when it traces destructiveness (whether it is bound in a symptom or character trait or expressed in a sublimated or aim-inhibited form) is not reached when it has been able to uncover a destructive biological drive, is not reached when the analysand has become aware of the fact that he wants (or wanted) to kill. This awareness is but an intermediate station on the road to the psychological "bedrock": to the analysand's becoming aware of the presence of a serious narcissistic injury, an injury that threatened the cohesion of the self,

---

[8] It goes without saying that conclusions about the significance of various aspects of man's behavior must also be drawn from the observation of man in his natural habitat, i.e., in the arena of history, in politics, as a member of his family, of his profession, etc. Such conclusions should assist the analyst in his investigative tasks as he attempts to discover new psychological configurations in the analytic setting and to explore them with analytic means. The same holds true in reverse. The social and political scientist, and, par excellence, the historian, should be aware of the analyst's findings and conclusions and should apply, test, and if necessary modify them in order to broaden their validity.

especially a narcissistic injury inflicted by the self-object of childhood.

The psychoanalytic reader will, of course, have recognized that I used the term "psychological bedrock" here in order to contrast my view with that voiced by Freud (1937, pp. 252-253) at the end of his profound final statement on the therapeutic effect of psychoanalysis. I do not believe that the castration threat (the male's repudiation of passivity vis-à-vis another male; the female's repudiation of her femininity) is the bedrock beyond which analysis cannot penetrate. The bedrock is a threat that to my mind is more serious than the threat to physical survival and to the penis and to male dominance: it is the threat of the destruction of the nuclear self.[9] For almost all people, it is true, the need to maintain the integrity of the body-self is a prevalent content of the nuclear self. And the same holds true with regard to an individual's initiative and assertiveness. But not of necessity and not without exceptions. If the self-objects' selective responses have not laid down the usual nuclear self in the boy or girl, but have led to the acquisition of nuclear ambitions and ideals that are not characterized by the primacy of phallic-exhibitionistic physical survival and triumphant active dominance, then even death and martyred passivity can be tolerated with a glow of fulfillment. And, in the reverse, survival and social dominance can be bought at the price of the abandonment of the core of the self and lead, despite seeming victory, to a sense of meaninglessness and despair.

Important though it is, not only in theory but also

[9] It bears mention that Freud's bedrock lies in the "biological" field, but concerns a psychological problem, the patient's inability to overcome a narcissistic injury.

and especially in clinical practice, to recognize the genetic-dynamic primacy of the narcissistic injury, let us focus
now on the developmental priority of complex psychological configurations that, from the beginning, contain
aggression—whether aggression is conceptualized as a
drive or as a reaction pattern—only as a subordinated
constituent, just as even the most primitive biological
anlagen are composed of complex organic molecules and
not of simple inorganic ones. (The former are the
primary configurations; the latter, although more primitive, are secondary: they are fragments of the former,
products of the former's disintegration.) The child's rage
and destructiveness should not be conceptualized as the
expression of a primary instinct that strives toward its
goal or searches for an outlet. They should be defined as
regression products, as fragments of broader psychological configurations, should be conceived as fragments of
the broader psychological configurations that make up
the nuclear self. Aggression, in brief, serves *ab initio* as a
constituent of these broader configurations—however
rudimentary they might be in the beginning of life.
Stated in descriptive terms: the behavioral base line with
regard to aggressiveness is not the raging-destructive
baby—it is, from the beginning, the assertive baby,
whose aggressions are a constituent of the firmness and
security with which he makes his demands vis-à-vis
self-objects who provide for him a milieu of (average)
empathic responsiveness. Although traumatic breaks of
empathy (delays) are, of course, experiences to which
every infant is unavoidably exposed, the rage manifested
by the baby is not primary.[10] The primary psychological

---

[10] The findings of F. Leboyer, a French pediatrician, should be considered in this context. Leboyer (1975) claims (and he supports his claims by
filmed evidence) that the raging cry of the newborn infant is not an unalter-

configuration, however short-lived, does not contain destructive rage but unalloyed assertiveness; the subsequent breakup of the larger psychic configuration isolates the assertive component and, in so doing, transforms it secondarily into rage. (How could it be in the reverse — after the successful survival period in utero?) I have no quarrel, in this context, with the behavioral formulation (Benedek, 1938; see also my remarks about the specific theoretical position taken by Benedek and others [1971, p. 219, fn. 1]) that the baby *develops* confidence in his environment. But while this, in essence, sociopsychological formulation describes a developmental sequence correctly, it is inexact because it leaves out of consideration the critical fact that the baby's confidence is innate, that it was there from the start. The baby does not *develop* confidence, he *re-establishes* it. Put in different words: in principle, the base line of *psychological* life is not revealed either in states of complete psychic equilibrium (the dreamlessly sleeping baby) or in states of seriously disturbed equilibrium, i.e., in traumatic states (the raging, hungry baby) — it is given in the experiential content of the first impulses toward the re-establishment of the psychic equilibrium at the moment it had begun to be disturbed (the healthily assertive baby who announces his wants).

Two points should be emphasized with regard to the opinion that aggression is a constituent of nondestructive primary configurations and that the isolated destructiveness — the "drive" — that appears after the breakup of these configurations is, psychologically speaking, a disintegration product.

---

able given. Aggression is initially absent in the baby if, from the beginning, he is responded to with empathy.

(1) At the beginning of life these nondestructive primary psychological configurations are very simple and have no ideational content; still, it must be stressed again: they are not isolated drives. If a depth-psychological theoretician at this point insisted that we here speak of a prepsychological state to be explored by the methods of biology or of behaviorism, he would not be forced to reject the tenet that isolated aggression is psychologically speaking a disintegration product. If he insisted on a biological approach, the question about the psychological essence of the baby's seemingly destructive behavior is simply postponed, and my conclusions would therefore have to apply from that point onward, when psychological life is said to have its beginning. If, however, on the basis of neurophysiological data, a simple behavioristic stance is advocated as the only valid scientific approach vis-à-vis the small infant, we must ask whether the behaviorist does or does not admit an admixture of empathy as he evaluates the infant's activities. If he does, then my conclusions may apply if he does not, then they are again postponed.

(2) The role played by elemental aggression within the context of the broader configurations I presume to exist from the beginning—however primitive they might be in the infant—should be seen as being, at first, in the service of the establishment of a rudimentary self and, later, in the service of its maintenance.[11] Nondestructive aggressiveness is, in other words, a part of the assertive-

---

[11] See in this context the remarks on pp. 274-275 about the parents who, not empathic with the needs of the rudimentary self of the child to define itself via anger, are unable to confront the child with a firm "no" that would be in tune with the child's developmental needs by calling forth his healthy anger.

ness of the demands of the rudimentary self, and it becomes mobilized (delimiting the self from the environment) whenever optimal frustrations (nontraumatic
delays of the empathic responses of the self-object) are experienced. Nondestructive aggressiveness, it should be
added here, has a developmental line of its own—it does
not develop out of primitive destructiveness by educational influences, but develops under normal circumstances from primitive forms of nondestructive assertiveness to mature forms of assertiveness in which aggression
is subordinated to the performance of tasks. Normal,
primary, nondestructive aggression, in its primitive as
well as in its developed form, subsides as soon as the goals
that had been striven for are reached (whether these goals
are related in the main to objects that are experienced as
separate from the self—as independent centers of initiative—or to the self and to self-objects). If, however, the
phase-appropriate need for omnipotent control over the
self-object had been chronically and traumatically frustrated in childhood, then chronic narcissistic rage, with
all its deleterious consequences, will be established. Destructiveness (rage) and its later ideational companion,
the conviction that the environment is essentially inimical
—M. Klein's "paranoid position"—do not therefore constitute the emergence of elemental, primary psychological givens, but despite the fact that they may, throughout
a lifetime, influence an individual's mode of perceiving
the world and determine his behavior, they are disintegration products—reactions to failures of traumatic
degree in the empathic responsiveness of the self-object
vis-à-vis a self the child is beginning to experience, at
least in its first, hazy outlines.

It will bear repeating at this point that the tenets I

propose with regard to the experiences of aggression and rage also apply to the libidinal drives. The infantile sexual drive in isolation is not the primary psychological configuration—whether on the oral, anal, urethral, or phallic level. The primary psychological configuration (of which the drive is only a constituent) is the experience of the relation between the self and the empathic self-object. (See in this context the description [pp. 75-76] of an imaginary interaction of a mother and her child.) Drive manifestations in isolation establish themselves only after traumatic and/or prolonged failures in empathy from the side of the self-object environment. Healthy drive-experiences, on the other hand, always include the self and the self-object—even though, as I pointed out before, if the self is not seriously disturbed we may omit it from our psychodynamic formulations without great harm.[12] If the self is seriously damaged, however, or destroyed, then the drives become powerful constellations in their own right.[13] In order to escape from depression, the child turns from the unempathic or absent self-object to oral, anal, and phallic sensations, which he experiences with great intensity. And these

[12] I have no hesitation in claiming that there is no mature love in which the love object is not also a self-object. Or, to put this depth-psychological formulation into a psychosocial context: there is no love relationship without mutual (self-esteem enhancing) mirroring and idealization.

[13] I am grateful to Dr. Douglas C. Levin for an evocative analogy between the formulations of modern physics and those which I am positing in the present context. Just as the splitting of the atomic nucleus, Dr. Levin maintains, is followed by the appearance of an enormous quantity of energy, so does the break-up of the self (the "nuclear" self) lead to the appearance of an isolated "drive," e.g., to the eruption of narcissistic rage. (It may be added that the most violent eruptions of isolated destructiveness after an injury to a fragmenting or already almost destroyed self occur in certain instances of catastrophic reactions [see Kohut, 1972, p. 383] or in the furor of catatonic schizophrenia.)

childhood experiences of drive-hypercathexis become the crystallization points for the forms of adult psychopathology that are in essence diseases of the self. Thus, here again, the deepest levels to be reached by analysis in, let us say, certain perversions do not concern the experience of the drive (e.g., in behavioral terms, the child's oral, anal, phallic masturbation). And it is not the aim of analysis to confront the patient with a now supposedly fully uncovered drive so that he can learn to suppress it, to sublimate it, or to integrate it in other ways with his total personality. The deepest level to be reached is not the drive, but the threat to the organization of the self (in behavioral terms, the depressed child, the hypochondriacal child, the child who feels that he is dead), the experience of the absence of the life-sustaining matrix of the empathic responsiveness of the self-object.

Returning once more to the consideration of the position of aggression in human psychology, let me emphasize again that rage and destructiveness — I am here also including the genetically decisive precursor experiences in childhood that account for the propensity for narcissistic rage which can be relived in the transference and recalled by our analysands who suffer from narcissistic personality disorders — are not primary givens, but arise in reaction to the faulty empathic responses of the self-object. True, a modicum of frustration of the child's trust in the self-object's empathic perfection is necessary, not only in order to usher in transmuting internalizations which build up the structures necessary for the tolerance of delays, but also in order to stimulate the acquisition of responses that are in harmony with the fact that the world contains real enemies, i.e., other selves whose narcissistic requirements run counter to the survival of one's own self.

If such a modicum of frustration is not present—i.e., if the self-object remains unempathically overly enmeshed with the child for too long—then the condition might supervene, which I have at times, in the clinical situation, jokingly referred to as a "pathological absence of paranoia." But an isolated striving to search for an outlet for rage and destructiveness is not part of the primary psychological equipment of man, and the guilt with regard to unconscious rage that we encounter in the clinical situation should not be regarded as a patient's reaction to a primal infantile viciousness.

The opposite—in my opinion, erroneous—view is held by the Kleinian school. I have elsewhere (1972) discussed the therapeutic attitude that is correlated to the basic theoretical view I am advocating here. In particular (again in contrast to those who are influenced by the Kleinian outlook), it leads (in the over-all strategy of the conduct of the analysis) to a shift of emphasis away from a set of psychological manifestations that lie closer to the psychological surface (the content of the rage, the patient's guilt about his destructive aims) to the deeper-lying psychological matrix from which the rage, and secondarily the guilt about the rage, have arisen. The rage, in other words, is not seen as a primary given—an "original sin" requiring expiation, a bestial drive that has to be "tamed"—but as a specific regressive phenomenon —a psychological fragment isolated by the breakup of a more comprehensive psychological configuration and thus dehumanized and corrupted—which arose as the result of a (pathological and pathogenic) deficiency in empathy from the side of the self-object. Although for tactical reasons the curbing of the rage and the dynamics of the rage-guilt cycle will often temporarily occupy a prominent position on the analytic stage—an analysand who is not conscious of his rage must first experience it before he can fruitfully examine the broader context in which it arises—it is in the long run the task of the analysis to allow the analysand to become sufficiently empathic with himself to recognize the genetic context in which the rage arose and in which the guilt had become reinforced (by the self-objects' blaming the child for their own inability to respond adequately to the child's emotional requirements). If rage and guilt are thus worked through in the transference against the background of the matrix of the pathogenic narcissistic frustrations to which those had been exposed in childhood who have developed narcissistic personality disorders (with secondary rage and guilt), then rage and guilt will gradually subside, the patient will view the parental shortcomings with mature tolerance in a more forgiving light (perhaps as the results of the childhood experience of the parents) and will learn to cope with the unavoidable frustrations of his need for the empathic responsiveness of the environment with the aid of an increasingly varied and nuanced set of responses.

The dynamic-structural relationship between self pathology, on the one hand, and drive fixation and infantilism of the ego, on the other, becomes especially clear in a certain type of sexual perversion in which the disturbance of the self is the center of the psychological illness.

Mr. A. (see Kohut, 1971, pp. 67-73), whose severely abnormal (latently schizophrenic?) mother provided grossly inadequate mirroring for him as a child and whose idealized father-image was shattered traumatically, recalled early in his analysis that as a child he drew

people with large heads supported by bodies consisting of
a pencil-line trunk and pencil-line limbs. Throughout his
life he had dreams in which he experienced himself as a
brain at the top of a substanceless body. As the analysis
progressed he became able to describe the causal (motiva-
tional) connection between the dreadful feelings of emptiness from which he suffered and certain intensely
sexualized fantasies to which he turned when he felt depressed, in which he imagined himself subduing a powerful male figure with his "brains," chaining him through
the employment of some clever ruse in order to imbibe,
via a preconscious fellatio fantasy, the giant's strength.
From early on he had felt unreal because he experienced
his body-self as fragmented and powerless (in consequence of the absence of adequate joyful responses from
the maternal self-object) and because the barely established structure of his guiding ideals had been severely
weakened (in consequence of the traumatic destruction of
the paternal omnipotent self-object). Only one fragment
of his grandiose-exhibitionistic self had retained a modicum of firmness and power: his thinking processes, his
"brains," his cleverness. It is against this background that
we must understand the nonsexual significance of the
perverse sexual fantasy that accompanied his masturbatory activities. The fantasy expressed the attempt to
use the last remnant of his grandiose self (omnipotent
thought: the ruse) in order to regain possession of the
idealized omnipotent self-object (to exert absolute control
over it — to chain it) and then to internalize it via fellatio.
Although the masturbatory act gave the patient fleetingly
a feeling of strength and heightened self-esteem, it was,
of course, unable to fill the structural defect from which
he suffered, and thus had to be repeated again and

again—the patient was indeed addicted to it. The successful filling in of the structural void could, however, ultimately be achieved in a nonsexual way via working through in the analysis. This resulted, not in the incorporation of magical power, but in the transmuting internalization of idealized goals which supplied narcissistic sustenance to the self.

This patient's sadistic fantasies—the chaining of the self-object in order to rob it of its power—became understandable when examined within the framework of the relation of the self to the self-object rather than from the point of view of the psychology of the drives. The puzzling nature of sexual masochism, too, is broadly illuminated if examined in the light of the explanation that, after the child's healthy merger wishes with the idealized self-object have remained unresponded to, the idealized imago breaks into fragments and the merger needs are sexualized and directed toward these fragments. The masochist attempts to fill in the defect in the part of the self that should provide him with enriching ideals through a sexualized merger with the rejecting (punishing, demeaning, belittling) features of the omnipotent parental imago.

Before leaving the topic of perversions, I will, in passing, add for the sake of completeness that there may well exist another type of sexual aberration in which the self is in essence intact. In these instances, the abnormal sexual aims would have established themselves because of a drive regression motivated by a flight from oedipal conflicts, especially under the pressure of castration anxiety. Cases of this type, however, in which a firm self participates actively in the search for specific pregenital pleasure—not, in other words, a self that attempts to gain cohesion and substance with the aid of perverse activities —are rarely encountered in the analyst's clinical practice; I would assume that such individuals will not feel the need for therapy as strongly as those whose central psychopathology is a fragmenting or enfeebled self.

In most perversions, then, that are seen by the analyst in his clinical work, the behavioral manifestations that appear to be the expression of a primary drive are secondary phenomena. The essence of sadism and masochism, for example, is not the expression of a primary destructive or self-destructive tendency, of a primary biological drive that can only secondarily be kept in check through fusion, neutralization, and other means; it is a two-step process: After the breakup of the primary psychological unit (assertively demanded empathy-merger with the self-object), the drive appears as a disintegration product; the drive is then enlisted in the attempt to bring about the lost merger (and thus the repair of the self) by pathological means, i.e., as enacted in the fantasies and actions of the pervert.

But it is not only the conceptualization of the primacy of an aggressive drive, in particular, and of "the drive," in general, that is inadequate with regard to large areas within the universe of complex mental states with which the depth-psychologist deals; the conceptualization of the way in which drives are "processed," particularly such concepts as repression, sublimation, or discharge, which are formed in analogy to gross mechanical action patterns (the damming up of a river, the passage of electricity through a transformer, or the draining of an abscess), do not do justice to a number of important, empirically ascertainable psychological facts. Such seemingly experience-distant issues as those raised by our questioning the concepts of the repression, the sublimation, the discharge of a drive, have important practical consequences; or—to put it in the obverse—the conceptual changes introduced by the psychology of the self influence not only our theoretical outlook but also, and especially, our outlook as therapists, educators, and social activists. If, for example, an analyst's perception of certain behavioral manifestations of his analysands is guided by an image that portrays repressed aggression in the form of a force held in check by a counterforce (defensive overidealization, for instance), then his aim will be to make the aggression conscious so that it can be suppressed, sublimated into characterological firmness, or discharged via realistic action. Or, turning to an example in the social field, a reformer who bases his advice on the classical psychoanalytic theory of the drives might advocate the discharge of the aggressions of slum-dwelling adolescents through institutionalized, socially harmless pursuits, such as sports, aggressive fantasies supplied by movies and television, and the like. But however elegantly simple and persuasive these conceptualizations are, they are not always appropriate. I am certain that, at least in some significant and important instances, aggression cannot be drained like an abscess or discharged like the man's semen in intercourse—severe chronic narcissistic rage, for example, can continue throughout a lifetime in the individual, unmitigated by any discharge, and the same holds true for certain of the most destructive propensities of the group. Kleist's *Michael Kohlhaas* and Melville's *Moby Dick* are artistic illustrations in the realm of the psychology of the individual; Hitler's followers with their vengeful destructiveness constitute a historical example in the realm of group psychology (cf. Kohut, 1972).

We come nearer to conceptual clarity in these instances, and, secondarily, we increase our leverage for eventual control, when we shift our focus from the image of the processing of a drive via a mental apparatus to the idea of the relation between self and self-object. It is the loss of control of the self over the self-object that leads to the fragmentation of joyful assertiveness and, in further development, to the ascendancy and entrenchment of chronic narcissistic rage. The consequence of the parental self-object's inability to be the joyful mirror to a child's healthy assertiveness may be a lifetime of abrasiveness, bitterness, and sadism that cannot be discharged—and it is only by means of the therapeutic reactivation of the original need for the self-object's responses that the actual lessening of rage and sadistic control and a return to healthy assertiveness can be achieved. And similarly with regard to possible remedial action vis-à-vis the aggressions of the group. As I said before, a social reformer influenced by imagery evoked by the concepts of untamed aggressive drives might advocate the furthering of sports in order to lessen the hostile tensions of slum-dwelling adolescents via sublimated and aim-inhibited drive-discharge. The social reformer influenced by the imagery of the fragmented self, however, will focus not on an aggressive-destructive drive but on the poor cohesion of the self of slum-dwelling youths; and he will attempt to institute remedial action by enhancing self-esteem and by supplying idealizable self-objects. It should give us food for thought, however, that a drive-oriented approach may be successful despite the fact that it bases itself on the less relevant theory. To speak in terms of the example just used: the introduction of institutionalized sports may indeed lead to a diminution of the aggressive-

destructive propensities of slum-dwelling youths — not because an outlet for a drive had been provided, but because of the heightening of self-esteem via the facts that a
parental self-object (a government agency) is interested in
the young people, that self-cohesion is increased by the
skillful employment of the body, and that idealizable
figures (athletic heroes) are offered. All these social re-
forms are effective, in other words, because they lead to a
firming of the adolescents' self and thus secondarily to a
diminution of the diffuse rage that had formerly arisen
from a matrix of fragmentation.

The Termination of Analysis
and the Psychology of the Self

As I stated at the beginning of this chapter, our
theoretical outlook will decisively influence our judgment concerning the question whether or not an analysis has reached the point of termination. Contrary to
what one might expect, however, the outlook of structural psychology on the question of termination, even with
the refinements of ego psychology, is not significantly different from the outlook correlated to the topographic
conceptualizations which preceded structural psychology — indeed, seen from the standpoint of the psychology
of the self, the two viewpoints are quite closely related to
one another. True, the "structural outlook" will evaluate
the degree of ego autonomy and ego dominance, of the
independence from or the domestication of man's unruly
drives, whereas the "topographic outlook" evaluates the
degree of accretion of knowledge (the disappearance of
the infantile amnesia, the recall of the pivotal childhood
events, and the grasp of dynamic interconnections). But

the two have this in common: they look upon man's condition as being characterized in essence by the conflict
between his pleasure-seeking and destructive tendencies
(the drives), on the one hand, and his drive-elaborating
and drive-curbing equipment (the functions of the ego
and superego), on the other.

And how, by contrast, does the psychology of the self
evaluate the analysand's readiness to terminate his analysis?

It seems to me that, viewed in broad perspective,
man's functioning should be seen as aiming in two directions. I identify these by speaking of *Guilty Man* if the
aims are directed toward the activity of his drives and of
Tragic Man if the aims are toward the fulfillment of the
self. To amplify briefly: Guilty Man lives within the
pleasure principle; he attempts to satisfy his pleasure-
seeking drives,[14] to lessen the tensions that arise in his
erogenous zones. The fact that man, not only because of
environmental pressure, but especially as the result of
inner conflict, is often unable to achieve his goals in this
area, prompted me to designate him Guilty Man when he
is seen in this context. The concept of man's psyche as a
mental apparatus and the theories clustered around the
structural model of the mind (superego conflict with regard to incestuous pleasure wishes is a classic example)
constitute the basis for the formulations analysts have
employed in order to describe and explain man's strivings

---

[14] In line with my proposition that the field that can be investigated by
depth psychology requires two complementary explanatory approaches (see
pp. 77-78), I am here outlining the psychology of Guilty Man without regard
to a participating self. (See, however, my argument on behalf of a psychology
of the self in the narrow sense, i.e., of a conceptualization of the self as a
content of the mental apparatus, on pp. 205-209.)

in this direction. Tragic Man, on the other hand, seeks to express the pattern of his nuclear self; his endeavors lie beyond the pleasure principle. Here, too, the undeniable fact that man's failures[15] overshadow his successes prompted me to designate this aspect of man negatively as Tragic Man rather than "self-expressive" or "creative man." The psychology of the self—especially the concept of the self as a bipolar structure (see pp. 171-191 below) and the positing of the existence of a tension gradient between the two poles (see p. 180)—constitutes the theoretical basis for the formulations that can be employed to describe and explain man's strivings in this second direction.

Having depicted—though only with the broadest of brush strokes—the two major aspects of the psychological nature of man that I can discern and the two depth-psychological approaches that are required to deal with them, let me round out these considerations by returning to our original questions: What yardstick must we use in order to assess whether a sufficient cure has been achieved through an analysis? And what yardstick must we use in order to assess whether an analysis has reached a

---

[15] Tragic Man's defeat and death do not, however, necessarily signify failure. Neither is he seeking death. On the contrary, death and success may even coincide. I am not speaking here (as did Freud [1920]) of the presence of a deep-seated active masochistic force which drives man to death, i.e., to his ultimate defeat, but of a hero's *triumphant* death—a victorious death, in other words, which (for the persecuted reformer of real life, for the crucified saint of religion, and for the dying hero on the stage) puts the seal of permanence on the ultimate achievement of Tragic Man: the realization, through his actions, of the blueprint for his life that had been laid down in his nuclear self. My delineation of Tragic Man's striving to express the basic pattern of his self, although it, too, refers to a function that lies beyond the pleasure principle, thus differs decisively from Freud's (1920) psychobiological formulations of the existence of a basic striving—a death instinct, Thanatos—that aims toward destructive aggression and death.

valid termination? While large segments of these questions have been answered before in different contexts, they should now take on new dimensions of meaning when re-examined in light of the preceding reflections.

In the case of a structural neurosis we can measure the progress and success of the analysis by estimating how much knowledge the patient has acquired about himself, particularly with regard to the genesis and psychodynamics of his symptoms and pathological character traits, and by estimating how much control he has achieved over his infantile sexual and aggressive strivings, especially over those genetically and dynamically involved in his symptoms and pathological character traits, and how firm and reliable the newly acquired controls are.

If we are dealing with a narcissistic personality or behavior disorder, however, the success of the analysis is to be measured primarily by evaluating the cohesion and firmness of his self and, above all, by deciding whether one sector of the self has become continuous from one of its poles to the other, and has become the reliable initiator and performer of joyfully undertaken activities. Stated in still different terms, in cases of narcissistic personality disorder, the analytic process brings about the cure by filling in the defects in the structure of the self via self-object transference and transmuting internalization. Often — as in the case of Mr. M. — the cure is not achieved through a complete filling in of the primary defect, but through the rehabilitation of compensatory structures. The decisive issue is not whether all structures have been made functional, but whether the exercise of the functions of the rehabilitated structures now enables the patient to enjoy the experience of his effectively functioning and creative self. And I will only add to this simple for-

mulation of a unidirectional cause-and-effect relationship—the filling in of structural defects leading to increased functional vitality—that a reverberating beneficial cycle is now also established: the strengthened self becomes the organizing center of the skills and talents of the
personality and thus improves the exercise of these functions; the successful exercise of skills and talents, moreover, in turn increases the cohesion, and thus the vigor, of
the self.

The preceding response to the interrelated questions
about what constitutes a psychoanalytic cure of a case of
narcissistic personality disorder, and what a valid termination, is in need of further elaboration. It may be criticized, for example, because it appears to neglect the
reference frame of cognition, i.e., because it fails to focus
on the content and on the extent of the knowledge that
the analysand acquired through his analysis, because it
fails to take into account—to evaluate and to measure—
the insight he obtained. It is probably true that the yardstick of knowledge-accretion does not loom as large nowadays as it did in the early days of psychoanalysis—even
with regard to the conflict neuroses. I believe, therefore,
that this shift is not primarily related to the fact that in
early times analysts focused on structural disorders while
today they are directing their major attention to the disorders of the self. The decisive change concerns, in other
words, the attitude of the observer—witness the shift
from the topographic point of view with its emphasis on
knowledge-accretion (to make the unconscious conscious)
to the structural point of view with its emphasis on the
expansion of the domain of the ego—and not the nature
of the subject matter, i.e., it does not concern the shift
from a predominance of the classical transference neu-

roses to a predominance of narcissistic personality disorders. It is in fact just as easy to apply the yardstick of
knowledge-accretion (insight-gain) with regard to the
evaluation of the analytic treatment of the narcissistic
personality disorders as it is with regard to the evaluation
of the analytic treatment of the classical transference
neuroses; only the content of what is to become known
and the resistances opposing the acquisition of knowledge
are not the same in the conflict neuroses as in the narcissistic personality disorders. In the conflict neuroses, the
hidden knowledge concerns—if we are willing to disregard the participating self—drive-wishes. And the resistances which emanate from unconscious infantile layers
of the ego try to protect the personality from experiencing
the fears of childhood concerning these drive-wishes,
e.g., from experiencing castration anxiety. In the narcissistic personality disorders the hidden knowledge concerns the aspirations of the nuclear self—the need to confirm the reality of the self through the appropriate responses of the mirroring and of the idealized self-object.
And the roots of the resistances reach into the most deeply buried unconscious layers of the personality: the resistances are the activities of the archaic nuclear self,
which does not want to re-expose itself to the devastating
narcissistic injury of finding its basic mirroring and idealizing needs unresponded to, i.e., the resistances are
motivated by disintegration anxiety.

Presented in these terms, the difference between the
models of the psychoanalytic process in the transference
neuroses and in the narcissistic personality disorders is
clearly discernible, but is not very great: in the former,
we are dealing with a conflict betwen psychological structures; in the latter, with a conflict between an archaic self

and an archaic environment — a precursor of psychological structure (cf. Kohut, 1971, pp. 19 and 50-53) — that is experienced as part of the self. Considered within this conceptual framework, the criteria to be employed in evaluating the successes and failures of our psychoanalytic endeavors in both structural neuroses and narcissistic personality disorders — and with regard to the question whether the appropriate time for termination has been reached — will essentially be the same. Still, because the repressed content is not the same in the two classes of disorders — incestuous drive-wishes vs. fear of punishment (castration anxiety) in the one; the needs of a defective self vs. the avoidance of the mortification of being re-exposed to the narcissistic injuries of childhood (disintegration anxiety) in the other — these criteria will have to be applied in a different way. While the narcissistic personality disorders are as analyzable as the classical transference neuroses, the self-object transferences these patients develop and the correlated working-through processes their resolution requires do not follow the pattern of the classical model. The essential psychopathology in the narcissistic personality disorders is defined by the fact that the self has not been solidly established, that its cohesion and firmness depend on the presence of a self-object (on the development of a self-object transference), and that it responds to the loss of the self-object with simple enfeeblement, various regressions, and fragmentation. (As I have emphasized before [Kohut, 1972, p. 370, n. 2; 1975b, n. 1], the reversibility of these untoward changes differentiates the narcissistic personality disorders from the psychoses and borderline states.) The termination of the analysis of the narcissistic personality disorders must therefore be evaluated with

the aid of conceptual yardsticks that measure the amelioration of the infirmities of the self that lie in the center
of the psychopathology. In other words, the analysis of a
case of narcissistic personality disorder has reached the
phase of termination when the analysand's self has become firm, when it has ceased to react to the loss of self-
objects with fragmentation, serious enfeeblement, or uncontrollable rage.

But whether evaluated in terms of knowledge accretion (insight) or—clearly a vastly more relevant approach—in terms of the degree of cohesion and stability
of the self that was achieved, I would like to say once
more (cf. pp. 19-20 above) that I attribute great significance to the patient's inner perception (often subtly but
convincingly expressed in his dreams) that the analytic
task is done. The patient's view must, of course, be carefully scrutinized, and the possibility of a defensive flight
into health must be considered. I have nevertheless become more and more convinced that in the narcissistic
personality disorders—and similar considerations also
apply to the classical neuroses—analogous to the spontaneous establishment of the transference (the beginning
of the analytic process), the patient's awareness that a
successful transformation of the self-object into psychological structure has been achieved is an intrinsic part of
a process we must beware of interfering with, one we can
foster and purify, but over the unrolling of which we have
essentially no control.

These considerations lead me to the following preliminary conclusion. The successful end of the analysis of
narcissistic personality disorders has been reached, when,
after a proper termination phase has established itself
and has been worked through, the analysand's formerly

enfeebled or fragmented nuclear self—his nuclear ambitions and ideals in cooperation with certain groups of
talents and skills—has become sufficiently strengthened
and consolidated to be able to function as a more or less
self-propelling, self-directed, and self-sustaining unit
which provides a central purpose to his personality and
gives a sense of meaning to his life. In order to emphasize
that this therapeutic success is achieved by a lasting alteration of psychic functions, I am suggesting the term
"functional rehabilitation" for this result of the process of
the recovery of the self. I am suggesting, in other words,
that the manifestations characterizing the stage of termination of an analysis of a case of narcissistic personality
disorder will being to appear in the analysand's free associations at the point when the self-objects (and their functions) have been sufficiently transformed into psychological structures so that they function to a certain extent (see
p. 187n.; see also Kohut, 1971, p. 278n.) independently,
in conformity with self-generated patterns of initiative
(ambitions) and of inner guidance (ideals).

CHAPTER THREE
Reflections on the Nature of Evidence in Psychoanalysis

One cannot approach the problem of proper termination and cure in analysis unless one first circumscribes the nature of the disturbance that is being treated. And one cannot convince anyone about the accuracy of the definitions of certain psychic disorders to be ameliorated or cured through analysis unless one has first succeeded in demonstrating that the framework into which these definitions are placed—in the present context, the framework of a psychology of the self—is both valid and relevant. The claim that a psychology of the self does indeed fulfill these criteria cannot be satisfactorily supported, however, through logical argument alone. Without empirical data, one can hardly do more than demonstrate the internal consistency of one's views.

Before I undertake arguing the case, on the basis of the examination of empirical data, that psychoanalysis does indeed need a psychology of the self, I would ask anyone wishing to make the serious attempt of evaluating

140

the explanatory power of this new step in theory first to set aside his established convictions that all psychological illnesses can be adequately explained within the framework of mental-apparatus psychology in general, and of modern structural-model psychology (ego psychology) in particular—or even on the maturational level of the Oedipus complex. In other words, the explanatory power and the heuristic value of a new theory, of a new way of viewing the empirical data in the field of complex mental states, can be gauged only if the evaluator can accept the difficult task of temporarily suspending his convictions to the contrary in order to expose himself to new configurations. (I am omitting here the issue of specific emotional resistances and am addressing myself only to the reluctance to give up the security provided by habitual modes of cognitive mastery.) The evaluator must be able to put aside the traditional way of seeing the data frequently enough and for sufficiently prolonged periods so that he can become familiar with the new theory.

Any beginner could of course tell me *ex cathedra,* for example, that Mr. M. broke off his analysis at the point when it really should have started, i.e., at the point when the yearning for the merger with the idealized father would have turned into oedipal competitiveness accompanied by castration fear. Clearly, I cannot deny with complete certainty that oedipal pathology was hiding behind Mr. M.'s narcissistic disturbance. I can only state that, while I remain open to considering such a possibility, it does not, on the basis of extensive clinical experience seem likely—although occasionally one is indeed surprised to discover that a centrally located oedipal pathology has been covered over by what seemed at first to be a primary disturbance of the self.

Further investigations of the various relations existing between self pathology and structural pathology
must, of course, still be undertaken. But they will be able
to shed new and perhaps unexpected light on human psychology only under the condition that the investigator's
mind is not closed to the idea that a whole sector of
human psychology is in essence independent of the child's
oedipal experiences and that the Oedipus complex is not
only the center of a certain type of psychological disturbance, but that it is a center of psychological health as
well—that it is a developmental achievement.

The assessment of the comparative significance—
with regard to normal development and psychopathology
—of the child's experiences with the objects involved in
the oedipal drama, on the one hand, and of the child's
experiences with the self-objects involved in the drama of
the formation of the self, on the other hand, warrants a
return to concentrated, unprejudiced clinical observation. Clinical descriptions given in essays and books, however, even in the form of extensive case histories, can
rarely by themselves supply convincing proof for the correctness of specific interpretations of specific psychological data, and they can never by themselves supply sufficient evidence in support of the claim that one viewpoint is more adequate, more encompassing, more accurately discerning than another. The enormous number
of variables contained in the psychological field dooms a
purely cognitive approach to failure. The refined empathy of the trained human observer, however, constitutes a potentially adequate instrument for the performance of the first step—understanding—of the two-step
procedure—understanding-explaining—that character-
izes depth psychology. The fact that I consider the

trained observer's empathy to be the irreplaceable step that leads to the meaningful grasp — understanding — of the psychological field[1] will illuminate two closely related features of the present work (and of some of my other writings): the use of personal expressions — such as, "I have become increasingly convinced" — and the emphasis in my clinical descriptions on the analyst's responses to the material — the various closures at which he arrives, the gradual conviction that one of them rather than any of the others is correct.[2] My clinical data are meant to be evocative. I want to demonstrate my viewpoint and offer it to my colleagues for experimental use in the laboratory of their own practice. Analysts will be able to acquire a solid conviction about the relevance and the vitality of a psychology of the self only as they employ it in their own work. The fact that the presentation of a case has succeeded in dispelling the reader's doubts about the correctness of the writer's thesis is a testimony to the writer's skill and intelligence — it is not a proof of the correctness of his thesis. An analysand can give fifty well-fitting associations whose ideational content would lead to a specific interpretation of the material — yet his tone of voice, the message emanating from the mood portrayed by his gestures and bodily posture will tell the analyst that the significance of the material lay elsewhere.

How, then, do analysts arrive at a valid understanding of the material under their observation? Depth psy-

---

[1] That the phase of "understanding" must be followed by a phase of "explaining" is of no significance in the present context.

[2] See two simple but important interrelated statements by Freud: his remark about the irreplaceable role of empathy in psychology (1921, p. 110, fn.2) (see p. 306n. below), and his comments on the procedures that lead to scientific solutions in the field of psychoanalysis (E. Freud, 1960, p. 396).

chology, after all, cannot support its claims with the kind of evidence available to such sciences as physics and biology that study the external world via sensory observation. Valid scientific research in psychoanalysis is nevertheless possible because (1) the empathic understanding of the experiences of other human beings is as basic an endowment of man as his vision, hearing, touch, taste, and smell; and (2) psychoanalysis can deal with the obstacles that stand in the way of empathic comprehension just as other sciences have learned to deal with the obstacles that stood in the way of mastering the use of the observational tools—sensory organs, including their extension and refinement through instruments—they employed.

The possibility of achieving valid results in our field must be evaluated against the background of two principles: one concerning the emotional state of the empathic observer, the other the cognitive aspect of his task. One might call the first of these the Emperor's-New-Clothes principle; it is the embodiment of the view that fact-finding in psychoanalysis requires at times the naïve courage of the observer rather than a very highly developed cognitive apparatus. The second principle—let us refer to it as the Rosetta-Stone principle—embodies the view that the validity of newly discovered meanings (or their significance) must be established in analogy to the validation procedure employed in the deciphering of hieroglyphics. If the observer-decipherer can demonstrate to himself that an increased number of phenomena can be combined to spell out a meaningful message when seen from a new point of view, that a broader range of data can now be understood and interpreted meaningfully, then one can indeed say that his conviction about the new mode of interpretation has become stronger.

The essential focus of interest of the psychoanalyst, furthermore, concerns the meaning and the significance of the material under scrutiny, rather than causal sequences. His comprehension of human experience is thus no more accessible to cause-effect considerations in time and space than is the validity of the assertions of a decipherer of hieroglyphics. Stated in different terms, the depth psychologist pursues psychological truth by three methods: by persistently examining empirical data via empathy from as many different viewpoints as he can discover; by singling out the specific empathic stance that allows him to see the data in the most meaningful way; and, last but not least, by removing obstacles to empathy — predominantly in himself, but also, through example and encouragement, on the one hand, and through repeated demonstration to his colleagues, on the other, that a new empathic stance will allow them to discern heretofore not recognized psychological patterns.[3]

The following illustrative clinical episodes — the purpose of their presentation and certain features of the form in which they are given — should be evaluated against the background of the preceding remarks. They are meant to demonstrate that the meaning and significance of certain clinical phenomena are more broadly and deeply understandable when viewed within the framework of the psychology of the self than when viewed within the framework of drive psychology, of the structural model of the mind, and of ego psychology.

---

[3] The future might bring a quantifying approach in which the increasing conviction of the empathic investigator is corroborated by means of a quantifying methodology that determines the number of data or counts the number of details that form meaningful configurations when seen from a particular point of view.

Clinical Illustrations

The Psychoanalyst's Child

In my practice I have, especially in recent years, encountered several patients who were the children of psychoanalysts.[4] They consulted me for reanalysis because
they felt that their previous analyses had been failures.
They were afflicted by a vague sense of not being real
(often in the form of their inability to experience
emotions), and they experienced an intense (yet conflictual) need to attach themselves to powerful figures in
their surroundings in order to feel that their life had
meaning, indeed, in order to feel alive. Their disturbance, as I came to see, was genetically related to the fact
that their parents had from early on communicated to
them, frequently and in great detail, their empathic
insights about what they (the children) thought, wished,
and felt. As far as I could judge—and there were instances in which I have cause to feel on firm ground with
regard to this conclusion—these parents were in general
neither cold nor rejecting. They did not, in other words,
cover over an underlying rejection of the child with the
aid of, in essence, hostile interpretations. These repeated
interpretations did not result in the child's feeling rejected. Nor did they give the child the feeling that he
was *overly* responded to. The pathogenic effect of the
parental behavior lay in the fact that the parents' participation in their children's life, their claim (often cor-

---

[4] The views presented here are not only derived from analyses of
children of psychoanalysts, but also of children of other psychoanalytically
sophisticated parents, such as psychologists, social workers, psychiatrists,
and others.

rectly made) that they knew more about what their children were thinking, wishing, feeling than the children themselves, tended to interfere with the consolidation of the self of these children, with the further result that the children became secretive and walled themselves off from being penetrated by the parental insights. The decisive issue, however, in the present context is the following. In the previous analyses, their analysts had regarded their strong reluctance to reveal themselves and their inability to give themselves over to free association either as a non-transference obstacle to the establishment of a therapeutic alliance or as a transference resistance opposing the emergence of incestuous libidinal wishes or as the manifestation of an object-instinctual negative transference — as a way of frustrating (defeating) the rival parent. In the first instance, the analysts seem to have reacted by exerting — in more or less subtle ways — a degree of moral pressure on the patients, exhorting them to commit themselves to the analytic task; in the second and third instances they had tried to deal with the problem by, as they saw it, appropriate interpretations.

One might easily surmise that these patients' ultimately achieved conviction that their previous analyst had been mistaken is no more than a manifestation of a positive transference to the subsequent analyst. The way the relevant material emerged, however, speaks against this conclusion. As a matter of fact, for a long time in the analysis with me, these patients did not complain about their previous analyst, but tended to take his approach for granted — just as they had never questioned the appropriateness of the parental intrusions. These had been a way of life with them when they were children; and the analyst's pressures and/or interpretations were, as far as

they recognized, similarly accepted by them as appropriate. In fact, it was against considerable resistance that the
patients began to realize—without any suggestion on my
part: indeed, at first to my surprise—that it was a deep
fear of the dissolution of the self that had prompted them
to wall themselves off against the danger of being understood.

The previous analysts of these patients were in all instances that I encountered competent, experienced, and
well-regarded members of the profession who were undoubtedly in tune with the constructive aspect of the resistances on which I am focusing here, or at any rate who
recognized that resistances are unavoidable and must be
treated with respect. I think, however, that the majority
of even these analysts would tend to see the resistance displayed by these patients as a reaction to a deficiency of an
ego that was damaged because it had been overtaxed in
early life. There is an essential and decisive difference between this outlook and the one I am advocating. The
conceptualization of a defective ego (whose boundaries
have not been firmly established) prompts the analyst to
take on a commendable attitude of cautiousness (in order
to preserve the ego boundaries still present), followed by
an educational approach (the attempt to establish cognitive mastery of the relation between ego and object
[cf. Federn, 1947]).

The conceptualizaton of an ego defect, in other
words, leads of necessity to an educational rather than a
psychoanalytic approach—however psychoanalytically
informed this educational approach may be. In view of
the fact that the mental apparatus itself is not an
experiential content for the analysand, the analyst who
conceptualizes the patient's illness as due to a defect of

the ego can do no more than teach the patient to recognize the malfunctions of his defective psychic apparatus. And the patient in turn can do no more than attempt through conscious effort to resist certain existing pathological trends (such as the tendency to believe that others know his thoughts) by the strained activation of opposing forces (by laying stress upon his conscious knowledge that others *don't* know his thoughts).

The conceptualization of a specific psychopathology of the self, on the other hand, leads to a psychoanalytic rather than educational approach. It leads to the emergence of the pathognomonic experiential contents, specifically to the re-experience of the claims of old psychic constellations—claims that had gone into hiding because they had been unempathically disregarded by the self-objects—and it permits these constellations to be re-experienced in the transference—in fact, to become the very center of the psychoanalytic process. The conceptualization of a pathology of the self leads in these cases to the recognition that the patient's resistance against being analytically penetrated is a healthy force, preserving the existence of a rudiment of a nuclear self that had been established despite the parents' distorted empathy; it also leads to the recognition that this nuclear self is becoming increasingly reactivated, i.e., the analyst witnesses the revival of the analysand's archaic conviction of the greatness of his self—a conviction that had remained unresponded to in early life and had thus not been available for gradual modification and integration with the rest of the personality; and, finally, it leads to the recognition that a working-through process is being mobilized which concerns the claims of the reactivated nuclear self in one (or several) of the varieties of a self-object transference.

This working-through process begins in most instances with the mobilization of archaic needs for mirroring and for merger; as working through is maintained, it gradually transforms the patient's ideas of archaic greatness and his wishes for merger with the omnipotent objects into healthy self-esteem and wholesome devotion to ideals.

I have no doubt that the central psychopathology in the cases under consideration concerned the insecure cohesion of the self (or other forms of self pathology). It was this central disturbance that formed the core of the self-object transference (a "mirror transference in the narrower sense" [see Kohut, 1971, pp. 115-125]) that established itself spontaneously in the psychoanalytic situation. The fact that the parents of these patients had continued to intrude via selectively empathic perceptions into their children's minds during the later, verbal stages of their development—i.e., long after the preverbal stage when near-perfect parental in-tuneness with the content of the baby's mind (the baby's needs and wishes) is indeed the prerequisite for the formation of the baby's rudimentary self—proves beyond doubt that they were out of tune with their children's maturational needs (that is, with the requirements of the child's whole self), even though their empathic grasp of certain details of their children's mentation was often quite accurate.[5] The development of the child's self—its clear delineation—was therefore ham-

---

[5] The distorted empathy of these parents for their children is distantly related to the paranoiac's correct but distorted perception of hostile impulses in other people (cf. Freud, 1922, pp. 223-232). In both instances a single tree is seen, but not the woods. I have elsewhere (1971, p. 121) remarked on the analogous distortion of empathy in the analyst who directs his interpretation at a single mental mechanism—at a defense, for example, or some other detail of the analysand's neurosis—at a time when the patient seeks a comprehensive response to his whole self concerning some important event in his life, such as a new achievement.

pered. What the child had needed were not fragmentation-producing interpretations concerning specific ideational and emotional contents of his mind, but interpretations leading to his increasing awareness of his persisting need for cohesion-enhancing responses to his total self. It was the childhood need for such responses (frustrated in childhood and thus intensified) that was revived in the self-object transference; and it was this need that required interpretation. The analyst should not have rejected the resistance against self-revelation as an untoward attitude to be overcome, the sooner the better, in the service of analysis (as the patients began to see it in retrospect, for the enhancement of the parent-analyst's self-esteem), but interpreted it without censure as an important shield against being penetrated by interpretations—a shield with which the patient was attempting to protect a small, coherent sector of his self. It was this barely maintained, secretly safeguarded, comparatively intact sector of the self, however, and not incestuous drive-wishes that now, after its existence had been acknowledged by the analyst's interpretation, became reactivated in the self-object transference. Slowly and against strong resistances, it offered itself to the analyst's view: wanting to be admired and confirmed in order to gain a sense of its reality and, secondarily, aspiring to carry to completion a frustrated developmental step, to expose itself to working-through processes (optimal frustrations) that would allow its integration into the patient's mature personality.

From the Analysis of Mr. W.

And now to another set of more detailed illustrations in support of the claim that a broadening of our focus—

relinquishing exclusive reliance on conflict psychology and the structural model of the mind—to include the conceptual framework of a psychology of the self, will in certain instances allow us to see the psychological data in a new light and increase our ability to activate and maintain specific beneficial working-through processes in the area of our patients' narcissistic disturbance.

Mr. W.,[6] a single man in his late twenties, after trying a number of different jobs, had in recent years been quite successful as a journalist. He had been analyzed before but wanted now to be reanalyzed. He said his first analysis (which had ended about three years earlier) had helped him a little by diminishing his pervasive restlessness. He felt, however, that it was not primarily the insights provided to him during the former treatment that had been responsible for the amelioration of his condition, but the steadying influence of his former analyst—a predictable, devoted, kindly, older man.

Although his complaints when he presented himself for reanalysis were quite vague—he experienced a general dissatisfaction with his life and said that he felt restless and generally "nervous" at times—I can say in retrospect, on the basis of insights gradually obtained in the course of his analysis, that he suffered from that sense of inner uncertainty and purposelessness concerning widespread sectors of his life so characteristic of diffuse disturbances of the self. And the more specific complaint of recurrent increases in his restlessness and nervousness can also in retrospect be seen as referring to episodic

[6] This patient was treated by an experienced colleague who had frequent (once-a-week) and regular consultations with the author during the first three years of this analysis and then continued the consultations, although with less frequency, for another four years until termination.

exacerbations in the weakness of his self-cohesion. Altogether, the most characteristic manifestation of Mr. W.'s psychological disturbance was the recurrence of a syndrome of irritability, hypochondria, and confusion.

On the basis of what we learned during the analysis about the meaning of Mr. W.'s episodically increased restlessness—especially with regard to the effect of separations from the analyst—there can be no doubt that these reactions had always occurred—before, during, and after his previous analysis—in response to events that gave him the feeling that he had been abandoned. At the beginning of the reanalysis, however, and for most of the first year of this analysis, the patient was completely unaware of any emotional responses to actual or impending separations from the analyst and, so far as could be ascertained, had never before been aware of such reactions either in his previous analysis or outside of treatment. Gradually, however, not only was it possible to establish that he was indeed strongly affected by such experiences, but the meaning of the psychological features of his reactions became increasingly understandable.

The initial clue was provided in a dream that occurred toward the end of the first year of the analysis, a few days before the analyst was to be away for a week—in New York, as the patient had learned by chance. In the dream, the patient was in an airplane flying from Chicago to New York. He was occupying a window seat on the left side of the plane, as he mentioned, looking out toward the south. When the analyst pointed out the inconsistency in his report of the dream: that, going from Chicago to New York, he would be looking north, not south, from the left side of the plane, the patient became utterly confused and spatially disoriented—to the point that he literally could not tell right from left for a short time. (I might add here that the spatial disorientations from which he suffered at such periods were not always as harmless as this one. Once, during the second year of the analysis, again in anticipation of a separation from the analyst, he exposed himself to considerable danger when he made a wrong turn into an expressway against fast-moving traffic—a turn, it must be emphasized, he had made correctly many hundreds of times before.) The associations to the spatial disorientation revealed by his dream led him to recall repeated incidents of his adult life and later childhood (of which he had never spoken earlier, although these memories had clearly not been repressed) when he had become spatially disoriented in unfamiliar places—with the dreadful feeling that he would never find his way back to familiar surroundings.

The analysis of Mr. W.'s dream opened the first significant path to the genetic-dynamic understanding of the core of his personality disturbance. When he was about three and a half years old his parents had been forced to leave him, their only child, for the span of more than a year. During that period the patient, who up to this time had known only the big-city surroundings of Chicago, lived on a farm in Southern Illinois with unfamiliar people, distant relatives of his mother. They seemed to have been conscientious people who took care of his physical needs but who otherwise paid only scant attention to him. He did not see his father at all during that year, and had only a very few brief visits from his mother. As the analysis progressed, each of the leading symptoms with which he reacted to separations in the transference led to the recall of significant precursor experiences from that fateful period of his early life.

Before separations and, in the earlier part of the analysis also in response to situations and events he experienced as emotionally analogous to separations — especially when the analyst (occupying the emotional position of the foster family on the farm) seemed distant or unempathic[7] — Mr. W. filled the sessions with more or less anxious descriptions of various physical sensations he was experiencing and accounts of illnesses he believed he was developing. Prominent among his preoccupations was concern about his eyes (which he thought were not focusing properly) and about his hemorrhoids. At such times during the early part of the analysis, he consulted ophthalmologists and proctologists and even considered surgical interventions. He never actually underwent surgery, but managed to exteriorize his obsessional doubts by finding experts who gave him opposing advice concerning treatment. Gradually, as the analysis progressed and made the patient more and more aware of the relation that existed between his hypochondriacal worries and the psychological effect of impending separations from the analyst, he began to recall the crucial mental states from his childhood that were the precursors of the present ones.

As soon as Mr. W. suffered the loss of the self-object analyst, he was deprived of the psychological cement of the narcissistic transference that had maintained the cohesion of his self. And, in consequence, he felt threatened by the fearsome perception that various parts of his body were isolating themselves and were beginning to be experienced as strange and foreign, and by the loss of the

---

[7] Ernest Wolf ("The Disconnected Self," 1976, unpublished) refers to such contingencies as "the functional absence of the self-object."

secure feeling of being a unit in space, a continuum in time, and a center for the initiation of actions and for the reception of impressions.

The choice of symptoms during these episodes was not determined by specific unconscious wish fantasies as are the somatic symptoms of conversion hysteria, but pre-existing minor physical defects to which the patient paid little attention when the cohesion of his self was not threatened became the foci of his attention when his self began to fall apart. The essential psychopathology in such instances is not the emergence of intensified specific sexual and aggressive fantasies in somatic form, but the diminution of the cohesion of the body-self in the absence of the mirroring self-object. The experience of the total self decreases while *pari passu* the experience of the frag-ments of the self increases—a painful process that is ac-companied by a mood of diffuse anxiety. But while the somatic symptoms do not express any specific meaning that could be verbalized and interpreted, the choice of symptoms is not entirely random: certain body parts become the carriers of the regressive development from the patient's yearning for the absent self-object to states of self-fragmentation and will, therefore, especially lend themselves to becoming crystallization points for hypo-chondriacal worry. Fantasies, for example, of a yearning to take in the absent self-object through the eyes and anus might at first have been transitionally experienced by a still cohesive self during the precursor stage in childhood when the hypochondria first occurred. But it is of crucial importance to realize that the eyes and the anus soon cease to serve as the executive organs of a still cohesive self that is longing to see the lost self-object or that wants the lost self-object's ministrations to the anal area. After the self has broken into fragments, the residual part of the self that experiences its own fragmentation, has no other power left to it as it alarmedly seeks some aid in its attempt to reconstitute itself, but to attach its anxieties and complaints to this or that fragment of the body.

We now turn to the deterioration (and temporary loss) of certain of Mr. W.'s basic mental faculties: his ability to orient himself in space, to differentiate right from left, to think precisely, and to express himself clearly. How can we explain these malfunctions as they occurred in the clinical situation and elsewhere—and as they had occurred during the crucial period of his childhood when the basic pathogenic foci were established in his personality? On gross inspection and in terms of social psychology, we could say that in the clinical situation these defects were caused by his being deprived of a symbiotic relationship with a care-taking person (the analyst) who had up to this point functioned as an auxiliary personality. And a similar statement could also be made with regard to other situations in his adult life that imposed an analogous deprivation on him, and with regard to his experiences at the age of four when he had been deprived of his parents at a time when they still performed certain mental functions for him. The empathic stance of the depth-psychological observer of the details of the transference, however, allows us to add a crucial new dimension to explain the patient's behavior. Careful observation of the regressions that took place in the self-object transference demonstrated that the hypochondriacal state always preceded the tendency to disorientation and confusion; that the hypochondriacal preoccupation with fragments of the body-self had to reach a certain intensity before the patient became liable to lose his orientation in space and to experience difficulties in verbal expression. Fragmentation of the self preceded deterioration of ego functions. And the same sequence appears to have occurred during the patient's childhood: the loss of the specific mental faculties that had occurred at that time also required a preceding step, the fragmentation of the self. These deficits were not the direct result of the separation, they were indirectly brought about via the temporary and partial fragmentation of his self. As was true in the transference, first came the absence of the self-object, then followed the fragmentation of the (body-mind) self (in the form of hypochondria and of the other symptoms to be discussed shortly), and finally followed the deterioration of the specific mental faculties mentioned before. This sequence in the causal chain is in harmony with the tenet that there exists a mutually supportive relation between self-cohesion and the optimal productivity and creativeness of the personality, a tenet that is corroborated, though in a pathological and distorted form, by the attempt made by some patients faced with serious self-fragmentation to prevent the total crumbling of the self with the aid of a temporary, frantic increase of various mental and physical activities.

It was in the context of the attempt to understand the bleakness in the patient's outlook on himself and his existence while the analyst was away — there had been no clear-cut change in his mood (he had not been depressed), but his life had seemed impoverished, his mind was not creative, and he had pursued his activities without zest[8] — that he began to speak about a tendency to lie

---

[8] Although one of the initial complaints with which Mr. W. had re-entered analysis had concerned a certain flatness of his outlook on life,

awake for hours during the first part of the night — a tendency that increased during the analyst's absence. And it
was in the context of assessing the change in his over-all
condition that his greater understanding of his hypochondriacal preoccupations and of his insomnia converged
and led to memories of the time when he was alone in the
country and was unable to fall asleep because he felt
vaguely threatened in an environment he experienced as
nonsupportive (nonempathic) and therefore inimical.

There can be no doubt that lacking an empathic environment, the boy had felt threatened by a beginning
fragmentation of his body-self and that he was therefore
unable to give up conscious control (was unable to go to
sleep) because of the fear that if his vigilance ceased his
body-mind self would break apart, never to mend again.[9]
A fantasy game which he played for hours at such times
demonstrates one of the countermeasures he employed to
allay his fragmentation fears. As he lay awake, he
imagined making long excursions on his body. Starting
from his nose, he would imagine himself walking over the
landscape of his body down to his toes, then back again to
his navel, shoulder, ear, etc.; thus reassuring himself that
his body had not fallen apart.[10] His trips from one part of
his body to another reassured him that all the parts were
still there and that they were still held together by a self
that inspected them. The hypochondria repeated these
early experiences: By talking in detail about his anus and

---

this previously pervasive disturbance receded significantly as soon as the new
transference was established.

[9] A considerable number of observations has convinced me that the fear
of a permanent loss of self-cohesion is the major cause of many cases of severe
disturbances of the ability to fall asleep.

[10] See in this context the interpretation of the "little-piggy" game in
Kohut, 1971, pp. 118-119.

about his eyes, he not only gave expression to his anal and visual incorporation needs and to the worry that these and other parts of his body were beginning to be experienced as not part of the self, but he also tried to maintain control over the totality of his body-self by focusing his attention on the parts that were becoming estranged from him.

Decisively important though the experiences on the farm were, the question can be raised whether they would have resulted in the lifelong disturbance of self-cohesion from which Mr. W. suffered had it not been for the influence of still earlier experiences — experiences that were not directly recalled in the analysis. What I have in mind is the influence of the mother's personality on the child in the years before the crucial separation took place. The mere fact that she could let go of the small boy for such a long period might be taken as indicative of a flatness of her maternal feelings; and her behavior during her visits — her apparently abrupt comings and goings — might be understood in a similar way. I would, however, not put too much stock in the reliability of these reconstructions on the basis of the patient's direct memories from childhood. And even the evidence that was obtained from the transference experiences — certain phases of the merger-mirror transference when the analyst was felt to be nonresponsive, unpredictable, and of a nonhuman, stony quality — was only suggestive, not conclusive. The mother's behavior during visits with the patient while the analysis was in progress, however, and the inconsistency of her behavior toward children, which the patient observed and reported to the analyst, allowed a more reliable assessment of her personality. The analyst concluded that, while her attitude had been one of dutiful caretaking, of a fulfillment of obligations, she had not been able to relate to the child with calming emotionality. She emerged as a woman who, deeply insecure about herself—especially about her own body—was also insecure and clumsy about her handling of others, particularly children—and was therefore unable to provide the kind of emotional support to a small child that sets up the central nucleus of self-acceptance and security that a mother with self-acceptance and free maternal emotionality is able to provide for her children.

As stated before, the worry about his physical defects and his appeal for the help of physicians were the adult replicas of the anxieties of childhood and his need for the attention of the missing self-objects. The remedial attempt enacted in his fantasy game, however, had no direct replica in adult life. The only adult behavior that, as analyst and patient came to view it, appeared distantly related to the body-game of childhood was his tendency, when he felt abandoned by self-objects in adult life, to engage in pleasureless sexual activities and to become compulsively interested in obscene photographs. The significance of these activities appeared to lie in the attempt to stimulate himself erotically in order to regain the sense of the aliveness and reality of his body-self. I might add here, even though it probably goes without saying, that, in many instances, the sexual activities of people who are away from home are not primarily due to the temporary diminution of the influence of the superego; they are rather, as in Mr. W.'s case, attempts to stimulate and thus to bring alive a lonely, threatened self.

The second symptom with which Mr. W. responded to separations from the analyst was great irritability. He was, for example, prone to becoming involved in angry arguments and ugly confrontations with comparative strangers—in restaurants, while driving his car, with neighbors. At first the analyst surmised that the irascibility (and the fact that Mr. W. actually provoked a number of bitter verbal arguments and confrontations) was due to an upsurge of aggressiveness (specifically, of death wishes directed against the analyst). But repeated observation of certain features of his mental state and careful scrutiny of his behavior during such times, to be described shortly, led to the conclusion that his mood and his reactions (both in the transference and, under emotionally analogous circumstances, in his childhood when he was temporarily abandoned by his parents) were manifestations of a traumatic state—of a mental condition, encountered with great frequency during the analysis of patients suffering from narcissistic personality disorders, in which he considered himself unsupported and overburdened and felt that his emotional powers were overtaxed. Two of these reactions were in fact quite typical for the condition of psychological overburdenedness that is the essence of a traumatic state. (In the later stages of his analysis, Mr. W. himself began to recognize them as signs indicating that a traumatic state was imminent.) The first of these behavioral manifestations was that the patient overreacted to strong sensory stimuli (in particular, he reacted with great irritability and anger to noises, smells, and bright lights), the second that he became sarcastic—indulging in cutting jokes and an annoying tendency to punning.[11] The most conspicuous behavioral manifestation of Mr. W.'s traumatic state *outside* the

---

[11] For a discussion of the psychology of the traumatic state, see Kohut, 1971, pp. 229-238, especially the interpretation of Hamlet's traumatic state (including his tendency to use sarcastic puns), pp. 235-237.

clinical situation was his irascibility—his tendency to become involved in arguments.

Mr. W.'s state of psychological overburdenedness—the inability of his mental apparatus to handle the stimuli intruding from the surroundings and to cope with external problems of average complexity—was due to the fact that, in consequence of the loss of the self-object, he was not sustained by the experience of a strong central self. His aggression was not (unconsciously or preconsciously) directed at a specific object, but the expression of a tendency to lash out indiscriminately against the whole environment, which had become strange and unsupportive (unempathic) and which he therefore experienced as an impersonal potential attacker. Among the fragmentation products appearing under these circumstances was not only aggressivity in general but aggressivity as it related to specific erogenous zones. His aggression was, in other words, expressed on a variety of drive levels. Anal aggression (e.g., the impulse to flatulate in social situations) was often prominent; but oral and phallic aggression (the former through biting verbal attacks; the latter as provocative exhibitionism, e.g., "fuck-you" signs at drivers who annoyed him) was also frequently in evidence. Because his fragmenting self did not function as effectively as before as the organizing center of his activities, did not adequately provide him with the synthesis required for efficient functioning, the patient was hard pressed on two counts: he confronted an unfamiliar environment which, in a revival of the crucial childhood experiences, was not empathically in tune with him and thus became anxiety-provoking; and his capacity to cope with his environment was much reduced—the mental mechanisms he usually employed had become disorganized. The patient's insecurity vis-à-vis his surroundings was further diminished because the emotional powers he could still muster were now deflected from the task of dealing with the environment and had to be committed to the task of holding the self together. External demands were therefore an unwelcome drain on his energies, and he reacted to them, whatever their content, as inimical intrusions.

In addition to irascibility, Mr. W. at these times of separation displayed obsessive-compulsive characteristics. When, in the beginning of the analysis, the analyst first became acquainted with the appearance or increase of obsessive-compulsive features in Mr. W.'s ideation and behavior, he formulated a tentative explanation in object-instinctual terms. He thought that the patient, when faced by the analyst's leaving him, became angry at him and wished him dead, but that, in order to preserve the analyst's life, he tried to deflect his anger onto others and erected defenses against the magical power that he unconsciously attributed to his death wishes by developing obsessional symptoms. But—analogous to the dynamic essence of his irascibility—the obsessive-compulsive features of Mr. W.'s ideation and behavior that appeared when he faced a separation from the analyst were not the manifestations of defensive psychological maneuvers designed to stem the tide of object-instinctual aggressions, not the manifestations of a countermagic which the patient had mobilized against the magical power of his unconscious death wishes toward an unfaithful love-object, i.e., toward the analyst.

The significance of one pseudo-obsessive-compulsive symptom was discovered almost accidentally in the course of an analytic session that took place several months after

the one in which the analyst first witnessed Mr. W.'s becoming disoriented in space. The preceding hour had
seemed especially devoid of content, and the analyst, who
admitted that he had been bored, assumed quite naturally that the patient was on strike against analysis or — a
mode of dealing with the trauma of abandonment frequently seen inside and outside the analytic situation —
that he was closing shop before closing time. In view of
the facts that this was again a session which took place
shortly before an interruption of the analysis and that
some important work had been done in the preceding sessions, it was not surprising that the patient appeared to
be unwilling to tackle new, emotionally taxing analytic
tasks. His thinking, however, had taken on the obsessional cast of which I spoke before; and, despite the insights
with regard to the significance of his hypochondria that
had previously been gained and that had again been sub-
stantiated in some recent sessions, he continued to rumi-
nate about his physical health. True, his worries were not
quite as poignant and his preoccupations not quite as intense as they had been during the first year of the analysis. Nevertheless, the analyst assumed, as he listened to
him droning on endlessly about seemingly irrelevant details, that the emotional impact of the forthcoming interruption, and/or the need for a respite after some difficult
analytic work, accounted for the present stagnation.

It was in the course of this dull session that Mr. W.
began to talk about the several items he kept in one of his
trouser pockets. The analyst (who happened to have his
consultation with me shortly after he had seen Mr. W.)
gave me a vivid description of his own reactions. He had
listened to the patient's account with bored resignation,
just as he had done in the past when, under similar cir-

cumstances, he had been annoyed by similar accounts, which, however, he had hardly noticed and which, at any rate, he had soon dismissed from his mind. And he thought again today that he was simply witnessing yet another manifestation of a preinterruption and/or post-progress resistance. He concluded, furthermore, that the patient's detailed enumeration of the various contents of the pocket was quite in tune with the generalized obsessional quality that characterized his thinking whenever he felt under stress. I recall that, listening to the analyst's report, I pondered the question whether the locus of the patient's preoccupations, so close to the genitalia, might indicate the presence of castration anxiety or — "everything is still there" — of a defense against it, and I therefore asked the analyst whether the patient's behavior or his tone of voice suggested the presence of some underlying anxiety. The analyst said he did not think so, adding after further reflection that, on the contrary, he had been struck by the quiet calmness of the patient's voice as he gave the inventory of his pocket, and by the fact that the secure finiteness of the complete listing of the details the patient presented to him (the exact number of coins; a piece of crumpled-up note paper; a small ball of woolly fuzz he had preserved; etc.) stood in strong and remarkable contrast to the general shiftlessness, hurry, restlessness, and insecurity that characterized Mr. W.'s emotional state at this time.

I remember that, following the description of Mr. W.'s behavior, the analyst and I sat for a while in silent contemplation. Somewhat unaccountably, although I had no inkling of the specific meaning of the patient's behavior, the impression grew on me that we were not witnessing a manifestation of the patient's negativism about the analysis but that his account expressed a positive attitude. Judging by the analyst's report, it seemed to me that the patient spoke about the contents of his pocket with the simplicity of a child who calmly and unhurriedly talks to a grownup about something he knows, and who is pleased with himself as he does so. I communicated my impressions to the analyst who said he could not supply any further data that would throw new light on the patient's symptom. He was, however, inclined to believe that I had put my finger on a possibly significant issue. Luckily, the patient continued his behavior in an almost unmodified way during the next session, and the analyst now listened not as if he were being exposed to boring gibberish, but perhaps to a potentially important message. Indeed, after a while, he felt prompted to tell the patient that it seemed to him that he heard a child's proud account to a grownup—just as it had been formulated during the preceding consultation. The analyst was rewarded by the patient's presenting him with some surprising insights and the recall of some important memories. Put succinctly, the psychological significance of Mr. W.'s preoccupation was that, in a world that had become insecure, unpredictable, unfamiliar—as fragmented as his fragmented self—he had taken refuge in an enclosed space which his mind was able to master completely because he knew everything about it and because everything that was within it was familiar and under his control. And in connection with these insights concerning the ongoing transference, a number of childhood memories began to emerge concerning the time when he was first on the farm, when no one had paid attention to him, and when he was often alone while everyone was working in the fields. It was at such times, when his unsupported childhood self began to feel frighteningly strange to him and began to crumble, that he had in fact surrounded himself with his possessions—sitting on the floor, looking at them, checking that they were there: his toys and his clothes. And he had had at that time a particular drawer that contained his things, a drawer he thought about sometimes at night when he could not fall asleep, in order to reassure himself. His preoccupation with the contents of this drawer might well have been the precursor of his preoccupation with the contents of his trouser pocket.

How can we be certain that our explanation of the observational data from Mr. W.'s analysis was correct? Could we not have understood the same data in a different way—for example, by seeing them in the light of oedipal psychopathology? What can the analyst do to avoid errors in his struggle to get nearer to the truth?

All analysts are surely aware of the danger of a possible skewing of their empathic perception by expectations arising from a matrix of learned (or otherwise acquired) theoretical views. But we also know that there is one attitude that, after it has become an integral part of our clinical stance, provides us with an important safeguard against errors arising in consequence of our instinctive commitment to established patterns of thought: our resolve not to be swept away by the comfortable certainty of the "Aha-experience" of intuited knowledge but to keep our mind open and to continue our *trial empathy* in order to collect as many alternatives as possible. Whereas empathy is the scientific analyst's greatest friend, intuition may at times be one of his greatest enemies—from which it follows that, while the analyst must of course not relinquish his spontaneity, he should learn to mistrust explanations that suddenly surge up in him with unquestioned certainty.

Although analysts are aware of the multiplicity of factors that can lead to an amelioration of a patient's condition and are therefore loath to adduce "cure" as proof for the correctness of explanatory formulations, I can say, in support of the correctness of our understanding and of the treatment strategy pursued in Mr. W.'s analysis, that the patient benefited from the treatment. True, neither the disappearance of symptoms nor even a broad change from maladaptive to adaptive behavior patterns constitutes proof that the insights gained in an analysis were correct, that the assessment of the structure of the personality of the analysand was accurate. But a gradual disappearance of symptoms and a gradual change in behavior patterns *pari passu* with increasing insight are indeed highly suggestive of the relevance and correctness of the latter. Mr. W. became a more firmly organized person: he became more thoughtful and deliberate and less inclined to act rashly, on the basis of impulse and hunch. To give an illustration: one area in which he was inclined toward rash action was in his financial dealings. Although he had for a long time occasionally invested in high-risk stocks, the ups and downs of the impulse to do so could be studied during the analysis. The increased urge to undertake risky stock market transactions occurred always when he felt deprived of the relationship to self-objects (e.g., the analyst). These swings are explained genetically in terms of the psychology of the self by the threat to his experience of the continuity of his self along the time axis whenever he lost the self-object, just as the experience of the con-

tinuity of the self, and thus the basic experience of normally unrolling time, had been disrupted in childhood
when he was deprived of the presence of his parents and
exposed to the unpredictable visits of his mother. By
gambling with high-risk stocks he asserted defensively a
magical control over the future at the very time he felt
that his capacity of experiencing himself as a continuum
in time, as a self that had a future, was slipping away.
The increasing understanding of the connection between
the disruptive impact of the loss of the self-object and his
defensive assertion of omniscient control over the future
led to a diminution of the latter need. (To be exact: it was
not only the tendency to engage in risky action that decreased — his obsessional ruminations about the possibility that he might engage in such actions also decreased,
leaving his mind free to engage in productive pursuits.)

Then, too, Mr. W.'s hypochondriacal preoccupations disappeared almost completely in the course of the
analysis. I would again lay stress not so much on the fact
that an important and bothersome symptom was ultimately dissolved, but rather that it receded gradually,
giving way *pari passu* with the working-through processes
with regard to the insights obtained about the significance of the loss of the self-object in the transference and
during his childhood.

CHAPTER FOUR
The Bipolar Self

Theoretical Considerations

I trust I have succeeded in demonstrating (see Chapter Two) the relevance and explanatory power of the hypothesis that the primary psychological configurations in the child's experiential world are not drives, that drive experiences occur as disintegration products when the self is unsupported. It is instructive in this context to examine the disintegration of the two basic psychological functions—healthy self-assertiveness vis-à-vis the mirroring self-object, healthy admiration for the idealized self-object—whose presence under normal, favorable circumstances indicates that an independent self is beginning to rise out of the matrix of mirroring and idealized self-objects. When the child's self-assertive presence is not responded to by the mirroring self-object, his healthy exhibitionism—experientially a broad psychological configuration even when single body parts, or single mental functions, are conspicuously involved as representatives

171

of the total self—will be given up, and isolated sexualized exhibitionistic preoccupations concerning single symbols of greatness (the urinary stream, feces, phallus) will take over. And similarly, when the child's search for the idealized omnipotent self-object with whose power he wants to merge fails, owing to either its weakness or its refusal to permit a merger with its greatness and power, then again, the child's healthy and happy wide-eyed admiration will cease, the broad psychological configuration will break up, and isolated sexualized voyeuristic preoccupations with isolated symbols of the adult's power (the penis, the breast) will take over. Ultimately, the clinical manifestations of an exhibitionistic or voyeuristic[1] perversion may arise in consequence of the breakup of those broad psychological configurations of healthy assertiveness vis-à-vis the mirroring self-object and of healthy admiration for the idealized self-object, to which—protractedly, traumatically, phase-inappropriately—the self-object did not respond. That the perversion, i.e., the sexualized

---

[1] I might well be told by some friendly critics—as has indeed been the case with regard to my having temporarily adhered to Freud's differentiating employment of the terms "narcissistic libido" and "object libido" (see, for example, Freud, 1923b, p. 257, and see also Kohut, 1971, p. 39n.) and with regard to my having temporarily used the term "narcissistic transference" (instead of the term "self-object transference" which I have now introduced) that I should drop such words as "exhibitionism" and "voyeurism" and thus avoid the confusion bound to result from the use of traditional psychoanalytic terminology within the framework of the psychology of the self. But there are a number of what I consider important reasons for retaining the classical terminology. First, I believe that we should do our best to ensure the continuity of psychoanalysis and should therefore whenever possible retain the established terms, even though their meaning may gradually change. Second, the direct confrontation between the new and the old meanings of the established terms allows us, indeed forces us, to be explicit with regard to the redefinitions and reformulations we feel obligated to introduce. Third, and most important, significant connections do indeed exist between the substance of the classical findings from which the old terms were derived and the substance of the findings we are dealing with now.

replica of the original healthy configuration, still contains fragments of the grandiose self (exhibitionism of parts of one's own body) and of the idealized object (voyeuristic interest in parts of the body of others) is to be understood as a vestige of one aspect of the original self-object constellation: it was, transitionally, subject oriented (*self*-object) in the one instance and transitionally object oriented (self-*object*) in the other. The deepest analysis of either one of these two clinical manifestations does not, however, lead to a bedrock of drives, but to narcissistic injury and depression.

Having shown that the responses of the mirroring self-object and the idealizability of the omnipotent self-object must not be viewed within the context of the psychology of drives, we are now in a position to throw further light on the development of the self during childhood by focusing on two processes that take place during the psychoanalysis of patients suffering from self pathology[2] — processes, I might add, that contribute decisively to a favorable outcome of an analysis, i.e., to the establishment of a firmly consolidated, functionally rehabilitated self.

[2] The traditional method by which the psychoanalyst draws his conclusions about his patient's childhood, and about the psychology of childhood in general, rests on Freud's hypothesis that the clinical transferences are at bottom a repetition of childhood experiences. The classical genetic reconstructions, in other words, concern the experiential content of the child's psychic life. By contrast, the method to which I am referring in the present context does not focus on the content of experiences but on the ways by which a specific psychological structure, the self, is laid down. In analyses of patients who suffer from narcissistic personality disorders, we observe the reactivation (in the form of self-object transferences) of structure-building attempts that had been thwarted during childhood. Our conclusions about the specific ways in which structure-building takes place via transmuting internalizations in childhood rests, therefore, on the hypothesis that the self-object transferences during analysis are in essence a new edition of the relation between the self and its self-objects in early life.

The first of these processes contributes to the establishment of a firm self by bringing about the separation of the psychological structures that ultimately form the self from those that will be excluded. In order to illustrate the mode of operations of these processes and to have a solid empirical base for our discussion of their significance, let us return to the termination phase of the analysis of Mr. M.

The questions we had asked ourselves earlier with regard to the conclusion of Mr. M.'s analysis was whether the end of the psychoanalytic process had indeed been reached when the functional rehabilitation of the compensatory structures had been achieved, i.e., when the working-through processes had resulted in the filling in of the defects of these structures of the self. Or, defining this question now even more exactly, we could ask ourselves, in the obverse, whether we should not rather consider the analysis incomplete and the termination premature, in view of the fact that there was another part of the self—the part that had not been fully consolidated because of the insufficiency of the responses from the side of the earliest mirroring self-object—regarding which the working-through processes had been incomplete and which therefore had remained incompletely consolidated.

From a practical point of view, we can be satisfied: Mr. M. seems now to be functioning well, he feels that his former lack of creative initiative has been overcome, and he appears to be happy and productive. Yet, and I am stressing this point again, a broad psychological area remains—one we might have expected to contain the nourishing soil for the deepest roots of the exhibitionism and ambitions emanating from his nuclear self—which was insufficiently explored. In the course of the analytic work, this area seemed to separate itself spontaneously into two layers. The more superficial one (corresponding to late preverbal and early verbal stages of development) became engaged in the working-through process; the other, the deeper one (corresponding to an early preverbal stage), receded.

These endopsychic processes are reminiscent of those apparently analogous ones that occurred in the Wolf Man after Freud had set a termination date, particularly after his analysand had come to see that the analyst "was in earnest" about adhering to it, come what may. "Under the inexorable pressure of this fixed limit," Freud said, "his resistance ... gave way, and ... the analysis produced all the material which made it possible to clear up his inhibitions and remove his symptoms. All the information, too, which enabled me to understand his infantile neurosis," Freud added, "is derived from this last period of work, during which resistance temporarily disappeared..." (1918, p. 11). Some twenty years later, Freud amplified this statement by explaining that the setting of a definitive termination date in an analysis, "this blackmailing device," as he now called it, "cannot guarantee to accomplish the task completely. On the contrary," he continued, "we may be sure that, while part of the material will become accessible under the pressure of the threat, another part will be kept back and thus become buried..." (1937, p. 218).

On first sight, the endopsychic cleavage in the Wolf Man and in Mr. M. may seem to be similar. Closer scrutiny, however, will show that in certain respects the two processes are essentially different. To point immediately to a decisive difference: it is of crucial importance that the separation into two layers—one accessible, the other

inaccessible — occurred in the Wolf Man under the pressure of the analyst's wish to penetrate cognitively into
the analysand's mind, while with Mr. M. it took place
spontaneously, not only without pressure from the analyst, but also — the importance of this fact may not be
obvious at this point, but I believe we will come to see
that it is indeed of great moment — in an analytic atmosphere that is in a subtle but crucial way different from
that created by Freud (or, perhaps, to put it more exactly, from that created by Freud in 1914, before the advent
of ego psychology). In contrast to the therapeutic atmosphere in which analyses were conducted in 1914, the
therapeutic atmosphere in which Mr. M.'s analysis took
place (see in this context Wolf, 1976) was, to state it in
the negative, not suffused by the absolute primacy of the
value system correlated to the model of unconscious and
conscious areas of the mind, i.e., by the primacy of the
value system that it is "good" to know (to know more),
that it is "bad" not to know (to know less).

But if it was Freud's insistence on cognitive penetration within a fixed time limit that overtaxed the resilience
of the Wolf Man's psyche and caused it to crack — a "vertical split, I believe, in contrast to the "horizontal split"
that occurred in Mr. M. — what is it that causes the
diseased grandiose self of Mr. M. to become split into
two layers during the working-through process? Why does
one layer become actively engaged in the therapeutic
work, while the other sinks into the darkness and remains
out of sight?[3] Is this horizontal split no more than the

---

[3] The possibility cannot be discounted that the untreated layer, surviving outside the cohesive structure of the active and productive self, may
serve as a stimulus to the self to persist relentlessly in its activities. I cannot
support this claim with detailed clinical data, but the fact that creativity

result of a healthy inertia from the side of the patient, the creation of a self-protective shield vis-à-vis the possibility of an attack by overly radical psychic surgery, which, by opening up the area of his deepest depression, of his most severe lethargy, and his most profound rage and mistrust, could, in a single-mindedly zealous attempt to establish complete mental health, endanger psychological survival?

Some such preconscious or conscious motivation from the side of the analysand might well have been involved. But it might not have been the only one, might not even have been the most important one. Here are my reasons for this view. In trying, again and again, in analysis after analysis, to determine the genetic roots of the selves of my analysands, I obtained the impression that during early psychic development a process takes place in which some archaic mental contents that had been experienced as belonging to the self become obliterated or are assigned to the area of the nonself while others are retained within the self or are added to it. As a result of this process a core self—the "nuclear self"—is established. This structure is the basis for our sense of being an independent center of initiative and perception, integrated with our most central ambitions and ideals and with our experience that our body and mind form a unit in space and a continuum in time. This cohesive and enduring psychic configuration, in connection with a correlated set of talents and skills that it attracts to itself or that develops in response to the demands of the ambitions and ideals of the nuclear self, forms the central

---

often has a compulsive, involuntary quality and in its absence depression may supervene can be adduced in support of such a hypothesis.

sector of the personality. And I have become convinced that, to some extent at least, a properly conducted analysis of patients suffering from a disturbance in the formation of the self creates a psychological matrix that encourages the reactivation of the original developmental tendency. In other words, the nuclear self of the patient is consolidated, the talents and skills of the analysand that are correlated to the nuclear self are revitalized, while other aspects of the self are discarded or recede.

Only the combination of an additional number of genetic reconstructions derived from careful empathic observation of the sequential transferences that establish themselves during analyses of individuals who suffer from narcissistic personality disorders with the information derived from the analysis and direct observation of children will allow us to provide a reliable answer to the question whether the foregoing description of the processes by which the self is formed is indeed in essence accurate. And only by using the aforementioned combination of research approaches will we be able to obtain the answers to a number of how-and-when questions, which can not yet be answered with certainty, questions such as: (1) *how* the constituents of the nuclear self are gathered and *how* they become integrated to form the specific energic tension arc (from nuclear ambitions via nuclear talents and skills to nuclear idealized goals) that persists throughout each person's lifetime; (2) *when* the several constituents of the nuclear self are acquired (*when,* for example, the nuclear ambitions are established through the consolidation of the central grandiose-exhibitionistic fantasies, *when* the nuclear structure of the specific idealized goals is set up which thereafter remains permanent, etc.), and (3) *when* the whole series of processes by which the nuclear self is laid down may be said to have in essence its beginning and *when* it has its end.

A number of more or less tentative answers to these questions can already be given, but as I said, they must await confirmation by other investigators using the extrapolative-reconstructive method and by still others using different research methodologies. It seems very likely, for example, that, while traces of both ambitions and idealized goals are beginning to be acquired side by side in early infancy, the bulk of nuclear grandiosity consolidates into *nuclear* ambitions in early childhood (perhaps mainly in the second, third, and fourth year), and the bulk of *nuclear* idealized goal structures are acquired in later childhood (perhaps mainly in the fourth, fifth, and sixth years of life). It is also more than likely that the earlier constituents of the self are usually predominantly derived from the relation with the maternal self-object (the mother's mirroring acceptance confirms nuclear grandiosity; her holding and carrying allows merger-experiences with the self-object's idealized omnipotence), whereas the constituents acquired later may relate to parental figures of either sex.[4]

It may well be, furthermore, that the sense of the continuity of the self, the sense of our being the same person throughout life — despite the changes in our body and mind, in our personality makeup, in the surroundings in which we live — does not emanate solely from the abiding *content* of the constituents of the nuclear self and from the *activities* that are established as a result of their pressure and guidance, but also from the abiding specific *re-*

---

[4] Freud's biological tenet of the essential bisexuality of man might be rephrased in psychological terms when re-evaluated against the background of a bipolar self that is derived from male and female self-objects.

lationship in which the constituents of the self stand to each other.

I have tried to express this hypothesis by the employment of an evocative terminology. Just as there is a *gradient* of tension between two differently charged (+ , −) electrical *poles* that are spatially separated, inviting the formation of an electrical *arc* in which the electricity may be said to flow from the higher to the lower level, so also with the self. The term "tension gradient" thus refers to the relationship in which the constituents of the self stand to each other, a relationship that is specific for the individual self even in the absence of any specific activity between the two poles of the self; it indicates the presence of an action-promoting condition that arises "between" a person's ambitions and his ideals (cf. Kohut, 1966, pp. 254-255). With the term "tension arc," however, I am referring to the abiding flow of actual psychological activity that establishes itself between the two poles of the self, i.e., a person's basic pursuits toward which he is "driven" by his ambitions and "led" by his ideals (ibid., p. 250).

If we turn from theoretical formulation to actual experience, we can say that the healthy person derives his sense of oneness and sameness along the time axis from two sources: one superficial, the other deep. The superficial one belongs to the ability—an important and distinguishing intellectual faculty of man—to take the historical stance: to recognize himself in his recalled past and to project himself into an imagined future. But this is not enough. Clearly, if the other, the deeper source of our sense of abiding sameness dries up, then all our efforts to reunite the fragments of our self with the aid of a *Remembrance of Things Past* will fail. We may well ask ourselves whether even Proust succeeded in this task. His creative effort, it is true, held him together for many years after the loss of the parental self-objects (especially of his mother) that had sustained the cohesion of his self. Yet, his monumental novel contains as much evidence of his persisting fragmentation—witness the narrator's recurrent preoccupation with such isolated experiential details as the taste of the madeleine, the perception of the theme by Vinteuil, and the sight of the milk-girl from the train to Balbec; his recurrent preoccupation with thought processes and bodily functions; and his preoccupation with names, particularly with the names of places and the etymology of these names—as it contains evidence of his reconsolidation.[5] Indeed, the reconsolidation achieved by Proust (and the narrator of *Remembrance of Things Past*—see the narrator's mysterious experience [Vol. II, pp. 991-992] after he lost and regained his *physical* balance) rested on a massive shift from himself as a living and interacting human being to the work of art he created. *The Past Recaptured,* the Proustian recovery of childhood memories, constitutes a psychological achievement significantly different from the filling in of infantile amnesia, which as Freud taught us, is the precondition for the solution of structural conflicts and thus for the cure of

---

[5] The effect of the loss of a self-object on Proust's self can be most convincingly demonstrated with regard to the narrator's relation to Albertine: the narrator does not love her, he needs her, he keeps her as his prisoner (even the title of the volume dealing with Albertine is *"La Prisonnière"*), and he molds her to a likeness of himself by educating her. When she leaves him (as described in the volume *Albertine Disparue*) he does not mourn her as a person would mourn a love object, but works through a protracted change in his self. His self breaks up into several fragments (see, for example, Volume II, pp. 683-684) and he merges into others (see p. 767. In this context, see also the similar experiences of Mr. E. in Kohut, 1971, p. 136). While he seems to be desperately preoccupied with regaining possession of Albertine, he is actually attempting to restore his own self.

a psychoneurosis. The Proustian recovery of the past is in
the service of healing the discontinuity of the self. The
achievement of such a cure is the result of intense psychological labors—whether in the analytic situation as
the result of working through a self-object transference or
outside the treatment situation as the result of the working-through performed by an artistic genius. Neither the
recurrent but only temporary self-discontinuities encountered in the narcissistic personality disorders, however,
nor the protracted loss of the self's sense of its past or
future encountered in the psychoses will yield to the
efforts of the sufferer to apply the historical point of view
to his life. In the last analysis, only the experience of a
firmly cohesive nuclear self will give us the conviction that
we will be able to maintain the sense of our enduring
identity, however much we might change.

Yet, as I said before, our sense of abiding sameness
within a framework of reality that imposes on us the
limits of time, change, and ultimate transience is not
based entirely on the lifelong sameness of our basic ambitions and ideals—even these will sometimes change without an ensuing loss of our sense of continuity. It may
ultimately be, not the content of the nuclear self, but the
unchanging specificity of the self-expressive, creative tensions that point toward the future—which tells us that
our transient individuality also possesses a significance
that extends beyond the borders of our life. *"Wer immer
strebend sich bemüht, den können wir erlösen* (Who
always striving efforts makes, for him there is salvation),
say Goethe's angels toward the end of *Faust* as they carry
the immortal core of Faust upward from earth to heaven
(Part 2, lines 11936-7).

Let me now retrace my steps and summarize my conclusions. On the basis of certain genetic reconstructions made during the psychoanalytic treatment of patients suffering from self pathology, I arrived at the hypothesis that the rudiments of the nuclear self are laid down by simultaneously or consecutively occurring processes of selective inclusion and exclusion of psychological structures. And, furthermore, I came to hold the view that the sense of abiding sameness along the time axis—a distinguishing attribute of the healthy self—is laid down early as the result of the abiding action-promoting tension gradient between the two major constituents of the nuclear self. If both of these hypotheses concerning the formation of the self are correct, then we can, in turn, posit now two tenets with regard to the psychoanalytic restoration of a formerly fragmented or otherwise faultily established self: (1) The disengagement from the working-through processes of certain ill-functioning structures indicates, under certain conditions, that the analytic work is nearing completion, that a functioning self has been formed; it does not indicate a flight-into-health incompleteness of the analysis—not even the kind of incompleteness that would be acceptable as a realistic compromise.[6] (2) Analogous statements can also be made with regard to the recovery of childhood memories. The re-

---

[6] It might be helpful to contrast this situation with the analogous one in a case of structural neurosis. Here we sometimes say that it is the better part of wisdom in a particular case not to try to promote further the transference reactivation of unmodified archaic drive-wishes—a reactivation that might lead to dangerous acting out or to other states of ego-insufficiency—if a point in the analysis has been reached in which the patient's defenses appear to operate reliably, and sufficient ego-autonomy in nonconflict areas has been achieved. While our decision to end the analysis in some such instances is fully justified on the basis of the realistic attitude of letting sleeping dogs lie (Freud, 1937), we will nevertheless have to admit that the analysis was *in principle* incomplete.

covery of the past has, in principle, come to its end in the analysis of some cases of narcissistic personality disorder when a sense of the abiding sameness of the self along the time axis has been established. The purpose of remembering in the analysis of disturbances of the self is not to "make conscious" the unconscious components of structural conflicts so that these conflicts can now be resolved in consciousness—a move from the system *ucs.* to the system *pcs.,* from primary process to secondary process, from the pleasure principle to the reality principle, from the id to the ego—but to strengthen the coherence of the self. The Proustian *Remembrance of Things Past* attempts to provide an experientially valid continuity for the self[7]—Proust laid out artistically what the modern psychology of the self attempts to give to man in scientific formulations.

We turn now to the second set of the processes which, as we can reconstruct on the basis of our observations in the therapeutic setting, determine the decision whether the nuclear self will be firmly consolidated during early development and, if so, in what specific form it will be established.

Once the rudiments of the self have been laid down by the first group of processes—the processes of selective inclusion and exclusion of structures—the decision

---

[7] The fact that historiography is in the service of the needs of the "group self" (Kohut, 1976) deserves careful consideration by the historian. He will be able to fight the distorting tendencies that are an outgrowth of this employment if he recognizes clearly that they are in the service of buttressing a pathological group self—pathological self-esteem disturbances of the group —by pathological means, just as is the case in the analogous disturbances of the individual. What is needed in both cases for the recovery of healthy self-esteem is the reactivation of the healthy grandiose self and of the healthy idealized object—of structures, in other words, that had not been integrated into the self of the mature organization.

whether, and, if so, in what form, the self will indeed be firmly established is often decisively influenced by a second one. This group of processes makes its specific contributions to the formation of an ultimately cohesive self by compensating for a disturbance in the development of one of the constituents of the self via the especially strong development of the other. Stated in different terms: the child has two chances as it moves toward the consolidation of the self — self disturbances of pathological degree result only from the failure of both of these developmental opportunities.

The two chances relate, in gross approximation, to the establishment of the child's cohesive grandiose-exhibitionistic self (via his relation to the empathically responding merging-mirroring-approving self-object), on the one hand, and to the establishment of the child's cohesive idealized parent-imago (via his relation to the empathically responding self-object parent who permits and indeed enjoys the child's idealization of him and merger with him), on the other. The developmental move frequently proceeds — especially in the boy — from the mother as a self-object (predominantly with the function of mirroring the child) to the father as a self-object (predominantly with the function of being idealized by the child). Not infrequently, however — especially in the girl — the child's successively mobilized developmental needs for different self-objects en route to the laying down of the nuclear self are directed toward the same parent. And, finally, exceptional circumstances in the environment may occasionally force a child to turn to his parents in the reverse order (from a mirroring father to an idealized mother). From the point of view of the child, the developmental movement (in the majority of cases) leads from the self's greatness being mirrored to the self's active merger with the ideal—from exhibitionism to voyeurism (in the broad sense discussed before); that is, the two basic constituents of the nuclear self which the child attempts to build up appear to have divergent aims. Still, insofar as concerns the whole nuclear self that is ultimately laid down, the strength of one constituent is often able to offset the weakness of the other. Or, expressed in developmental terms, a failure experienced at the first way station can be remedied by a success at the second one. Briefly, we can say that if the mother had failed to establish a firmly cohesive nuclear self in the child, the father may yet succeed in doing so; if the exhibitionistic component of the nuclear self (the child's self-esteem insofar as it related to his ambitions) cannot become consolidated, then its voyeuristic component (the child's self-esteem insofar as it is related to the child's ideals) may yet give it enduring form and structure.

The definition of the bipolarity of the nuclear self and the correlated outline of its genesis is no more than a schema. Yet, although it is an abstraction—or perhaps because it is an abstraction—it permits the meaningful examination of the complexities of the empirical material the psychoanalyst observes in his clinical work. With its aid not only can we understand the many shades and varieties or types of nuclear selves (whether primarily ambitious or idealistic, charismatic or messianic, task-oriented or hedonistic), apart from evaluating their relative firmness, weakness, or vulnerability, we can also grasp the significance of the variety of environmental factors (again, not only gross events and broadly outlined factors in the child's early life, but also—and principally—the pervasive influence of the personalities of the parents and of the atmosphere in which the child grew up), which, singly or in combination with each other, account for the specific characteristics of the nuclear self and for its firmness, weakness, or vulnerability.

I believe that psychoanalysis will move away from its preoccupation with the gross events in the child's early life. There is no doubt that gross events—such as the births, illnesses, and deaths of siblings, the illnesses and deaths of parents, the breakups of families, the child's prolonged separations from the significant adults, his severe and prolonged illnesses, etc.—can play an important role in the web of genetic factors that lead to later psychological illness. But clinical experience tells us that in the great majority of cases it is the specific pathogenic personality of the parent(s) and specific pathogenic features of the atmosphere in which the child grows up that account for the maldevelopments, fixations, and unsolvable inner conflicts characterizing the adult personality. Stated in the obverse: the gross events of childhood that appear to be the cause of the later disturbances will often turn out to be no more than crystallization points for intermediate memory systems, which, if pursued further, lead to truly basic insights about the genesis of the disturbance. Behind the seeming importance of a child's sexual overstimulation and conflicts with regard to his observations of parental sexual intercourse, for example, often lies the much more important absence of the parents' empathic responses to the child's need to be mirrored and to find a target for his idealization.[8] It is, in

---

[8] The phrase "the child's need to be mirrored and to find a target for his idealization" has a categorical sound that I might do well to modify. What a child needs is neither continuous, perfect empathic responses from the side of the self-object nor unrealistic admiration. What creates the matrix for the

other words, deprivation in the area of the sustaining
matrix of empathy, not the pressure of the child's curiosity (which is not pathogenic) that, via depression and
other forms of self pathology, leads him to an excessive
(pathological and pathogenic) involvement with the
sexual life of his parents. Or, to mention briefly a related
matter: the seductive parent is not primarily harmful to
the child because of his seductiveness; it is his disturbed
empathic capacity (of which the grossly sexual behavior is
only a symptom) that, by depriving the child of matura-
tion-promoting responses, sets up the chain of events
leading to psychological illness. And it can also be ascertained, in the obverse, that if a child grows up in a family
in which there is no healthy sex between young and loving

---

development of a healthy self in the child is the self-object's capacity to
respond with proper mirroring at least some of the time; what is pathogenic
is not the occasional failure of the self-object, but his or her chronic incapacity to respond appropriately, which, in turn, is due to his or her own
psychopathology in the realm of the self. As I have repeatedly pointed out, it
is the optimal frustration of the child's narcissistic needs that, via transmuting internalization, leads to the consolidation of the self and provides the
storehouse of self-confidence and basic self-esteem that sustains a person
throughout life. The endopsychic narcissistic resources of normal adults
remain, however, incomplete. The apparent exceptions—some instances of
unshakable inner certainty about the power of the self and about the
righteousness of its values—may be the manifestation of specific forms of serious psychopathology. The psychologically healthy adult continues to need
the mirroring of the self by self-objects (to be exact: by the self-object aspects
of his love objects), and he continues to need targets for his idealization. No
implication of immaturity or psychopathology must, therefore, be derived
from the fact that another person is used as a self-object—self-object relations occur on all developmental levels and in psychological health as well as
in psychological illness. That the difference between health and disease is
here seen to be relative, is exemplified by our reaction to depressed people:
The depressed person's inability to respond to us—our incapacity to infect
him with even a minimum of joy in response to our presence and to our
efforts in his behalf—inevitably creates a lowering of self-esteem in ourselves,
and, feeling narcissistically injured, we react to it with depression and/or
rage.

parents, he may well be forever deprived of certain zestful aspects in his personality. He may then remain emotionally dry and impoverished throughout life — not primarily because he is inhibited, but because he had not been exposed to the subtle influence of that pervasive healthy atmosphere so invigorating to the personalities of those lucky children who grow up in families where a young mother and father are engaged in enjoyable sexual activities. I also believe that some of the sexual traumata of early life (e.g., the boy's castration fears and the discovery of what he interprets as the castrated state of the woman) are not the bedrock of that nexus of factors that bring about certain psychological illnesses, particularly the narcissistic personality disorders, but that more deeply buried and beyond them lies the fear of the cold, unempathic, often latently psychotic, at any rate psychologically distorted, self-object. True, behind the head of the Medusa lies the supposedly castrated genital of the woman. But behind the dreadful genital of the woman lies the cold, unresponding, nonmirroring face of a mother (or of a psychotic father who has usurped the mother's self-object functions) who is unable to provide life-sustaining acceptance for her child because she is depressed or latently schizophrenic or afflicted with some other distortion of her personality.[9] Hence, to reconstruct specific features of the pathogenic parents' personality, of the pathogenic atmosphere in the childhood

---

[9] The pathogenic personality disorder of the self-object is not always easily discerned. In the case of Mr. U., for example (see pp. 55-58; 79-80), the mother seems to have been completely in tune with her son's needs when he was an infant, but because of a pervasive lack in her own self-esteem she was unable to mobilize the empathic tolerance for her child's self-assertiveness (including the growing child's need for approving responses to his increasing ability to stand frustrations) that he required in his later childhood.

family, and to establish a dynamic connection between these genetic factors and the specific distortions of the patient's personality most frequently constitute the principal therapeutic task of analysis.

A wide variety of genetic constellations can interfere with the development of a firmly cohesive and vigorous self in the child. Perhaps the father is seriously disturbed and the mother's influence is weak (as in the case of Schreber—see Kohut, 1971, pp. 255-256); or the mother's serious psychopathology is combined with the traumatic breakdown of the idealized father imago (cf., the discussion of the psychopathology of Patient A. [Kohut, 1971, pp. 57-73]); or a serious disturbance of the mother's personality is combined with a traumatic separation from both parents (cf. the discussion of Mr. W., pp. 151-170, above); or any one of many other combinations of factors can be responsible. However different from each other all these noxious circumstances may be, they all seem to have in common the fact that the child had been deprived of *both* chances in the developmental sequence of events: either the idealized self-object failed the child after the mirroring one had failed or the mirroring self-object failed again when the child attempted to return to it for remedial sustenance after the destruction of a tentatively delimited self by the traumatic failure of the idealized self-object.

The preceding statement is in need of amplification in one respect. When we speak of the failure of both self-objects or of the failure of either the one or the other, the term "failure" and the opposition implied by the use of the words "either" and "or," must not be taken in an absolute sense. It is the more-or-less of the self-object's failures in fulfilling the child's needs, the relative failure of one as compared with the failure of the other that, disregarding other causal factors, determines the ultimate state of the child's self—whether, and if so to what degree, it has suffered a disturbance, has become ill. And these, too, are the circumstances we must investigate when we are examining the question of specificity—in other words, when we are confronting the question why a patient has fallen ill of one type of self pathology rather than of another.

With respect to the last-mentioned contingency, it will be helpful at this point to enumerate and describe the various forms of self pathology as accurately as our present knowledge concerning this new field of investigation allows.

A Classification of Self Pathology

I suggest that we first subdivide the disturbances of the self into two groups of vastly different significance: the *primary* and the *secondary* (or reactive) disturbances. The latter constitute the acute and chronic reactions of a consolidated, firmly established self to the vicissitudes of the experiences of life, whether in childhood, adolescence, maturity, or senescence. They are not important in the present context. The entire gamut of emotions reflecting the state of the self in victory and defeat belongs here, including the self's secondary reactions (rage, despondency, hope) to the restrictions imposed on it by the symptoms and inhibitions of the psychoneuroses and of the primary disorders of the self. Still, even though heightened and lowered self-esteem, triumph and joy, dejection and rage at frustration are part and parcel of the human condition and are, in and of themselves, not pathological, they can be understood only within the framework of the psychology of the self—explanations of these affective states that disregard the ambitions and goals emanating from the pattern of the self will tend to be flat or irrelevant.

But now to the classification of the primary disturbances of the self. This group of disorders of the self includes five psychopathological entities: (1) *the psychoses* (permanent or protracted breakup, enfeeblement, or serious distortion of the self), (2) *the borderline states* (permanent or protracted breakup, enfeeblement, or serious distortion of the self, which is covered by more or less effective defensive structures), and (3) *the schizoid* and the *paranoid personalities,* two defensive organizations employing distancing, i.e., keeping at a safe emotional distance from others—in the first instance via emotional coldness and emotional shallowness, in the second instance via hostility and suspiciousness—which protect the patient against the danger of incurring a permanent or protracted breakup, enfeeblement, or serious distortion of the self. The deepest roots of these pervasive defensive positions reach back to the time when the small child's psyche had to wall itself off against the noxious penetration by the self-object's depression, hypochondria, panic, etc. (See pp. 88-90 for a discussion of the pathogenic sequence of the child's attempt to merge with a soothing self-object, the self-object's pathological reaction to the child's need, and the child's being flooded by the self-object's pathological affective state.)

The preceding three forms of psychopathology are in principle not analyzable, i.e., while a rapport between patient and therapist may be established, the diseased (or potentially diseased) sector of the self does not enter into the limited transference amalgamations with the self-object imago of the analyst that can be therapeutically managed by interpretation and working through.

Two forms of primary self disturbance, however, are in principle analyzable. They are (4) *the narcissistic personality disorders* (temporary breakup, enfeeblement, or serious distortion of the self, manifested predominantly by autoplastic symptoms [Ferenczi, 1930], such as hypersensitivity to slights, hypochondria, or depression), and (5) *the narcissistic behavior disorders* (temporary breakup, enfeeblement, or serious distortion of the self, manifested predominantly by alloplastic symptoms [Ferenczi, 1930], such as perversion, delinquency, or addiction). In these last two forms of psychopathology, the diseased sector of the self enters spontaneously into limited transference amalgamations with the self-object analyst — indeed, the working-through activities concerning these transferences constitute the very center of the analytic process.

I believe that only the last of these definitions requires further elaboration. In order to clarify the reason for assigning to the narcissistic behavior disorders a special place in the classification of the disorders of the self, distinct from that occupied by the narcissistic personality disorders, let me turn to the comparative examination of two frequently occurring instances of self pathology in men.

The comparison I have in mind is between the frequent instances of self pathology in men where the primary defect — the diseased unmirrored self — is covered over by promiscuous and sadistic *behavior* toward women and the equally frequent instances in which the defensive cover consists of *fantasies*.

Why, to focus our attention on two concrete clinical instances, did Mr. M. (see Chapter One)—a narcissistic personality disorder—restrict himself in the main to sadistic fantasies about women, while Mr. I. (Kohut, 1971, pp. 159-161; pp. 167-168)—a narcissistic behavior disorder—engaged in actual relations with many women whom he controlled and dominated and whom he treated sadistically.[10] The answer to this question—however incomplete and tentative it may be—should be regarded as an attempt to make a contribution to a very difficult chapter of psychoanalytic theory and practice, an attempt to solve a vexing problem of neurosogenesis: why some people become neurotic or develop narcissistic disturbances of a neurotic type, while others act out and become perverts, delinquents, or addicts.

If we compare Mr. M. and Mr. I. in this respect, we can immediately say that their defensive structures have this in common: their sadism toward women is motivated by the need to force the mirroring self-object's response to them. We can, in other words, define the function of the defensive structures of these two patients by applying to them a formula akin to one I advanced, in a different context, for the phenomenon of "narcissistic rage" (Kohut, 1972, pp. 394-396). Mr. M.'s sadistic fantasies and Mr. I.'s Don-Juan behavior may be considered manifestations of the variant of narcissistic rage wherein the dominant propelling motivation is less the revenge motif and more the wish to increase self-esteem.

But what is the evidence for our conclusion that

[10] The *Don Juan* syndrome can undoubtedly be motivated by a variety of divergent psychological needs. I speak here only of those patients to whom, as with Mr. M. and Mr. I., it constitutes the attempt to provide an insecurely established self with a continuous flow of self-esteem.

Mr. M.'s fantasies and Mr. I.'s behavior are psychological activities that are maintained by defensive and not by compensatory structures? It is not difficult to answer this question: our conclusion is based on the fact that in both instances the psychological activities are only *one* step removed from the underlying defect in self-esteem. In the dynamics of the transference, for example, it was easily observed that Mr. M.'s fantasies and Mr. I.'s promiscuous behavior always became activated when the patients felt that the analyst did not empathically respond to them; Mr. M.'s fantasies and Mr. I.'s promiscuous activities subsided as soon as they felt that the analyst had re-established empathic contact, had understandingly responded to their sense of narcissistic deprivation—in other words, as soon as the cohesion of their self had been reinforced or their self had become stronger by virtue of the analyst's correct (empathic) interpretation.

Against the background of aspects of these two patients' defensive structures that were identical, I can now outline those that were different. In brief, the essential sameness of the structures suggests that the differences in their manifestations have to be explained not within the framework of the dynamic point of view of classical metapsychology but within the framework of the psychology of the self. Specifically, I advance the hypothesis that the demands made by the diseased self were more intense, more urgent, more primitive in Mr. I.'s case, than in Mr. M.'s. But what accounts for these differences? They are at least partly explained by the fact that Mr. I. was lacking even the minimum of goal-setting structures that Mr. M. had indeed obtained—albeit incompletely—from the idealized self-object, his father. *Both* of Mr. I.'s parents failed to respond empathically to his narcissistic needs; he

was not only exposed to a highly unempathic mother
(who, for example, discussed the boy's brother's genitals
with her friends while he was present), but also to a self-
absorbed, self-esteem-hungry father who needed to out-
shine the son and to take the limelight away from him
and who was incapable of taking pride in the boy's
achievements. Mr. I. did not therefore develop the compensatory structures (i.e., a system of ideals and of correlated executive ego functions) that Mr. M. had developed at least to some extent.

A technical note might be in order here. In the
clinical treatment of such cases, I believe that little is
gained by the analyst's disapproval of the self-esteem-
enhancing behavior of personalities for whom acting
out is the manifestation of defensive structures. Instead of exerting moral pressure, the analyst should
explain to the patient that his behavior is motivated
not by libidinal but by narcissistic needs. He should,
in particular, demonstrate repeatedly to the patient,
by examining the increase or decrease of the patient's
sadistic promiscuous activities, how his defensive behavior is related to the increase or decrease of the manifestations emanating from the primary defect in the narcissistic sphere (his lethargy or depression, his low self-
esteem); and he should, above all, allow the working
through of the various narcissistic transferences to bring
about the gradual diminution of the patient's need for
the asocial behavior through the amelioration of his
primary defect and the increased efficacy of his compensatory structures.

In the very center of the clinical attitude I am advocating lies the analyst's recognition that the analysand's defensive activities are not effective. Instead of dis-

approving on ethical grounds, the therapist should demonstrate to the patient that his behavior does not lead
to the result he is craving. The analyst might, in other
words, tell the patient at the appropriate moment that his
attempt to raise his self-esteem with the aid of his defensive promiscuity is like the attempt of a man with a
wide-open gastric fistula to still his ravenous hunger by
frantic eating.[11] Put differently, it is the very inefficiency
of the defensive maneuvers that explains why they are so
incessantly pursued. The size of Leporello's register (Mr.
I. had, indeed, a similar notebook of telephone numbers
of available women) is an indication of the intensity of the
unsatisfied needs in the realm of their self-esteem experienced by at least some Don Juans. (Not, however, by the
Don Juan of Mozart and Da Ponte. The behavior of this
immortal figure seems to be initiated by a firmly cohesive, defiant, and vigorous self. [Cf. in this context
Moberly's (1967) analysis of Mozart's *Don Giovanni*.])

The examination of the psychopathology of Mr. M.
and Mr. I. was undertaken to explain the dynamic and
economic differences existing between narcissistic personality disorders and narcissistic behavior disorders. Yet,
despite these differences, the cases have much in
common. Not only, as I said before, is the dynamic sig-

---

[11] The employment of the eating simile should not, of course, mislead
us—or the patient—to assume that it is oral craving that lies behind the
genital one. It is the structural void in the self that the addict tries to
fill—whether by sexual activity or by oral ingestion. And the structural void
cannot be filled any better by oral ingestion than by other forms of addictive
behavior. It is the lack of self-esteem of the unmirrored self, the uncertainty
about the very existence of the self, the dreadful feeling of the fragmentation
of the self that the addict tries to counteract by his addictive behavior. There
is no pleasure in addictive eating and drinking—the stimulation of the
erogenous zones does not satisfy. To sum up: the problems of the self cannot
be adequately formulated in terms of drive psychology.

nificance of their defensive psychological activities in essence identical, but they also share the same genetic background. Specifically, they both belong to a particular genetic constellation in the realm of self pathology — a characteristic and instructive one — which I have encountered with some frequency. It consists of several interrelated factors: a serious disturbance in the grandiose-exhibitionistic component of the nuclear self due to grossly distorted mirroring from the side of a mother who had a very serious narcissistic personality disturbance or was even latently psychotic, and a moderately severe disturbance in the component of the nuclear self that contains the idealized guiding values — this disturbance was more severe in Mr. I. than in Mr. M. — due to the fact that the father to whom the child attempted to turn in his search for a sustaining merger with the idealized parent imago was not sufficiently available to the child.

Similar instances are frequently encountered in modern psychoanalytic practice, especially in those pathogenetically decisive family constellations wherein the mother has serious self pathology and the father abandons the family emotionally (e.g., by withdrawing into his business or profession, or by spending all his time in his recreational activities and with his hobbies). The father, in other words, in attempting to save himself from the destructive influence of his wife, sacrifices the child, who remains under the mother's pathogenic influence. My principal reason for singling out this constellation is not the frequency of its occurrence, but rather that it shows with great clarity that the disturbance in the self occurs as the result of the child's having been deprived of the wholesome relation with self-objects in *both* of the crucial areas of the development of the nuclear self — that a wholesome interaction with the idealized self-object did not heal the damage done by the pathogenic interaction with the mirroring one.

From the Analysis of Mr. X. — Clinical Data

When he presented himself for analysis, Mr. X.,[12] twenty-two years old, had been rejected by the Peace Corps, which he had wanted to join in order to obtain the fulfillment of a lifelong wish-fantasy: to help under-privileged, suffering people. He admitted to the analyst that, although the rejection had been the immediate stimulus for his seeking treatment, he had contemplated undergoing psychotherapy even before applying to the Peace Corps, but then decided he would spend several years in the Peace Corps first. The real motive for his wish for treatment appeared to be shame about his sexual dis-turbance[13] and, perhaps as a consequence of his shame, his social isolation and a pervasive sense of loneliness. His sex life, from early adolescence to the beginning of ther-apy, consisted of frequent masturbatory activities (several times a day, with addiction-like intensity) accompanied by homosexual fantasies. He had never had any actual sexual experiences — homosexual or heterosexual.

[12] This patient was in analysis with a young colleague who, shortly after her graduation from the Institute, consulted me toward the end of the third year of the patient's analysis. Her primary motive for the consultation was a desire to obtain first-hand information about my theoretical views. Second-arily, I believe she may also have been motivated by the wish for advice in order to mobilize a rather slow-moving analysis. My information about the case stems from these interviews and several brief conversations later on, as well as from a written report describing the progress of the case.

[13] Although Mr. X. did not reveal his perverse preoccupations to the examiners of the Peace Corps, they may have suspected their presence. At any rate, they rejected him and advised him to seek psychotherapy.

Mr. X.'s mother had idealized him and supported his open display of grandiosity — but only, as we will see, so long as he did not remove himself emotionally from her. Her attitude toward the boy's father had been strongly depreciative. Beginning in latency, the patient, a Lutheran, had felt a desire to enter the ministry, a desire that became even stronger during his adolescence. Although I am not certain that his mother explicitly supported this vocational choice, it was undoubtedly related to the sphere of her influence over him. At any rate, it was the carrier of consciously entertained grandiose ideas (an identification with Christ), which, however, implicitly deprived him of independence and of masculine goals. The patient's mother had often read the Bible to him when he was a child, laying stress on the relation between the boy Jesus and the Virgin. One of their favorite Bible stories — it later became a focus of many of the patient's daydreams — was of the boy Jesus in the temple (Luke 2:41-52); and particular emphasis seems to have been given to the implication that ("sitting in the temple surrounded by the teachers") Jesus was even as a child superior to the father figures ("and all who heard him were amazed at his intelligence and the answers he gave").[14] Although the patient's attempt to enter the Peace Corps was undoubtedly motivated by an offshoot of

---

[14] The atmosphere of family relationships indicated by the biblical passages quoted here is that of the constellation in which the mother belittles her husband, aggrandizes the son as long as he remains attached to her, but unconsciously harbors a deep awe of her own father. When his parents reproach him for his disappearance from home, Jesus replies, "Did you not know that I was bound to be in my Father's house?", referring to the temple as the house of the God-Father. (Translated into the language of depth psychology, he alludes here to the unconscious image of his maternal grandfather.)

the original identification with the figure of the Saviour, Mr. X. did not actually undertake steps that would have led him to the ministry. Without investigating in detail the endopsychic obstacles that stood in his way, I can give the following psychodynamic summary: Mr. X. could not fit his earlier grandiose preoccupations into the life pattern of a clergyman because his relation to religion had become sexualized. Beginning in late adolescence, many of his masturbatory activities were accompanied by fantasies of homosexual relations with the officiating pastor, particularly at the moment of receiving Holy Communion. Although Mr. X.'s desire for sexualized oral incorporation was thus quite close to the psychological surface, his deeply felt need for paternal psychological structure was not expressed through *conscious* fellatio fantasies. The manifest content of the relevant masturbatory fantasies—a fascinating synthesis of the sublimated symbolism of the Church and the patient's primary processes—concerned the crossing(!) of the powerful penis of the priest with his own at the moment of receiving the Host. Thus, at the moment of climactic ejaculation, the patient's preoccupation with a powerful man's penis, with oral incorporation, and with the acquisition of idealized strength found an almost artistically perfect expression in his sexualized imagery about the consummation of the most profoundly significant symbolic act of the Christian ritual.

On the basis of Mr. X.'s conscious memories, the analyst had at first surmised that he had hardly been in any meaningful emotional contact with his father as a child and that the relationship to his father had therefore become unimportant to him. It could be discerned in retrospect, however, that in the initial diagnostic inter-

views Mr. X. had alluded to a deep disappointment he
had experienced concerning his father. The analyst had
not recognized the significance of these references to Mr.
X.'s father, and the patient, too, was completely unaware
at that point that he was alluding to an important emotional need from his childhood. On the contrary, he presented the relevant communication—the complaint that
his mother had deprived him of his rightful share of the
father's estate—entirely with reference to an issue of the
more recent past (the disposition of the inheritance after
his father's death) and expressed it with such bitterness
and resentment that the analyst entertained the possibility of the presence of a hidden paranoia and was for a
while in doubt whether the patient would be suitable for
analysis. (In retrospect, it was possible to explain the
meaning of this complaint: behind the manifest accusa-
tion that he had been short-changed with regard to his
father's *financial* estate lay hidden the deeper reproach
that his mother had deprived him of the opportunity of
his rightful *psychological* inheritance by preventing him
from relating admiringly to his father and from thus
forming a self-structure guided by paternal ideals, values,
and goals.)

The patient began to develop the theme of his attempt to turn from his mother to his father—to avail
himself of a second developmental chance of acquiring a
reliably cohesive self—comparatively late in the analysis.
During the first two and a half years the analyst had
focused her attention almost exclusively upon the patient's overt grandiosity (his arrogance, his isolation, his
unrealistic goals); and she attempted to show Mr. X. that
his grandiosity was, on the one hand, part of an "oedipal
victory" and, on the other, that it was defensive—that it

was buttressing the child's denial of the fact that, despite
the mother's seeming preference for him, the father was
still her real possessor, that he could punish (castrate) the
little boy. Put briefly, she had tried to tell him that be-
neath his overt grandiosity lay the depression of an "oedipal defeat." In other words, the analyst's attention and
interpretations had been focused on the overt grandiosity
in which, as she and I came to recognize, the patient was
no more than the agent of his mother's ambitions. What
had remained disregarded was the patient's latent grandiosity, emanating from the boy's repressed grandiose-
exhibitionistic self — an independent boyish self that had
first yearned in vain for confirmation from the side of the
mother and had then attempted to gain strength by
merging with an idealizable, admired father.

But patients do not give up easily, and their unfulfilled childhood needs continue to assert themselves. Mr.
X. was somehow able to indicate to the analyst that he
had been misunderstood. One of the clues he provided
was the following. Several weeks after the summer interruption marking the end of the second full year of
analysis, he reported a touching sequence of events. He
recalled that at the beginning of his vacation he had
driven alone into a mountainous region, far from Chicago. While driving, he daydreamed a good deal of the
time, as had been his wont throughout his life. The analyst assumed that Mr. X. was now beginning to tell her
about how lonely he had felt when he was away from her.
But his associations moved into a different direction. He
recalled a very vivid daydream which apparently had
almost the features of a real dream. The patient
imagined that his car was not running smoothly, that the
engine was beginning to work irregularly and finally

stopped altogether. He looked at the fuel gauge and realized he had run out of gas. He then saw himself pulling the car over to the side of the road, coming to a stop on the shoulder of the expressway. In his fantasy he got out of the car and tried to signal to the passing cars that he needed help. But one after the other they kept rushing by, and his anxiety grew as he felt himself alone, helpless and powerless. But then a thought came to him. Had he not, long long ago, stashed away into the trunk of his car a can filled with gasoline? Could it be that it was still there and that he could find it and thus get moving again? He saw himself opening the trunk, looking at a heap of luggage and tools and a great variety of other, nondescript, discarded old objects. He dug into the heap and, by God!, here indeed was the old can—rusty, battered, dilapidated, yet still filled with gasoline—just what he had hoped to find, just what he needed. The daydream ended with his pouring the gasoline into the tank and driving off again.

He followed the recall of this daydream by an account of his wanderings through the wooded landscape of the beautiful region to which he had driven. Again he was alone, and again his mind was active during his walks. In particular, he kept reminiscing about an aspect of his childhood about which he had never before spoken in the analysis. He remembered that on very rare occasions he and his father had gone on walks through the woods, that during these walks there had been an intimacy, a closeness between father and son which otherwise had seemed to be totally absent from their relationship. And there was another feature that seemed immediately to be of potentially great significance: in contrast to the depreciated image of his father the patient had presented in the analysis up to that point, he now told the analyst that during these walks the father impressed him as a remarkable man, as an admirable teacher and guide. The father knew the names of the trees, he identified the tracks made by various animals, and he told his son about his having been a good hunter in his younger years who knew how to approach the game and how to kill it with a well-aimed shot. Needless to say, the boy had listened with delighted admiration to his father's stories and was an enthusiastic and attentive pupil when his father thus taught him the rudiments of the woodsman's craft. There was, however, another side to these experiences. Not only did they occur but rarely, they also remained isolated; they had not become integrated with the rest of Mr. X.'s personality, had existed only as enclaves in the boy's life (and in the father's relation to his son). Father and son never talked about these walks afterward, and, as if by a silent agreement, they never mentioned them in front of the mother.

From the Analysis of Mr. X.—Excursion into Theory

The structural basis of the patient's psychological disturbance was a vertical split in his personality. (See chart, p. 213.) One sector functioned by virtue of a still unbroken merger with his mother. The other sector harbored two not fully integrated constituents of his nuclear self—an unresponded-to grandiose-exhibitionistic fragment, and a fragment characterized by idealized-goal structures related to certain admiring attitudes toward his father. As we shall see shortly, the first of these two fragments of the nuclear self (the grandiose-exhibition-istic pole) was even more paralyzed than the second one (the pole that carried the masculine ideals). The nuclear self was, however, not only fragmented and weak, it was also out of touch with the functioning surface of the personality; it had gone into hiding. It had no communication with and no access to the conscious self-structures, but was separated from them by a horizontal split in the personality—it was repressed.

I must explain here why I have in the foregoing—in the context of an account otherwise set firmly within the framework of the psychology of the self—referred to repression, i.e., to a concept that belongs to the armamentarium of classical metapsychology wherein the human psyche is seen as a mental apparatus. I could have avoided it because, as I said earlier (cf. p. 132), self psychology and classical (mental-apparatus) psychology do not need to be integrated; in accordance with a psychological principle of complementarity, they accommodate, side by side, both major aspects of man's total psychology: the psychology of Guilty Man (conflict psychology) and the psychology of Tragic Man (self psychology). Although it is not necessary to integrate these two depth-psychological approaches, it can be done if one wishes to do so, albeit to the detriment of the scope of the explanatory power of sometimes the one and sometimes the other. In the present instance, I chose to fit the self and its constituents into the framework of the structural model of the mind, knowing full well that in doing so I reduced the self to a content of the mental apparatus and thus temporarily abandoned the comprehensiveness of the explanatory powers of an independent psychology of the self. These are permissible inconsistencies because, to my mind, all worthwhile theorizing is tentative, probing, provisional—contains an element of playfulness.

I am using the word playfulness advisedly to contrast the basic attitude of creative science from that of dogmatic religion. The world of dogmatic religion, i.e., the world of absolute values, is serious; and those who live in it are serious because their joyful search has ended — they have become defenders of the truth. The world of creative science, however, is inhabited by playful people who understand that the reality that surrounds them is essentially unknowable. Realizing that they can never get at "the" truth, only at analogizing approximations, they are satisfied to describe what they see from various points of view and to explain it as best they can in a variety of ways. As scientists, we can thus look up to the stars, the macrocosm, and we can look into the infinitesimally small microcosm of particles of matter. And in moving in either direction we can arrive at similar endless worlds of equal significance. The same holds true for the "psychology of the self" and the "psychology of the self within a mental apparatus." We can look at the self as the center of Tragic Man and can study its genesis and its vicissitudes. And we can look at the self as a content of the mental apparatus of Guilty Man and can study its relation to the structures of this apparatus.[15]

But let us shift back from the general to the specific. As I said before, Mr. X.'s personality was divided into two sectors by a vertical split. In one sector, characterized by

[15] Formerly, although the psychology of the self in the broad sense of the term was implicit in all my writings on the subject of narcissism, I defined the self exclusively in what I now call the psychology of the self in the narrow sense of the term, i.e, a psychology in which the self is a content of the mental apparatus. The additional conceptualizations of the psychology of the self in the broad sense of the term, i.e., a psychology in whose theoretical framework the self occupies a central position, is spelled out consistently for the first time in the present work.

a sense of superiority, arrogant behavior, unworldly and religious aims, and identification with Christ, he maintained the old merger with his mother who permitted, and even encouraged, his expression of ideas of greatness—and his pursuit of life goals that were in harmony with them—so long as he did not break the merger-bond with her, so long as he remained the executor of her grandiosity.[16] In the present context, however, we are not focusing on this sector, but on the second one where we encounter the condition to which I referred earlier as the "repression" of the structure that yearned for merger with the idealized parent imago and contained some rudimentary foci of already internalized nuclear ideals. The conditions present in this sector can, as I said, easily be depicted within the theoretical framework of the psychology of the self in the narrower sense of the term: we will say that the nuclear self, especially that part of its nuclear

[16] It could not be decided on the basis of the material at our disposal whether a preconscious fantasy that her son was her phallus belonged to the nexus of the mother's motivations. If so, I would assume such a fantasy to be only the tip of a whole, largely submerged, iceberg of causal psychological constellations. On the basis of my clinical experience, I have to conclude that the maternal need in such instances is not due to any intense wish for a penis, but to the need to remedy a serious defect in the self—witness the fact that the occasionally occurring emancipation of a son or daughter (during adolescence, young adulthood, or even later in life) from a long-standing and seemingly unbreakable merger with one of the parents is often followed by the development of serious self pathology (psychotic depression, paranoia) in the parent. (Compare these formulations concerning the enmeshment between parent and child that is established on the basis of structural *defects* in the parental self with the contrasting remarks by Aichhorn [p. 237n. below] concerning the entanglement that occurs on the basis of unsolved structural *conflicts* in the parents.) These considerations will also explain the nature of the deepest fear of the merged child vis-à-vis the possibility of breaking the ties to the parent. It is not the fear of the loss of love or the loss of the love object but the fear of the permanent disintegration of the self (psychosis) in consequence of the loss of an intense archaic enmeshment with the self-object.

greatness that is acquired through a merger with the idealized self-object, is walled off by repression (i.e., by a "horizontal split") from contact with the consciously perceived self. If we attempt to depict these relationships without a self concept, however, i.e., by employing only the framework of the structural model of the mind and without a self that is conceived as a mental content, then we face greater difficulties. It is, for example, very hard to provide, within the framework of the structural model of the mind, a simple pictorial rendition of the repression of the structures of the superego (the ego ideal)—Freud's drawings could not express his meaning unambiguously here, and he was forced therefore on a number of occasions to add to it the verbal explanation that parts of the superego are unconscious, or, as he expressed it, that the superego dips into the unconscious (1923a, pp. 39, 52; 1933, pp. 69-71, 75, 78-79). The greater ease with which the model of the psychology of the self is here able to deal with the pictorial rendition of these relationships is, I believe, an indication of its greater appropriateness and relevance with regard to the psychological conditions prevailing in the narcissistic personality disorders. (See chart, p. 213.)

A disturbing question confronts us at this juncture: In view of the bipolar organization of the nuclear self (and taking into account the corresponding duality of the pathogenic factors), is there just one or are there two—or perhaps even more—valid solutions to the problems arising from an analysand's need to reconstitute a functioning self through psychoanalysis? On first sight it might appear that this question should be brushed aside and that the answer should be: of course, why not? And one might well be tempted to justify an acceptance of the fact that analysis offers the patient a choice of health possibilities on the basis of Freud's statement that analysis gives "the patient's ego *freedom* to decide one way or the other" (1923a, p. 50n.). But I am afraid that to t..ke this course would be the easy way out, would be resorting to a subterfuge. It is one thing to say that analysis gives the patient a new choice (a "freedom to decide"), so long as we restrict the definition of the goals of analysis to the field of knowledge (to make the unconscious conscious); it becomes another matter when we speak of filling in structural defects, of the restoration of the self.

If we look at the problem with the aid of our clinical illustration, the answer to our question, in principle at least, seems easy. If the analyst does not actively interfere with spontaneous developments, the analytic process will deal with the preanalytic constituents of the patient's personality; after removing obstacles (defense-resistance analysis), it will lead to the freeing of structures that although formerly unavailable to the patient had nevertheless been present. The course of Mr. X.'s analysis, in other words (see chart on p. 213; see also the similarly constructed case of Mr. J. in Kohut, 1971, pp. 179-186, especially the diagram on p. 185), can be described in schematic approximation as unrolling in two phases.

The first phase will focus on breaking down the barrier that maintained the vertical split in his personality. The removal of this barrier has the result that the patient will gradually realize that the self-experience in the horizontally-split sector of his personality—a self-experience of being empty and deprived which, although underemphasized, had always been present and conscious —constitutes his authentic self, and that the up to now predominant self-experience in the nondichotomized sector—the self-experience of overt grandiosity and arrogance—did not emanate from an independent self but from a self that was an appendage to the self of his mother.

The second phase of the analysis may be said to begin when, after the removal of the vertical barrier, the patient's attention has shifted from the nondichotomized to the dichotomized sector.[17] Now the analytic work will focus on the horizontal barrier (the repression barrier) in the pursuit of the principal task of the analysis: to make conscious the *unconscious* structures that underlay the conscious self-experience. We can describe the goal of this second phase with the aid of the beautiful symbolic imagery Mr. X. employed in his daydream: the analysis should uncover the hidden supply of gasoline that can get him going again on the road of his life. Mr. X., in other words, is helped to discover the presence of a nuclear self that had been formed on the basis of his relation with the idealized self-object, his father.

The disturbing doubt, however, whether more than one valid solution to an analysis can exist is not allayed by the foregoing considerations. True, in a case such as that of Mr. X., a properly conducted analysis will unearth the patient's buried unconscious self which was derived from the idealized self-object, leading to this self's ascendancy and thus to the expression of hitherto unavailable am-

---

[17] In speaking of a second phase of the analysis, of a "removal" of the vertical barrier, and of the patient's turning his attention from one sector of his psyche to the other, I am, of course, presenting not the actual sequence of events but a schema of their unrolling. In reality the focus of the analytic work will from time to time—at first frequently, later more and more rarely —return to the vertical barrier, even after the "second phase" of the analysis has begun.

bitions and ideals. And indeed, as a result of the analytic work, the patient's personality underwent a gradual change, clearly in the direction of greater psychological health. *Pari passu,* furthermore, with the greater inner freedom and resilience he thus attained, he was able to make certain decisions that led to the adoption of new goals. He gave up the thought of entering the ministry (or the Peace Corps) and turned toward goals more in tune with being a "teacher and guide"—a pattern that had molded his nuclear self in accordance with his merger with the idealized parent imago represented by his father on their walks through the woods. Nevertheless, compelling as the preceding formulation may be, I will play devil's advocate and ask whether another analysis, concentrating its efforts on the mirror transference and interpreting it correctly, might not have succeeded in disentangling the patient's persisting merger with the mirroring self-object, his mother, and might thus have given Mr. X. greater mastery over the structures that had arisen in the area of his overt grandiosity. We could ask, in other words, whether such an analysis might not have led to success via this other route, opening a path to valid but different psychological solutions, e.g., to the decision to become a minister (and to the ability to reach this goal). Expressed in still different terms, we can ask whether such a result could have been attained if the analyst had further pursued the investigation of the area of overt grandiosity—but not, in accordance with the classical approach, by trying to make Mr. X. conscious of the experience of an oedipal defeat (which was not a psychodynamically active constellation in his personality), but by concentrating on the existing merger with the mother (the psychodynamic essence of his overt grandiosity).

THE CASE OF MR. X. — HIS PSYCHOPATHOLOGY AND THE COURSE OF HIS ANALYSIS

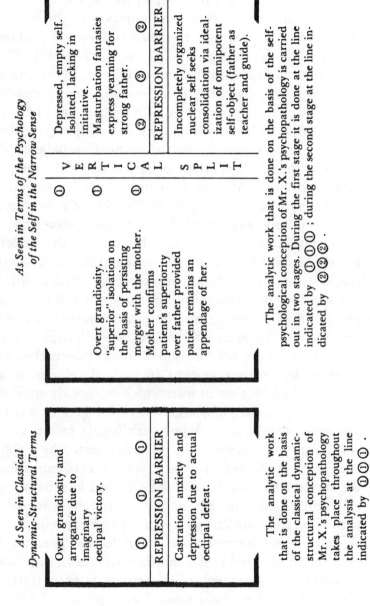

As Seen in Classical Dynamic-Structural Terms

Overt grandiosity and arrogance due to imaginary oedipal victory.

① ① ①

REPRESSION BARRIER

Castration anxiety and depression due to actual oedipal defeat.

The analytic work that is done on the basis of the classical dynamic-structural conception of Mr. X.'s psychopathology takes place throughout the analysis at the line indicated by ① ① ① .

As Seen in Terms of the Psychology of the Self in the Narrow Sense

Depressed, empty self. Isolated, lacking in initiative.

Masturbation fantasies express yearning for strong father.

V E R T I C A L — ① ② ② ②

S P L I T

Overt grandiosity, "superior" isolation on the basis of persisting merger with the mother. Mother confirms patient's superiority over father provided patient remains an appendage of her.

REPRESSION BARRIER

Incompletely organized nuclear self seeks consolidation via idealization of omnipotent self-object (father as teacher and guide).

The analytic work that is done on the basis of the self-psychological conception of Mr. X.'s psychopathology is carried out in two stages. During the first stage it is done at the line indicated by ① ① ① ; during the second stage at the line indicated by ② ② ② .

Cases of analyses do exist in which I would be inclined to answer the foregoing question in the affirmative—indeed I present an example of such an analysis later on (cf. the case of Mrs. Y. on pp. 244-266). These are instances where, at the point in life when the analysis is taking place, two divergent developmental potentialities are apparently about equally strong, or where the possibilities of a healthy unfolding in two divergent directions are about equally available. Such a balance can occur as the result of many different sets of factors. To give an analogy. Melting snow has created a current of water that is now running down the side of a mountain. In most instances there will be preformed unevenesses in the terrain which predetermine the course of the rivulet— but there may be instances when the terrain is such that a single stone, a tree trunk lying there by chance, will be decisive in determining whether the water will turn right or left—thus changing the whole later course of an eventual stream. In some patients, this equilibrium of potentialities occurs because some innate talents that had received less encouragement in early development are now matched by a set of gifts which, although originally not equally strong, had received much greater encouragement in childhood. A boy with innate talents in the employment of his muscular skills is rejected by his athletic physician father. His lesser, yet still adequate gifts in the verbal-conceptual area are nourished by a pathological enmeshment with his mother. Throughout school he withdraws from athletic competition and participation in shop work and concentrates on intellectual pursuits, especially in the field of literature (mother), but also, though to a lesser extent, in the natural sciences (father). Having entered medical school, as expected of him by family tradition, he soon becomes depressed and unable to study. At this point, our fictitious young man seeks analysis. It is not hard to see that, given the equilibrium of forces of which I spoke earlier, a functioning self can now develop in two different ways. One analyst, elucidating the pathological enmeshment with the mother, might enable the patient to emancipate himself from her; and the analysand will build up an independent self that is joyfully seeking praise, recognition, and success—yet he will not discard the ideals he had acquired while merged with his mother. Let us say he will now become a creative, productive psychiatrist. Another analyst, however, to pursue our somewhat playful fantasy, might concentrate on the pathological enmeshment with the mother only up to a certain depth, but will then focus on the then reactivated yearnings for a merger with the paternal ideal. (If indeed the balance is so even, in an exceptional instance, that it allows a choice.) Such an analysis might enable the patient to form an independent self by freeing himself from the pathological enmeshment with the mother *and,* overcoming the injury of paternal rejection, develop and strengthen the surviving minimal nuclei of paternal idealized goals, despite the fact that much of value had already developed in him in harmony with the maternal ideals. In this case the patient might decide to become a surgeon, i.e., after the healing of the narcissistic injury with regard to the father, he will be enabled to reawaken his innate talents in the area of coordinated movement and mechanical skill that, up to this point, had been largely blocked.

In the overwhelming majority of cases, however, the course of the analysis, if correctly pursued, is essentially predetermined by endopsychic factors. In Mr. X.'s case, in particular, the working-through processes of the spontaneously emerging central transference—an idealizing transference toward the father—, empathically interpreted by the analyst, would always lead, after the analysis of both sectors of the personality, to the type of solution to which, in Mr. X.'s case, analysis indeed did ultimately lead: to life goals related to the idealized pole of the self—life goals, in other words, that were only *modified* by the patterns that stemmed from the archaic mirroring experiences.

To be accurate, I should state that it was not any remaining influence of ideals acquired from the mother that helped shape the patient's ultimate personality. But the long-term merger relationship with her had indeed bequeathed on him a specific proficiency in certain areas of knowledge and a correlated set of intellectual skills. That he did not simply discard these abilities and interests (as he was temporarily inclined to do), but retained them, albeit now in the service of newly defined life goals, indicates, I believe, the strength of his integrative capacities and the reliability of the psychic equilibrium he was able to establish. The *actions* required of him in his profession related to the (paternal) idealized self-object, whereas the *contents* related to patterns of knowledge and interest acquired while he was under the influence of the (maternal) mirroring self-object.

On the basis of the preceding considerations we can now conclude that—as holds true with very few exceptions for all analyzable disorders, whether structural neuroses or self disturbances—the structure of Mr. X.'s psychopathology set the pattern for his analysis, that the specific course his analysis took and the specific remedial solution ultimately reached by it were predetermined.

The essential transference (or the sequence of the essential transferences) is defined by preanalytically established internal factors in the analysand's personality structure, and the analyst's influence on the course of the analysis is therefore important only insofar as he — through interpretations made on the basis of correct or incorrect empathic closures — either promotes or impedes the patient's progress on his predetermined path. In Mr. X.'s case, the essential transference related to the reactivation of the needs of the unconscious nuclear self — a nuclear self that attempted to gain strength via specific working-through processes concerning one of its constituents, namely, the pole that carried its masculine ideals. Specific disturbances of the relation between the developing self and the self-objects during the patient's childhood had not permitted the completion of the developmental sequence of (a) merger with the paternal ideal, (b) de-idealization and transmuting internalization of the idealized omnipotent self-object, and (c) integration of the ideals with the other constituents of the self and with the rest of the personality. The essential transference thus related to the reactivation of a specific incompleted developmental task — a Zeigarnick phenomenon (Zeigarnick, 1927) in the transference, one could say —, i.e., to the reintensification of the attempt to fill in a specific structural defect. Before the analytic process began to offer the patient truly effective means to fill in the structural defect, he could do no more than obtain fleeting relief through concretized erotized enactments.[18]

[18] The increased sexual activities and especially the so-called sexualization of the transference encountered in the early phases of some analyses of narcissistic personality disorders are usually manifestations of the intensification of the patients' need to fill in a structural defect. These manifestations

These found their most poignant expression in the patient's feeling suffused with male strength when he imagined the act of crossing his penis with the penis of the priest at the moment of receiving the Host. It was the task of the analysis to move this need for a firm self—particularly for the pole of the self that was able to carry his idealized goals—from its addictive-erotic representation, which provided only a temporary sense of strength, back to the underlying need to reactivate the relation with the idealized self-object. Mr. X., in other words, had to reactivate the relation with the real father of his childhood; he had to shed the Christ-identification his mother had fostered in him, and simultaneously he had to disengage himself from the father-surrogate (the Father of the Trinity—the mother's unconscious imago of her own father) offered him by his mother. It was with the aid of the analytic work focused on the sector of his personality that harbored the need to complete the internalization of the idealized father imago and to integrate the paternal ideal, after the analysis had shifted away from preoccupation with Mr. X.'s overt grandiosity, that structures began to be built, that a firming of the formerly isolated, unconscious self could take place through gradual transmuting internalizations.

I believe that I have adduced sufficient evidence in support of the claim that, in the case of Mr. X., a correctly responsive analysis would always, on the basis of intrinsic factors, become focused on the rehabilitation of the idealized parent imago and would in this way enable the patient to build up a properly functioning sectorial

---

should not be understood as an eruption of drives but as the expression of the patients' hope that the self-object will now supply them with the needed psychological structure.

unit of his self. I especially hope that I have been able to demonstrate the correctness of my approach to those of my colleagues who are wont to place the essentials of psychopathology in earliest infancy and who may thus be inclined to look on the rehabilitation of later structures as only a secondary and peripheral task. Once more let me say: the earliest layers of the psychopathology will often recede from the self — a process that is in essence different from repression — after a modicum of work has been done with them, allowing the crucial work to proceed spontaneously. I am convinced that any interference with this unrolling analytic process from the side of an analyst who insists that the patient continue to deal with the archaic material is in error — however well-meant and carefully buttressed by theories the analyst's actions might be.

I know that there is another group of analysts who will say that I need not have put so much serious effort to the task of demonstrating that the archaic layers of the grandiose self should be allowed to recede — that the archaic material should indeed have been given short shrift because all the material dealt with in this analysis, and especially that dealing with the patient's earliest entanglement, is only defensive. The real analytic material, they will say, has not even entered the analysis; and it is the analyst's principal task to see to it that the patient confronts it. The material these colleagues have in mind, the material that, in accordance with their theoretical views and convictions, always lies at the center of psychopathology, whatever the nature of the disturbance, is of course the Oedipus complex. And it is to the examination of this nuclear complex of the structural neuroses and its relation to the psychology of the self that we must now turn.

CHAPTER FIVE

The Oedipus Complex and the Psychology of the Self

Miss V. was an artist in her early forties. The investigation of penis envy had played a considerable role in a previous analysis, and her low self-esteem and tendency toward feelings of discouragement and hopelessness had been interpreted in accordance with Freud's formulation (1937) that the woman's inability to accept her femaleness constitutes the bedrock of analysis—in other words, that the patient was still yearning to acquire a penis and that her hopelessness related to her inability to reach this goal. During the third year of Miss V.'s analysis with me, she dreamed that she was standing over a toilet urinating and, vaguely, that someone was watching her from behind.[1] Her first associations concerned the fact

[1] With regard to the allusion to the transference (someone watching from behind), which is not important in the present context, I will merely say that the vague image of the analyst is the point of convergence for two lines of associations—the first leading to the need for the constructive presence of the self-object father, the second leading to the fear of the destructive presence of the self-object mother.

that she had had similar dreams in her previous analysis, which, in combination with many other bathroom dreams, had led to the repeated interpretation that she wanted to have a penis and to urinate standing up like a boy. Then she spoke about her previous analyst, a woman who held very strong beliefs about the correctness of her interpretations and had presented them with a certitude that allowed for no doubt from the side of the patient. The associations next turned to the patient's voyeuristic interests, in particular to her interest in her father when he was in the bathroom; and she remembered clearly (as she had always remembered) that as a little girl she had yearned to see her father's body, especially his genitals. The patient became silent, and, when I asked her what she was thinking and feeling, said that she felt depressed, diffusely anxious, and hopeless. On the basis of her pre- ceding associations and the broad knowledge about her personality and childhood I had acquired over the years, I ventured the opinion that the dream and her associ- ations constituted a point of convergence between her feelings about the analysis and the analyst and some crucial issues of her childhood experiences. And I added that I thought that her dream of urinating standing up and her wish to see the father's penis were not primarily related to sexual matters, but to her need—familiar from other memories that had emerged in preceding sessions— to extricate herself from her relation with her bizarre and emotionally shallow mother and to turn toward her emo- tionally more responsive and down-to-earth father. The associations elicited by these remarks brought us some unexpected confirmatory memories. The tip of the ice- berg was the memory that her mother had warned her never to sit down on a toilet outside their own house because of vaguely defined dangers having to do with dirt, infections, bacteria, and the like. The most important understanding, furthermore, to which these associations led was that these fears which were inculcated into the child did not in their essence relate to sexual wishes and conflicts concerning anal or phallic-genital drives but to the mother's hidden paranoid outlook on the whole world. The toilet seat was the world—an inimical, dangerous, infected world. And the child's healthy move toward the world—in sexual and nonsexual directions— was made impossible by the infiltration of the mother's paranoid beliefs into the child's psychic organization. Her wish to see her father's penis was the sexualized rendition of her attempt to turn to him for a positive, vigorous, nonparanoid attitude toward the world. And her essential wish in the analysis was not primarily the wish to obtain a penis-baby from an oedipal father, but to gain his support in order to overcome her mother's influence over her so that she could "sit down on the toilet," that is, to gain his support to be in direct and strong contact with the world. She wanted from him psychological structures that would allow her to be joyful and alive in sexual and nonsexual areas of experience, not shallow, empty, and suspicious like her mother.

The preceding case vignette, illustrating the shift in the meaning of clinical data—in my opinion a shift toward a deeper and more encompassing meaning—when we approach them from the point of view of a self struggling to maintain its cohesion—i.e., from the point of view of a self motivated by disintegration anxiety—rather than from the point of view of a psychic apparatus trying to deal with drives and structural conflict—i.e., from the point of view of an ego motivated by castration anxiety— raises certain theoretical questions.

Freud described and explained the child's oedipal experiences in conformance with his general theoretical outlook—an outlook he had adopted from the physical sciences of his day—in terms of forces (drives), counter-forces (defenses), and interaction of forces (compromise formations, such as the symptoms of the psychoneuroses) within a hypothetical space (the psychic apparatus). Two principles will guide us in our task of re-evaluating the Oedipus complex from the point of view of the psychology of the self: that we are not questioning the data of Freud's discovery, but the adequacy of the theoretical framework into which they were put and, thus, their significance; and that we are not necessarily denying the truth of the classical theory of the central position of the Oedipus complex, but only the universal applicability of this theory. We are, in other words, employing the approach I referred to earlier (p. xv) as the psychological principle of complementarity, a term meant to indicate that the explanation of the psychological field may require not one but two (or more) theoretical frameworks.[2]

The classical theory of drives and objects explains a good deal about the child's oedipal experiences; par excellence it explains the child's conflicts and, in particular, the child's guilt. But it falls short in providing an adequate framework for some of the most important experiences of man, those that relate to the development and vicissitudes of his self. To be explicit: notwithstanding the admirable effort by generations of psychoanalysts to extend the theories of drives and defenses and of the structures of the psychic apparatus to their utmost limits —including the ultimate heroic attempt by Freud (1920)

[2] Edelheit has recently (1976) applied the concept of complementarity to the "relationship between psychological description and neurophysiological description."

to give the drive theory a cosmological dimension—these theories fail to do justice to the experiences that relate to the crucially important task of building and maintaining a cohesive nuclear self (with the correlated joy of achiev- ing this goal and the correlated nameless mortification [cf. Eidelberg, 1959] of not achieving it) and, secondarily, to the experiences that relate to the crucially important striving of the nuclear self, once it is laid down, to express its basic patterns (with the correlated triumph and dejec- tion at having succeeded or failed in this end). As I said earlier, drive theory and its developments explain Guilty Man, but they do not explain Tragic Man.

Our examination of the Oedipus complex in the light of the preceding considerations can best be ap- proached from two different sides. We must first ask how the disturbances of the self and the oedipal psycho- neuroses are related to each other; and we must then ask whether—and if so, how—our conception of the Oedipus complex itself is altered when it is seen from the point of view of the psychology of the self.

We turn first to the question of how the disturbances of the self and the oedipal neuroses are related to each other.

There exist in theory—and indeed in practice—two possibilities: (1) the emotional retreat from the conflicts and anxieties of the oedipal period may lead to the chronic adoption of defensively held narcissistic positions; and, in the obverse, (2) the mortification to which the child is exposed by feeling that his self is fragmenting or lacking in vitality may lead him to the chronic adoption of defensively held oedipal positions. I have elsewhere (1972, p. 369) referred to the first group of disturbances as pseudonarcissistic disorders and to the second group as

pseudotransference neuroses. To this schematic classification I will add here that, apart from the clear-cut instances of layered pathology (i.e., the pseudonarcissistic
and the pseudotransference disorders), there exist also
mixed forms in which primary narcissistic pathology and
oedipal pathology are present side by side and are activated in the transference, either alternatingly or successively. These cases, however, are not frequent. In my clinical experience, at any rate, I have found to my surprise
that cases of pure pathology are much more frequent
than those of truly mixed pathology. Finally, I should say
that for the investigation *of the relation* between self pathology and structural pathology (though not for the investigation of the disorders of the self per se) the framework of classical metapsychology should be more or less
adequate — just as it is adequate for the traditional drive-
psychological investigations of the relation between oedipal and preoedipal psychopathology.

We turn now to our second question: whether — and
if so: how? — our conception of the Oedipus complex itself
is altered when it is evaluated from the point of view of
the psychology of the self.

I must ask the reader's forbearance if, to lay the
groundwork for my attempt to reply to this question,
I present a summary of the classical position in order
to bring certain of its features into sharp relief. The
classical position holds that, after an important series of
preliminary steps, the child enters a psychological stage
in which, on the basis of intrinsic psychological factors
(such as drive maturation), it is inexorably drawn into a
psychological situation — sexual desire for the heterogenital parent, rivalrous murderous wishes toward the
homogenital parent — that confronts it with conflicts

which it cannot solve on the basis of conscious choice and decisions through external action, but to which it responds by massive autoplastic adaptations. As a result of these events the psychic apparatus undergoes certain important changes: the repression of the desire for the heterogenital object is decisively important among the factors that determine the form and content of the id; the internalization of the imago of the hated homogenital rival plays the same role vis-à-vis the form and content of the superego. If the archaic structures are not firmly walled off from the ego and the modulating action of the intercalated semipermeable psychic structures is insufficient, then a central focus of psychopathology is established: the infantile (oedipal) neurosis. The latter may itself quickly be walled off, either temporarily or permanently (i.e., the entrenchment of the manifestations of a neurosis is prevented or delayed), and thus the ego is given some room for its learning tasks—though at a price in available energy. But in many instances the infantile neurosis will make its influence felt in childhood, with the deleterious absence of a clear-cut latency period. Under these circumstances the expansion of the range of intellectual and social learning is halted. In summary, then, classical analysis depicts the unsolvable aspects of the oedipal situation and sees the ensuing pathological consequences as due to the inability of the psychic apparatus to deal with the conflicts.

Psychological health, too, although less emphasized in the classical formulations, can be defined in oedipal terms. It is established by virtue of the ability of the psychic apparatus to deal with the conflicts by instituting effective autoplastic changes—a well-functioning psychic organization is established that can cope with the problems of adaptation. If, in other words, the barriers vis-à-vis the repressed id and superego are not only firm but also appropriately permeable, i.e., if the forces of the archaic id and superego are either securely walled off or neutralized by intercalated psychic structures, then the ego can function autonomously—a new phase of psychological development begins, relatively undisturbed by infantile sexuality and aggression: the ego is ready to confront a broadened range of intellectual and social problems—the child goes to school.

It does not indicate any lack of respect for the great explanatory power of the classical formulations, or any lack of appreciation for their beauty and elegance, when I affirm now that it is possible, from the viewpoint of the psychology of the self in the narrower sense—i.e., from the viewpoint of a theory that considers the self as a content of the mental apparatus (see pp. xv, 132, 206 above) —to enrich the classical theory by adding a self-psychological dimension. To state explicitly what has been implicit all along: the presence of a firm self is a precondition for the experience of the Oedipus complex. Unless the child sees himself as a delimited, abiding, independent center of initiative, he is unable to experience the object-instinctual desires that lead to the conflicts and secondary adaptations of the oedipal period. Furthermore, if we acknowledge the presence of an active self during the oedipal period, then our conception of the oedipal strivings themselves, as well as of the functions of the psychic structures that are the heirs of the oedipal experience, will reflect psychic reality more accurately. As I pointed out earlier, however, we can within certain clearly defined limits (e.g., in psychopathology, with regard to the area of structural disorders; in normal functioning, with regard to the area of conscious and preconscious psychic conflict) explain psychological life in a satisfactory manner on the basis of explanations that disregard the self. Once more aphoristically: Because the self is present on both sides of structural conflicts, it can be left out of the equation.

But, having summarized the classical position, we have now arrived at the crucial point of our considerations: the scrutiny of the significance of the Oedipus complex from the point of view of the psychology of the self in its broader sense, i.e., from the point of view of a psychology in which the concept of the self is supraordinated to that of the mental apparatus and its agencies.

Occasionally a distinct but brief oedipal phase appears in the transference at the end of many years of analytic work that was focused entirely on working through the relation between the self and the self-objects. In earlier years I simply assumed I was dealing with the revival of an oedipal conflict from childhood, that a developmental level, a *phase* tentatively reached in childhood, had been shattered by phase-specific fears and had led to a defensive, regressive retreat. But after several similar experiences, I have come to change my mind. I now believe it highly probable that these oedipal constellations are new, that they are a positive result of a consolidation of the self never before achieved, that they are not a transference repetition. I have formed my view on the basis of these observations: First, the analysand experiences the terminal oedipal phase in these instances almost entirely in terms of fantasies about the analyst and the analyst's family, and, while some associations may allude to a parental triangle, no intensely charged memory systems concerning oedipal conflicts in childhood are activated. Second—and this observation is of crucial evidential significance—despite some simultaneous anxiety, the brief oedipal phase is accompanied by a warm glow of joy—a joy that has all the earmarks of an emotionality that accompanies a maturational or a developmental achievement. I take the license of supporting my argument by retelling a lovely anecdote Freud told long ago, in a different context (1900, p. 157), of the girl who was yearning to be married. On being told that her suitor "had a violent temper and would be sure to beat her if they were married," she replied: "If only he'd begun beating me already!" The same attitude so charmingly portrayed in this little story prevails in the narcissistic personality disturbances and in other primary disturbances of the self vis-à-vis the conflicts that emanate from the Oedipus- complex. Any person afflicted with serious threats to the continuity, the consolidation, the firmness of the self will experience the Oedipus complex, despite its anxieties and conflicts, as a joyfully accepted reality, and he will say, with the girl in Freud's story, "if only I'd already begun to suffer the anxieties and conflicts of the oedipal period."

It is evident that, seen from the point of view of self psychology in the broader sense of the term, our focus is drawn to the positive aspects of the oedipal period. True enough, the classical theory is fully compatible with an appreciation of the positive features of the oedipal experience. But it sees the positive qualities that the psychic apparatus acquires at that period as the result of the oedipal experience, not as a primary, intrinsic aspect of the experience itself. Or to state it in other words: classical theory is limited by its focus on structural conflict and the structural neuroses. Psychoanalytic theory will come closer to fulfilling its legitimate aspirations of becoming an encompassing general psychology if it now expands it borders and places the classical findings and explanations within the supraordinated framework of a psychology of the self.

Let me now give a description of the oedipal phase from the point of view of self psychology. Reconstructing the experiential world of the oedipal child on the basis of those instances in which an oedipal phase is reached *de novo* at the end of an analysis of a case of narcissistic personality disorder that had achieved the restoration of a formerly fragmentation- and discontinuity-prone self, we can say that if a child enters the oedipal phase with a firm, cohesive, continuous self, he will then experience assertive-possessive, affectionate-sexual desires for the heterogenital parent and assertive, self-confident, competitive feelings vis-à-vis the parent of the same sex. We must immediately add, however, that it would be psychologically misleading to consider the child's oedipal experiences in isolation. As was true with regard to earlier phases of development, the child's experiences during the oedipal phase become understandable only when they are considered within the matrix of the empathic, partially empathic, or unempathic responses from the side of the self-object aspects of his environment.

The affectionate desire and the assertive-competitive rivalry of the oedipal child will be responded to by normally empathic parents in two ways. The parents will react to the sexual desires and to the competitive rivalry of the child by becoming sexually stimulated and counteraggressive, and, at the same time, they will react with joy and pride to the child's developmental achievement, to his vigor and assertiveness. Although under normal cir-

cumstances these seemingly inconsistent parental attitudes are fused, I will in the following discuss them as if
they could be neatly separated.

Concerning the first-mentioned parental responses,
little needs to be said—indeed, little can be said that is
not implicitly contained in the teachings of classical analysis, or, to say the least, that is not easily integrated with
the classical tenets concerning this phase of development.
We will say then that the empathic heterogenital parent
will, consciously or preconsciously, grasp the fact of having become the target of the child's libidinal desires and
will respond in an aim-inhibited libidinal fashion to the
child's advances. The homogenital parent, too, will consciously or preconsciously grasp the fact of having become
the target of the child's rivalrous aggression and will respond in aim-inhibited counteraggression to the child's
hostility. It is evident that both the parents' correct perception of the child's intentions and the fact that their appropriate responses are aim-inhibited are important with
regard to the child's growing capacity to integrate his libidinal and aggressive strivings—that, in terms of mental-apparatus psychology, the child acquires psychic
structures that modulate drive expression. It is clearly
deleterious for the child's maturing psychic apparatus if
the parental responses to the oedipal manifestations are
grossly sexual or grossly counteraggressive. But, apart
from declaring these extremes unacceptable, we must
admit that a wide variety of parental responses should be
regarded as—even if not actively promoting health and
development— at least nonpathogenic and not interfering with psychic development. We shall consider parental
responses that can be characterized in this way as lying
within the normal range of parental behavior. Thus,

within the limits indicated, we can say that a whole
spectrum of parental reponses lies within the realm of
normalcy. In patriarchally organized groups, for
example, the parental attitudes toward the oedipal boy
foster, as a result of his oedipal experiences, the development of a mental apparatus that is characterized by a
firm superego and a set of strong masculine ideals. This
type may be specifically adapted to the tasks of a frontier
society or at least to a society in which the values of a
frontier society still hold sway. Parental attitudes in
groups in which gender differentiation has lessened, may
produce, in consequence of different responses to the
oedipal child, girls whose superego firmness and ideals
correspond more to that normally found in boys of the
patriarchal group. And such girls may well be specifically
adapted to the tasks of a society that is nonexpansive—
perhaps the societies of the stabilized populations of
tomorrow.

These are broad issues that I will discuss later on—
covering areas, I might add, where the cooperation of
sociologists and psychoanalysts is indispensable—but on
which, in the present context, I need not expand. I will
only say here once more that the developments I have
sketched out can be described in terms of a slightly
extended classical metapsychology—in other words, the
results of our brief survey of the normal oedipal situation
can be presented in terms of self psychology in the narrower sense of the term. We can in this way give an explicit
self-psychological dimension to our formulations; the essence of the classical position, however—the formulation
that the beneficial result of a successfully lived-through
oedipal phase is a firm mental apparatus—remains un-
changed.

There is also no need here to focus on the failures of these developments, described by classical analysis in terms of the weakness of the borders of the psychic macrostructures that make up the mental apparatus, or in terms of their regression, or both. However modifying and enriching the introduction of self psychology in the narrower sense of the term might be, the end result remains that of classical analysis: a conception of man as endowed with either a well-functioning or a malfunctioning psychic apparatus — of man spurred on by his drives and shackled by castration anxiety and guilt. It is, to repeat once more, a concept that, in the narrow clinical field, does adequate justice to the problems of the structural neuroses, and, in the broad arena of societal and historical development, encompasses the conflicts of *Guilty Man*.

We are now turning to the discussion of a topic that — I might affirm this fact at the beginning — is not encompassed by the framework of classical theory, not even when it is given greater depth through the addition of self psychology in the narrow sense of the term: we shall examine the second aspect of the responses of normal (in the sense of being nonpathogenic) parents to their oedipal children. What, we ask, is the essence of parental nonpathogenicity during the oedipal period? As I said earlier, it is given by the crucially significant fact that, amalgamated to their sexual and aggressive reactions, normal parents experience joy and pride concerning the developmental progress of their oedipal children.

While these important responses from the parents of the oedipal child are comparatively silent, especially when they are deep-rooted and genuine, they are nevertheless all-pervasive. They are an expression of the fact that the parental selves are fully consolidated, that the parental selves have formed stable patterns of ambitions and ideals, and that the parental selves are experiencing the unrolling of the expression of these patterns along a finite life curve that leads from a preparative beginning through an active, productive, creative middle to a fulfilled end. It makes no difference at which point of the life curve the parental selves are during the oedipal phase of the child; so long as the pattern of the parental self is clearly designed and well consolidated and is in the process of expressing itself, the fulfilling peak and the fulfilled end are already implied. The oedipal child then is the beneficiary of the fact that the parents are in narcissistic balance. If the little boy, for example, feels that his father looks upon him proudly as a chip off the old block and allows him to merge with him and with his adult greatness, then his oedipal phase will be a decisive step in self-consolidation and self-pattern-firming, including the laying down of one of the several variants of integrated maleness—despite the unavoidable frustrations of his sexual and competitive aspirations and despite the unavoidable conflicts caused by ambivalence and mutilation fears. If, however, this aspect of the parental echo is absent during the oedipal phase, the child's oedipal conflicts will, even in the absence of grossly distorted parental responses to the child's libidinal and aggressive strivings, take on a malignant quality. Distorted parental responses are, moreover, also likely to occur under these circumstances. Parents who are not able to establish empathic contact with the developing self of the child will, in other words, tend to see the constituents of the child's oedipal aspirations in isolation—they will tend to see (even though generally only preconsciously) alarming sexuality and alarming hostility in the child instead of larger configurations of assertive affection and assertive competition — with the result that the child's oedipal conflicts will become intensified — just as a mother whose own self is poorly consolidated will react to the feces and the anal region and not to the total vigorous, proudly assertive anal-phase self of her child. A mother whose self is well consolidated, however, will not experience in isolation the object-libidinal and narcissistic (exhibitionistic) constituents which, alloyed with nonsexual constituents, make up the little boy's total oedipal self; and she will therefore not react to them either with intense sexual responses or by defending against them — just as she had not responded by focusing her exclusive attention on the feces of her proudly assertive anal-phase child. She will respond in both instances to the total cohesive and vigorous self. And the normal father will not respond with intense counteraggressions (either directly or defensively) to the constituents of aggression (whether they support object-libidinal or narcissistic strivings) that are alloyed with his little boy's total oedipal self, just as he would not have reacted by focusing his exclusive attention on the child's developing musculature when the child proudly displayed his newly discovered ability to crawl, to stand, to walk.

And what is the result of these self-cohesion-furthering attitudes of the parental self-objects vis-à-vis their oedipal child — how does a child who is the recipient of these wholesome responses experience his oedipal phase? What, in other words, is the Oedipus complex of the child who has entered the oedipal phase with a firmly cohesive self and who is surrounded by parents who themselves have healthy cohesive and continuous selves? It is my impression, on the basis of inferences that I believe can be drawn from the observation of the quasi-oedipal phase at the end of some successful analyses of narcissistic personality disorders, that the normal child's oedipal experiences—however intense the desire for the heterogenital parent, however serious the narcissistic injuries at recognizing the impossibility of their fulfillment; however intense the competition with the homogenital parent, and however paralyzing the correlated castration anxiety—contain, from the beginning and persisting throughout, an admixture of deep joy that, while unrelated to the content of the Oedipus complex in the traditional sense, is of the utmost developmental significance within the framework of the psychology of the self. I believe, again on the basis of inferences drawn from the observation of the terminal phase of certain successfully analyzed cases of narcissistic personality disorder, that this joy is fed from two sources. Let me here, somewhat artificially, separate them one from the other in order to elucidate the composition of the amalgam of the essentially unitary experience. They are: (1) the child's inner awareness of a significant forward move into a psychological realm of new and exciting experiences, and—of even greater importance—(2) his participation in the glow of pride and joy that emanates from the parental self-objects despite—indeed, also because of—their recognition of the content of their child's oedipal desires.

It is true, of course, that many parents are limited in their capacity to respond only with optimal empathic failures to their oedipal children—that many respond with overt or covert seductiveness (or with defenses against such tendencies) and that many respond with overt or covert hostility (or, again, with the correlated defenses).

It was one of Freud's greatest achievements to have discovered these facts. And his courage in revealing his own death wishes toward his son (1900, pp. 558-560) must be counted among the examples of heroism in science. But are the reactions of a genius, with his near-inescapable enormous narcissistic involvement in his own creativeness, representative examples of optimal parental attitudes?[3] I think they are not. The optimal parent is on neither end of the spectrum of self organizations. He is not the genius whose self is absorbed by his creative activities and whose self extensions relate only to his work and to those people who can be experienced by him as aspects of his work. Nor is he the borderline personality or the schizoid or paranoid personality — one of the parents, in other words, whose fragmented or fragmentation-prone selves are closed to that empathic merger with their children that would allow them to delight in their children's growth and assertiveness. Optimal parents — again I should rather say: optimally failing parents — are people who, despite their stimulation by and competition with the rising generation, are also sufficiently in touch with the pulse of life, accept themselves sufficiently as transient participants in the ongoing stream of life, to be able to experience the growth of the next generation with unforced nondefensive joy.[4]

[3] I believe that the investigation of the narcissistic disturbances of the sons of many great men could be fruitfully pursued in the context of their father's creative narcissism (cf. Hitschmann, 1932, p. 151) rather than from the traditional viewpoint of competition and failure. Why did so many of them fare poorly? And why did some of them escape this fate?

[4] A symbolic rendition of those parental figures who cannot experience themselves as participants in a meaningfully transient life is contained in the myths that depict the inability to die (the stories of *The Flying Dutchman* and of *The Wandering Jew*).

Classical metapsychology, the psychology of large-scale inner forces clashing with each other, illuminated and explained a vast area of human psychic life that had heretofore been covered by darkness. The excitement, however, that we felt as the recipients of the new insights has made us reluctant to face the fact that the new system left a significant and important layer of human experience essentially untouched. True, we tried to apply the theories that stood us in such good stead with regard to the transference neuroses, man in conflict, Guilty Man, also to this other level of human experience. But I believe that we have not succeeded—indeed, I believe that by relying on the classical conceptual armamentarium we could not have succeeded. Classical theory cannot illuminate the essence of fractured, enfeebled, discontinuous human existence: it cannot explain the essence of the schizophrenic's fragmentation, the struggle of the patient who suffers from a narcissistic personality disorder to reassemble himself, the despair—the guiltless despair, I stress—of those who in late middle age discover that the basic patterns of their self as laid down in their nuclear ambitions and ideals have not been realized. Dynamic-structural metapsychology does not do justice to these problems of man, cannot encompass the problems of Tragic Man.

It is in the light of these considerations that the re-evaluation of Freud's great discovery must be understood. Seen from the point of view of classical analysis, the oedipal phase is par excellence the nucleus of neurosis; seen from the point of view of the psychology of the self in the broad sense of the term, the Oedipus complex—whether or not it leaves the individual beset by guilt and prone to neurosis—is the matrix in which an important contribution to the firming of the independent self takes place, enabling it to follow its own pattern with greater security than before.

These formulations do not imply a contrast between a pessimistic and an optimistic philosophy. Classical metapsychology, on the one hand, can, of course, describe the Oedipus complex as the psychological battleground from which the lucky child emerges with a firmly organized mental apparatus that will enable him to lead a life unhampered by paralyzing conflicts and neurosis. And self psychology, on the other hand, can stress the ultimate failure in the formation and consolidation of the self at this period. As I said earlier, realism prompted me to adopt the negative terms Guilty Man and Tragic Man because man's failures in both realms do overshadow his successes. But, while self psychology takes cognizance of the self-destroying potentialities of an oedipal phase lived out in a matrix of parental self-objects who are not in touch with the tragic aspects of life, and while classical metapsychology takes cognizance of the wholesome structuralization of the psychic apparatus that results from the successfully transacted oedipal phase, the emphasis in self psychology is—and for good reasons—more on the growth-promoting aspects of this period and in classical conflict psychology more on the pathogenic ones.

The Re-evaluated Oedipus Complex—and Beyond

If we take into account that the oedipal situation cannot even become genuinely engaged without the presence of a previously consolidated self, it becomes clear that the oedipal period is more apt to be the breeding ground for paralyzing neurotic conflicts than a central focus for serious self disturbances. The self is already well on its way, we might say; and while a shakily formed self may perhaps not be able to weather the storms of this period, particularly when the oedipal self-objects are cold and destructive, and while a nuclear self already firmly laid down will now receive an important imprint determining its shape—it will par excellence henceforth be more definitely a male or female self—the oedipal phase is nevertheless not the pivotal point regarding the fate of the self that it is with regard to the formation of the psychic apparatus.

Is there, then, a point in the child's life as significant with regard to the early development of the self as is, with regard to early psychosexual development, according to classical psychoanalytic theory, the point at which the Oedipus complex comes to its resolution? All I can say, on the basis of reconstructions from the material obtained in the analysis of adults, is that, if such a point exists, it would be much earlier in psychological life than that at which the oedipal period turns into latency. Having given this admittedly imprecise reply, however, I do not feel inclined to commit myself further—not only because I think that a more precise answer, if any, would have to come from child analysts and analytically trained observers of children, but especially because I do not want self psychology to be hampered by the confining effect of an overly concrete and seemingly definitive presentation—a fallacy, I might add, to which analysis had indeed regrettably been exposed by the dramatic term Oedipus complex, however excusable an evocatively concrete nomenclature might be, considering the pioneering atmosphere of the period in which it was introduced.

But while I am thus reluctant to dramatize the establishment of the self by specifying a definite point at which it is said to be born, I believe that there is, later in life, a specific point that can be seen as crucially significant — a point in the life curve of the self at which a final crucial test determines whether the previous development had failed or had succeeded. Is young adulthood the crisis that faces the self with its most severe test? The incidence of the most destructive disorders in this realm, the schizophrenias soon after the age of twenty, would support this view. But I am inclined to put the pivotal point even later — to late middle age when, nearing the ultimate decline, we ask ourselves whether we have been true to our innermost design. This is the time of utmost hopelessness for some, of utter lethargy, of that depression without guilt and self-directed aggression, which overtakes those who feel that they have failed and cannot remedy the failure in the time and with the energies still at their disposal. The suicides of this period are not the expression of a punitive superego, but a remedial act — the wish to wipe out the unbearable sense of mortification and nameless shame imposed by the ultimate recognition of a failure of all-encompassing magnitude.

It is easy to see against this background that the psychology of the self provides us now with the means of explaining a related fact which, to my mind, has hitherto been unexplained, even though it has, I believe, been recognized by analysts for a long time. Some people can live fulfilling, creative lives, despite the presence of serious neurotic conflict — even, sometimes, despite the presence of a near-crippling neurotic disease. And, in the obverse, there are others, who despite the absence of neurotic conflict, are not protected against succumbing to the feeling of the meaninglessness of their existence, including, in the field of psychopathology proper, of succumbing to the agony of the hopelessness and lethargy of pervasive empty depression—specifically, as I said before, of certain depressions of later middle life.

I will even entertain the hope that the psychology of the self will some day be able to explain the fact that some people regard the inevitability of death as proof that life is utterly meaningless—the only redeeming feature being man's pride in his capacity to face life's meaninglessness without embellishing it—while others can accept death as an integral part of a meaningful life.

There are those, of course, who might say that the aforementioned issues are not a legitimate subject matter of science; that by dealing with them we are leaving the areas that can be illuminated through scientific research and are entering the foggy regions of metaphysics. I disagree. Such issues as experiencing life as meaningless despite external success, experiencing life as meaningful despite external failure, the sense of a triumphant death or of a barren survival, are legitimate targets of scientific psychological investigation because they are not nebulous abstract speculations but the content of intense experiences that can be observed, via empathy, inside and outside the clinical situation. True, these phenomena are not encompassed within the framework of a science that looks upon the mind as an apparatus that processes biological drives. But must we therefore conclude that an additional theoretical framework with another concept of mind cannot serve us here? It can—and, I will stress once more: it does so without discarding the old.

It will now be obvious, too, why self psychology does not assign a person's basic ambitions and basic ideals to his mental apparatus, specifically, to id and superego, but considers them, as I said, the two poles of his self. As seen from the point of view of the psychology of the self in the broad sense of the term, they are the essential constituents of that nuclear tension-arc which, having become independent of the genetic factors that determined its specific shape and content, strives only, once it has been formed, to live out its intrinsic potentialities.

In summary, then: The (sexual and destructive) id and the (inhibiting-prohibiting) superego are constituents of the mental apparatus of Guilty Man. Nuclear ambitions and ideals are the poles of the self; between them stretches the tension arc that forms the center of the pursuits of Tragic Man. The conflictual aspects of the Oedipus complex are the genetic focus of the development of Guilty Man and of the genesis of the psychoneuroses; the nonconflictual aspects of the Oedipus complex are a step in the development of Tragic Man and in the genesis of the disorders of the self. The conceptualizations of mental-apparatus psychology are adequate in explaining structural neurosis and guilt-depression—in short, the psychic disturbances and conflicts of Guilty Man. The psychology of the self is needed to explain the pathology of the fragmented self (from schizophrenia to narcissistic personality disorder) and of the depleted self (empty depression, i.e., the world of unmirrored ambitions, the world devoid of ideals)—in short, the psychic disturbances and struggles of Tragic Man.

Let us now move for a moment beyond clinical issues and examine, in the light of self psychology, a problem I confronted many years ago (Kohut, 1959, pp. 479-482) and found unmanageable. It gives me some satisfaction to see that the pieces of a puzzle that had stumped me then, now fall into place. Being at that time fully committed to the traditional acceptance of the fact that the domain where the authority of absolute determinism holds sway was unlimited, and clinging to Freud's model of the mind depicted as an apparatus that processes forces within a hypothetical space, I could find no place for the psychological activities that go by the name of choice, decision, and free will—even though I knew that these were empirically observable phenomena. I was already firmly convinced then that introspection and empathy were important instruments of observation in the science that deals with complex mental states—that indeed these operations *define* the science and its theories, that the field of psychoanalytic depth psychology *is* the dimension of reality that is perceived via introspection and empathy. And I knew, therefore, that the phenomena of choice, decision, and free will, being observable via introspection and empathy, were legitimate inhabitants of the psychological aspects of reality which are the domain of the depth psychologist. Still, I had to acknowledge that the theoretical framework at my disposal—classical mental-apparatus psychology, which conceived of the mind as a reacting machine—could not accommodate them within its realm.

Determinism holds limitless sway so long as the observer conceives of man's psychological activities as being performed in analogy with the processes in the external world that are explainable with the aid of the laws of classical physics. This is mental-apparatus psychology, governed by the laws of psychic determinism—and it explains a great deal. But while it is thus true that many psychological activities and interactions lend themselves to being satisfactorily explained within this framework, it is equally true that there are some phenomena that require for their explanation the positing of a psychic configuration—the self—that, *whatever the history of its formation*, has become a center of initiative: a unit that tries to follow its own course. The physicist's outlook on the aspects of reality that he investigates—"external" reality—is similarly governed by two contrasting theories: the processes *within* the boundaries of the known universe can be explained in the terms of cause-and-effect or probability theory (analogous to the work performed by and the processes taking place within the mental apparatus); the universe *in toto,* on the other hand—*however it came into being*—is conceived as a unit that runs its course from energic disequilibrium toward ultimate energic equilibrium and total quiescence (analogous to the course taken by the self throughout the lifetime of each individual).

But let us now return from our excursion into the realm of experience-distant theory to the more experience-near area that is the central target of our present inquiry: the re-evaluation of the significance of the Oedipus complex in the light of the psychology of the self. Our investigations here have thus far led us to one result: from the point of view of the psychology of the self we will look upon the oedipal period more as a source of potential strength than weakness. By itself, this shift in emphasis does not connote a disagreement with the classical formulation, it means merely that we are looking on the same childhood experiences from a new side, and recognize that the previously discovered facts take on an additional, a changed significance. But is this shift in emphasis concerning the significance of the oedipal events the only result of our re-evaluation of this period in the light of self psychology? Or does the new viewpoint lead us also to a different perception of the very content of the child's oedipal experiences? I must admit that I cannot give a definitive answer to this question. Does the psychology of the self, in other words, simply add a new dimension to our grasp of the experiences of the oedipal child because it permits us to take into account the support, or the lack of support, of the self-objects during this period? Or do the conceptualizations of self psychology cast doubt on the essential correctness of the oedipal reconstructions themselves?

I will not carry coals to Newcastle by giving the evidence — transference reconstructions, the observation of the behavior of children, the analysis of myths and works of art — that support the traditional view of the oedipal drama. But I believe that the analysis of the oedipal phase in the terminal stage of some cases of narcissistic personality disorders does cast serious doubt concerning the accuracy of our descriptions of the normal oedipal phase. I shall say no more here than that our observations of a joyfully entered quasi-oedipal phase should prompt us to re-examine our traditional conceptions in the light of the question whether the Oedipus complex of classical analysis that we take to be a ubiquitous human experience[5] is not in fact already the manifestation of a pathological development, at least of one *in statu nascendi*? Could it not be, we should ask, that the normal Oedipus complex is less violent, less anxious, less deeply narcissistically wounding than we have come to believe — that it is

[5] I am here not complicating the issue by taking into account the culturists' point of view that the Oedipus complex of classical analysis belongs only to certain organizations of society.

altogether more exhilarating and, to speak in the language of mental-apparatus Guilty Man, even more pleasurable? Could it not be that we have considered the dramatic desires and anxieties of the oedipal child as normal events when, in fact, they are the child's reactions to empathy failures from the side of the self-object environment of the oedipal phase?

We know that the self-objects' failures to be empathic with the whole self of the young child has disintegrating results, that in consequence of the incapacity of the self-objects to respond to the whole self, the complex experiential configurations of which it is originally made up begin to fragment, and that, in further consequence, isolated drive experiences (and conflicts about them) begin to manifest themselves. We need think only of the lonely masturbation of the unresponded-to preoedipal child and of his secondary conflicts about his masturbation, to see these conditions clearly. Could it not be that the same conditions prevail with regard to the oedipal child? That it is only the self of the child whose self-objects are severely out of touch with his newly forward-moving oedipal self that begins to break apart? That it is only the self of the child whose primary affectionate and competitive assertiveness is not responded to that is then dominated by unassimilated lust and hostility? That, in other words, the dramatic, conflict-ridden Oedipus complex of classical analysis, with its perception of a child whose aspirations are crumbling under the impact of castration fear, is not a primary maturational necessity but only the frequent result of frequently occurring failures from the side of narcissistically disturbed parents? As I said before, I do not know the answer to these questions with certainty, but I do know that analysts must take a fresh look at the experiences of their patients in the oedipal transference and that analytically trained observers should re-evaluate the behavior of children during the oedipal phase with these questions in mind.

CHAPTER SIX

The Psychology of the Self and the Psychoanalytic Situation

The theoretical framework that defines our understanding of psychopathology and normal psychology will influence not only our specific technical activities (especially with regard to the content of our interpretations), but also, via subtle innuendos and gross moves, our general attitude vis-à-vis analytic process and patient. The point of view, for example, taken with regard to such seemingly esoteric questions as whether it is correct to say that man is born helpless because he is not born with a significantly functioning ego apparatus — rather than that he is born powerful because a milieu of empathic self-objects *is* indeed his self — or whether man's untamed drives are the primary units in the world of complex mental states with which introspective-empathic depth psychology deals — rather than that the primary units are *ab initio* the complex experiences and action patterns of a self/self-object unit — is closely connected with the attitude (manifested in concrete behavior) that the depth-psychologist chooses to adopt as the most appropriate one for the therapeutic setting.

All psychoanalysts subscribe in principle to the tenet that the structure of the patient's personality (particularly his nuclear psychopathology and the genetically decisive experiences of his early life) will emerge optimally in a neutral analytic atmosphere. I fully agree with this tenet —indeed, I believe that it was only by a strict adherence to it that I was able to discern the specific form of psychopathology of the narcissistic personality disorders and that I could recognize the dynamic essence of this disturbance and delineate its genetic determinants. When I try to conduct myself in accordance with the principle of analytic neutrality, however, i.e., of being the neutral screen upon which the personality of the analysand, with its needs, wishes, and desires, can delineate itself, I do not attempt to approach a zero-line of activity.

I have wondered how psychoanalysts who in general are endowed with far-above-average ability to be empathic, could ever commit the error, as I think they sometimes do, of equating neutrality with minimal response. Could the analyst's training in the nonpsychological sciences be responsible for this misinterpretation of a sound psychological principle? Someone who was first trained in the physical sciences might well be inclined to compare the analytic situation with an experiment in chemistry or physics or with a surgical operation. And he might define the analyst's attempt to create a neutral psychoanalytic atmosphere in analogy to, let us say, the attempt to keep a sensitive scale insulated from any vibrations produced by noise or other uncontrolled sources. But appealing as such an analogy might be on first sight, it is misleading.

During the analytic process the analyst's psyche is engaged in depth. The essence of his evenly hovering attention is not to be defined in the negative, as a suspension of his conscious, goal-directed, logical thought processes, but positively, as the counterpart of the analysand's free associations, i.e., as the emergence and use of the analyst's prelogical modes of perceiving and thinking. Evenly hovering attention, in other words, is the analyst's active empathic response to the analysand's free associations, a response in which the deepest layers of the analyst's unconscious from the area of progressive neutralization (Kohut, 1961; Kohut and Seitz, 1963)[1] participate. The concept of the analyst's passivity, as Freud occasionally called the analyst's basic therapeutic attitude, is therefore in need of elucidation. The analyst's human warmth, for example, is not just an adventitious accompaniment of his essential activity — to give interpretations and constructions — which is performed by his cognitive processes. It is an expression of the fact that the continuous participation of the depth of the analyst's psyche is a *sine qua non* for the maintenance of the analytic process. Expressed in metapsychological terms, the analyst's responses to the analysand — his interpretations and constructions — are the activities of a *sector* of his psyche, not of a *layer;* and what is called for in the analyst's work is not *ego autonomy* but *ego dominance* (see Kohut, 1972, pp. 365-366). Ego autonomy, I should add, is required occasionally — transitionally — at moments when

---

[1] The diagram on p. 136 in Kohut and Seitz (1963) illustrates that these deep layers in the analyst's psyche are not repressed or otherwise separated from the psychic surface by a horizontal split, and it depicts the nature of the connection between surface and depth.

the analyst is trying to surmount an endopsychic obstacle that blocks his empathic understanding.

But if analytic neutrality or passivity is not to be defined in analogy to the attempt to protect the accuracy of a sensitive scale, how *is* it to be defined? I believe that, psychologically speaking, it should be defined as the responsiveness to be expected, on an average, from persons who have devoted their life to helping others with the aid of insights obtained via the empathic immersion into their inner life. Although this average empathic responsiveness lies within a broad band in the spectrum of possibilities and allows many individual variations, it is not — *in principle* — an approximation of the functions of a psychologically programmed computer that restricts its activities to giving correct and accurate interpretations. The conclusion that it is "in principle" true that the analyst must not try to function like a well-programmed computer rests on two premises: that the analyst's responses require the participation of the deep layers of his personality and, as I shall elaborate shortly, that the responses of a computer would not constitute an average expectable environment for the analysand.

These statements are, it seems to me, in full harmony with the basic principles of analysis; and the attitude they advocate is one that furthers the analyst's recognition of the emerging unconscious material. If, for example, a patient's insistent questions are the transference manifestations of infantile sexual curiosity, this mobilized childhood reaction will not be short-circuited, but, on the contrary, will delineate itself with greater clarity if the analyst, by first replying to the questions and only later pointing out that his replies did not satisfy the patient, does not create artificial rejections of the analysand's need for empathic responsiveness. These considerations hold true especially in the analyses of narcissistic personality disorders, where such seeming derivatives from infantile drives as the manifestations of sexual curiosity are merely the channel through which a more deeply lying striving for the responses of the self-object finds expression. And they also apply to some extent in the classical transference neuroses because the transference nature of the analysand's object-instinctual demands will become illuminated more sharply if the normal average needs of the patient are not rejected out of hand as defensive disguises or as derivatives of infantile drive-wishes, but are first taken at face value and responded to.

As I said earlier (see p. 85), man can no more survive psychologically in a psychological milieu that does not respond empathically to him, than he can survive physically in an atmosphere that contains no oxygen. Lack of emotional responsiveness, silence, the pretense of being an inhuman computer-like machine which gathers data and emits interpretations, do no more supply the psychological milieu for the most undistorted delineation of the normal and abnormal features of a person's psychological makeup than do an oxygen-free atmosphere and a temperature close to the zero-point supply the physical milieu for the most accurate measurement of his physiological responses. Appropriate neutrality in the analytic situation is provided by average conditions. The analyst's behavior vis-à-vis his patient should be the expected average one—i.e., the behavior of a psychologically perceptive person vis-à-vis someone who is suffering and has entrusted himself to him for help.

An objection might be raised here that I am carrying coals to Newcastle, that it goes without saying that the

analyst must behave humanly, warmly, and with appropriate empathic responsiveness, and that analysts do
indeed behave warmly and humanly vis-à-vis their
patients.[2] I am inclined to believe that, to a certain extent, this criticism is accurate, for the simple reason that
it would be an almost impossible feat, in the long run, to
behave otherwise in this so deeply human constellation we
refer to as the analytic situation. But I also know that a
theoretical bias exists that makes it hard for the analyst to
behave in a natural, relaxed way, and that, in the
obverse, analysts tend to feel vaguely uneasy or guilty

---

[2] Analysts tend to be sensitive about contributions that deal with the
difficult question of what constitutes an appropriate therapeutic attitude in
the analytic situation. I believe our sensitivity here is not so much due to de-
fensiveness about revealing hidden countertransferences, but is rather an
outgrowth of our tendency to value narcissistically our therapeutic activity,
our individual style, the mastery we have achieved—that derivatives of ideas
of omnipotence and omniscience are involved. At any rate, I would say that
we tend to react with wounded pride to those who question our prized therapeutic skill and the theory of technique on which it rests. And those who
question the traditional attitude of muted responsiveness and emotional reserve will soon hear that they are advocating "wild analysis" and "corrective
emotional experience"—and, simultaneously, that they are shooting at straw
men.

I was for some time inclined to take the incompatibility of these two sets
of reproaches as proof of their irrationality. As in the famous story of the
broken pitcher that could not possibly have been both returned whole *and*
have been originally received in a broken condition, those who criticize the
analyst's adherence to an attitude of strictly maintained reserve could not
possibly be wrong both because they are advocating cure through love *and*
because analysts are really warm and relaxed with their patients. I have
come to the conclusion, however, that the inconsistency of the two replies is
not primarily a manifestation of irrationality engendered by wounded pride
but an expression of the fact that there exists indeed an increasingly wide
gap between the analyst's behavior as prescribed, directly or by implication,
by the classical theory of technique, which is experienced as unrefuted—
see, however, the valuable contributions of Loewald (1960) and Stone (1961)
—and the actual behavior of most modern analysts in the psychoanalytic
situation.

when they behave thus with their patients. In consequence, a certain stiffness, artificiality, and strait-laced reserve are not uncommon ingredients of that attitude of expectant "neutrality" analysts bring to the analytic situation. And when the analysand reacts with anger to what is by no means a neutral but in reality a grossly depriving atmosphere, the analyst will assume that he is confronted with the emergence of resistances against the analytic procedure — resistances he interprets as manifestations of underlying drives (aggressions) — when he is in fact dealing with artifacts. If the analyst does indeed feel so much as a trace of guilt whenever he does not behave according to Freud's (1912, p. 115) famous dictum that analysts should "model themselves during psycho-analytic treatment on the surgeon, who puts aside all his feelings, even his human sympathy," then his emotional spontaneity will be restricted.

Freud's *informally* expressed views, it should be added here, were clearly at variance with the injunction cited above. In a letter (October 22, 1927) to Pfister, for example, he expressed himself in a way that is in harmony with the attitude I am delineating as the appropriate one in the context of the psychology of the self: "You know the human propensity to take precepts literally or exaggerate them. I know very well that in the matter of analytic passivity that is what some of my pupils do. Of H. in particular I am willing to believe that he spoils the effect of analysis by a certain listless indifference, and then neglects to lay bare the resistances which he thereby awakens in his patients. It should not be concluded from this instance that analysis should be followed by a synthesis, but rather that a thorough analysis of the transference situation is of special importance. What then remains of the transference may, indeed should, have the character of a cordial human relationship" (E. L. Freud and Meng, 1963, p. 113).

I know that the weight of a statement made in a carefully formulated basic contribution to the technique of analysis is quite different from that of an informal, relaxedly chatty remark made in a letter to a friend. But I would venture the guess that the points in Freud's life at which the two views were given are not without significance. We must first of all take into account that, between the first and second of the two contrasting views, Freud had added fifteen years to his clinical experience. And there may yet be another explanation for the change, namely, that Freud was in the main exposed to analysands suffering from structural neuroses during the early years of his analytic career, while, later, a shift in the dominant psychopathology may increasing have taken place—a shift to the form of pathology to which we are now referring as narcissistic personality disorders—and that Freud's second statement was a preconsciously determined response to this change.

In general, I have come to hold the view that an attitude of emotional reserve and muted responsiveness from the side of the analyst is often in tune with the needs of analysands who suffer from the classical transference neuroses. This view is based on the conclusion that these patients had been overstimulated as children, that they had been involved in the emotional life of their parents to a degree that overtaxed the capacity of their immature personality organization. Indeed, I believe that having been overstimulated as children by the adult environment is a genetic determinant of the type of their later psychopathology, namely, structural neurosis.[3]

An analyst's inclination to react with muted responsiveness vis-à-vis an analysand who had been traumatized as a child by an unempathically overstimulating adult environment could hence be indicative of his understanding of his patient's personality. And it could even be argued that, in view of the prevalence of such patients, the classical position was correct at that earlier period. But the fact that muted responsiveness was held to be the correct attitude with all cases argues against this conclusion. Because the classical analyst lacked conscious comprehension of the reasons for the validity of his position, his muted responsiveness cannot be evaluated as an appropriately empathic response — even in those instances where the patient experienced it as providing him with a wholesome therapeutic atmosphere. Whereas the correct empathic response is an intrinsic aspect of the first phase of the two-phase essential activity of the psychoanalyst in the therapeutic situation (cf. pp. 85-93), it must eventually be followed by verbal interpretations (in this case con-

[3] The differentiation of the two distinct types of empathy-failures from the side of the self-objects of childhood — one leading through overstimulation by the self-objects to structural neuroses, the other through the emotional distance of the self-objects to disturbances of the self — will be discussed in the final chapter of this book. I shall mention here only that by "overstimulation" I do not have in mind the gross sexual seductions that Freud's hysterical patients claimed to remember — memories that Freud unmasked as the manifestations of wish-fantasies from childhood. The manifestations of the unempathic seductiveness of adults vis-à-vis children of which I speak are subtle, and they are not easily remembered or reconstructed in analysis. Still, I believe that they are pervasive because they are an outgrowth of a certain type of adult psychopathology. And I believe that the childhood fantasies Freud discovered behind the memories of gross seduction are therefore not spontaneously arising, ubiquitous psychic formations, but that they are the manifestations of the distorted fantasy life of overstimulated children.

cerning the dynamics of the patient's sensitivity to over-stimulation and concerning the reconstruction of the genesis of this sensitivity, i.e., concerning the unempathically overstimulating self-objects of the patient's childhood). But, so far as I can tell, the interpretive focus of the classical analyst lay elsewhere. I am thus inclined to hold the view that even with regard to structural neuroses the classical attitude of emotional reserve and muted response cannot be unequivocally regarded as creating the average expectable analytic milieu that constitutes true neutrality, even though it happens to be in harmony with the needs of the analysand's overstimulated childhood self. The analyst's muted response is not adopted in consequence of the specific need of his analysand, is not adopted in consequence of his deep comprehension of the genetic core of the analysand's disturbed personality, it is adopted in obedience to the tenet that contamination of the transference has to be avoided. The analyst's muteness and reserve would therefore be experienced as unempathic even by the analysand who suffers from a structural neurosis—were it not for the fact that it is frequently softened decisively by emotional undertones and overtones, which, arising from the depths of the analyst's psyche, make themselves heard despite the analyst's conscious theoretical convictions.

The conceptual changes brought about by the viewpoints of the psychology of the self thus lead to conclusions that lend theoretical support to the way analysts —some analysts at least—really act in their clinical pursuits, even though theory and theory-bound technical prescription are in their way, and even though they therefore feel obliged to play down the significance of the attitude they adopt in dealing with the manifestations of some of the most central sectors of their analysand's psychopathology by relegating it to a peripheral position and by referring to it cautiously as analytic tact.

The analyst's tactful behavior may thus be taken as the manifestation of his awareness of the vulnerability of the analysand who suffers from a disorder of the self, of his awareness of the analysand's tendency to retreat or to respond with rage. But even the most sensitively responsive behavior from the side of the analyst, based on the analyst's correct but only preconsciously achieved assessment of the psychopathology of analysands who suffer from disorders of the self, cannot replace the reconstructive-interpretive approach based on the analyst's conscious grasp of the patient's structural defects in the self, and of the self-object transferences that establish themselves on the basis of these defects. And if, in addition to the analyst's failure to grasp the essence of the analysand's psychopathology and to interpret it appropriately, he insists on behaving with an attitude of cautious reserve and overly muted responsiveness vis-à-vis his analysands with narcissistic personality disorders, there will be further deleterious consequences. The analysand will feel that the germinally displayed exhibitionism of his self or the cautiously offered tendrils of his idealization have been rejected; these delicately constituted configurations, which have just barely begun to be remobilized, will again break down; the analysand's behavior will be characterized by a mixture of disappointed lethargy (enfeeblement of the self) and rage (regressive transformation of the self's assertiveness); and, in further elaboration, the analyst's interpretations will begin to focus on a supposedly reactivated interplay of infantile aggression and guilt[4]—the lethargy of the rejected self is often mistakenly considered to be the result of a structural conflict (guilt over destructive impulses)—and they will disregard the more profoundly significant repetition of the analysand's childhood experience: his reaction to the faulty responses of his self-objects. The analyst's reassessment of the significance of his analysand's rage and destructiveness in the light of the psychology of the self—a reassessment, I would like to stress once more, that is fully compatible with the analyst's complete intellectual and emotional acknowledgment of the ubiquity and importance of aggression and hostility inside and outside the clinical situation—tends not only to prevent the creation of an artificial adversary position between analyst and analysand, but, by changing the emphasis of the interpretations, it leads gradually to an analytic dissolution of the total pathogenic configuration that is the matrix of the analysand's propensity toward rage. The analysand, in brief, is not "confronted" with a bedrock of hostility which he now has to learn first to recognize in himself and then to tame, but with the task of realizing that, while he has the right to expect a modicum of empathic responses from the self-objects of adult life, he must ultimately realize that they cannot make up for the traumatic failures of the self-objects in his childhood. It is the revival in the transference of the pathogenic self-objects of the analysand's childhood—the reconstruction of the noxious childhood environment—and the working through of the traumatic states of early life that were the result of their failures,

---

[4] I believe that this sequence—a kind of self-fulfilling prophesy—is encountered especially in analyses that are conducted by those whose therapeutic attitude is influenced, directly or indirectly, by the theoretical tenets of Melanie Klein.

which, *pari passu* with the laying down of new psychological structures, will reduce the analysand's propensity for rage.

To summarize my views on the analyst's attitude in the analytic situation, I will say first that it must never become the goal of the analyst to provide an *extra* measure of love and kindness to his patients—he will provide substantial help to his patients only through the employment of his special skills and through the application of his specialized knowledge. The nature of his specialized knowledge, however—his specific theoretical outlook—is an important factor in determining the way in which he conducts himself vis-à-vis his patients. It influences not only to some extent the kind of phenomena he will observe, but also the way in which he evaluates and interprets them. If the analyst is of the opinion that it is the level of drives (whether libidinal or aggressive) that constitutes the greatest depth to which analytic observation can penetrate, that, after overcoming resistances, analysis uncovers drive-wishes so that they can be suppressed or tamed or sublimated, he will be in tune with those of the problems of his analysands who suffer from structural neuroses, and he will be able to help them solve their unconscious conflicts in a satisfactory manner. Although I would maintain that his theory is incomplete if he disregards the psychology of the self in the narrow sense of the term, this incompleteness does not decisively interfere with therapeutic efficacy because, as I said earlier, a cohesive self is present on both sides of the conflict and can therefore be left out of the psychological equation without great loss. If the analyst, however, is dealing with patients who suffer from defects in the structure of the self, the incompleteness of the theory—I am speaking here not only of the absence of the psychology of the self in the narrow but also in the broad sense of the term — becomes a serious obstacle. Instead of recognizing that, on the deepest levels, the analysand tries to establish a transference to a self-object by moving from certain disintegration products (libidinal experiences concerning erogenous zones, rage concerning the lack of control over the self-object) to the basic psychological configurations that preceded them (the reactivated attempt to build a cohesive self by means of the empathic response of the self-object), the analyst will focus on conflicts regarding drives — the analysand's erotic and destructive aims and his guilt about them — and become either educational (urging self-control) or — often accompanied by a display of prideful realism — unnecessarily pessimistic, on the basis of the conviction that the analysis has now reached the "biological bedrock" beyond which it cannot penetrate.

There is a problem — I have already discussed its theoretical significance (pp. 209-219 above) — to which I must now return, even though I consider it of much greater theoretical than clinical importance. Although I claim that the analyst's participation in the analytic process as defined and described in the preceding pages provides the analysand with a matrix of true neutrality for the development of a — purely endopsychically determined — undistorted transference, even though I claim, in other words, that the analyst's participation as defined will do away with artifacts — i.e., with experiences and modes of behavior that are not endopsychically determined — that do indeed distort the transference, I will, paradoxical as it may seem, admit to the possible occurrence of rare instances in which the analyst's personality contributes to influencing the choice between two (or several) equally available and equally valid patterns of structural rehabilitation of a defective self. Although it should be obvious, it may need to be said that I am not speaking about gross identifications with the analyst's personality. Whereas these do occur and have a legitimate place as a temporary phase of the working through that ultimately leads to *transmuting* internalizations (cf. Kohut, 1971, pp. 166-167), their persistence clearly indicates that the analysis is not complete, that the patient's self has been supplanted by a foreign self and has not been rehabilitated. Nevertheless, even if these pseudocures are carefully taken into account and weeded out, there may yet be rare instances where the selective responsiveness of the analyst will indeed influence the target of the working-through processes and thus the specific form of the ultimately rehabilitated self.

I have not been able to find indubitable evidence of the influence my own personality may have had on an analysand's available choices. As a matter of fact, I have naturally taken pride in the fact that my analysands find solutions to the problems of their disturbance of mental health that are unequivocally their own and that—however the intrinsically predetermined patterns of their selves may be temporarily distorted by transitionally occurring gross identifications with me—they will ultimately emerge with the knowledge that they have found themselves.

But while I am unable to adduce persuasive evidence from my own practice in support of my conjecture—the objectivity required for this task is very difficult to attain —I have as a supervisor and consultant occasionally observed analyses in which the sequence and the comparative intensity of the analyst's reactions to the emerging transference material appeared to influence the analysand's choice of direction in working through.

I recently had the opportunity, for example, to study an extensive and expertly presented report of the analysis of a case of narcissistic personality disorder which led to a favorable result. The analysand, Mrs. Y., a woman whose psychopathology included a fairly severe diminution of the liveliness and buoyancy of her exhibitionism and a moderate disturbance of the cohesion of her body-self, reached an acceptable degree of firmness of her body-mind self and experienced a modicum of enjoyment from the display of its functions. This allowed her to feel much more accepting of herself and, as an outgrowth of this improvement, to establish much better relations with her husband and, especially, with her children. The new balance was in essence achieved via working through the transference toward the maternal mirroring self-object.

At the beginning of the analysis, however, an interchange had taken place between the patient and her analyst (a woman) that I believe to be relevant in the present context. Mrs. Y. mentioned that she had been suffering from a bowel disorder which had been diagnosed as ulcerative colitis, and she was emphatic about wanting to get at "the psychological cause" of this disorder. The analyst expressed caution regarding this goal, suggesting that psychological insights might well be ineffective here. The patient immediately complied with the analyst's realism by saying that she did not expect the analysis to make "a new person" of her. And she added — a non sequitur, the significance of which, it should be noted, escaped the attention of the otherwise very perceptive analyst — that she did not expect "the analysis to make an author" out of her.

Is it possible that another analyst, unconsciously in tune from the beginning with the patient's aspirations to express the exhibitionism of her grandiose self through creative pursuits, would have reacted differently to her hope that the analysis would be able to deal with her bowel disease? That another analyst, even if prompted by defensive realism to caution the patient about the limits of the efficacy of analysis, would still have become alerted by the analysand's subsequent remark, which despite its expression in the negative (see Freud, 1925), indicated a connection between the bowel disturbance and her wish to become an author? And, therefore, the working through would have been channeled not only toward the faulty mirroring to which her body-self had been exposed in childhood, but also toward the insufficiently offered opportunities for a merger with an idealized omnipotent self-object who stood for goals that were the precursors of achievements in the realm of literary creativity? And is it not possible that such a shift of focus of the analysis would have led to a different analytic result? A result, it should be added, that would have been equally solid and equally valid psychoanalytically as the one in fact achieved. Such an analysis might have brought about a narcissistic equilibrium of a different sort — it might have led to the analysand's increasing awareness of her self-expressing exhibitionistic needs, to her increasingly firm idealization of the task of shaping beautiful and/or significant replicas of her grandiose-exhibitionistic self instead of the replicas of the feeble, ill-defined, nonmirrored self extruded by her diseased bowels. The ultimate result of such an analysis would also be the analysand's increased ability to achieve narcissistic homeostasis—not, however, on the basis of the sense of peaceful perfection that resulted from the analysis that was actually carried out, but on the basis of her sense of proud and triumphant achievements, accompanied by the joy that comes from having lived up to idealized goals.

CHAPTER SEVEN

Epilogue

The Changing World

There is a point after some course has been completed — a journey from which one has returned, a phase of life that is now in the past — when, relaxing from the strenuous efforts that lie behind us and allowing our attention to drift away from the details of the tasks that had to be done, we can look back on what we have experienced to see it whole and to extract a broader meaning.

This is the point I feel I have reached. However broad my subject matter may seem to have been, however free-minded my theorizing, the most important results of my inquiry were, up to here, obtained through investigations made within a strictly defined framework: the framework of empirical-clinical research. In the following, however, I will permit myself a glance at some broader vistas — allow myself to raise questions that cannot be answered by research that limits itself to a clinical approach — even though I know that I will be on less secure ground than before, that the views I now present will concern areas that are, at best, at the periphery of my professional competence or relate to subject matters that, in general, allow only a speculative approach.

Seen in a different perspective, the reflections contained in the forthcoming pages are an attempt to answer a question that has not only an impersonal scientific meaning but also a personal one. Why, to put the question in personal terms first, in the face of my long-term commitment to the theories of classical psychoanalysis, the science that I studied and taught for a professional lifetime, why, in the face of my deep-rooted conservative instincts which tell me that a functioning system should not be tampered with — why did I feel forced to suggest an expansion, a change? Why, to put the question into the broader framework where it belongs, does analysis now need, in addition to classical theory and technique, a psychology of the self and a technique in tune with it? It needs them, I say, because man is changing as the world in which he lives changes; it needs them because if psychoanalysis is to remain the leading force in man's attempt to understand himself, and indeed if it wants to stay alive, it must respond with new insights when it is confronted with new data and thus with new tasks.

What are these new data, these new tasks that analysis is confronting, these changes to which analysis must respond? And, furthermore, if analysis does change, will it still be analysis? True, some of these questions have already been answered in the preceding pages, directly or by easy inference, based largely on the observation of the spontaneously unrolling sequences of self-object transferences during analyses of narcissistic personality disorders. But now I shall turn to a field that lies "beyond the bounds of the basic rule": the field where the scrutiny of psychological factors and the scrutiny of social factors converge.

I shall go directly to the heart of the matter by making the claim that the psychological danger that puts the psychological survival of modern Western man into the greatest jeopardy is changing. Until comparatively recent times the dominant threat to the individual was unsolvable inner conflict. And the correlated dominant interpersonal constellations to which the child of Western civilizations was exposed were the emotional overcloseness between parents and children and intense emotional relationships between the parents—perhaps to be looked upon as the unwholesome obverse of such corresponding wholesome social factors as firmness of the family unit, a social life concentrated on the home and its immediate vicinity, and a clear-cut definition of the roles of father and mother.

Today's child has fewer and fewer opportunities either to observe its parents at work or at least to participate emotionally, via concrete, understandable imagery, in the parents' competence and in their pride in the work situation where their selves are most profoundly engaged and the core of their personalities is most accessible to the empathic observer. Today's child can, at best, observe the parents' activities during their leisure hours. And here are then indeed opportunities for the child to participate emotionally in parental competence and pride—when son or daughter, for example on a camping trip, can participate in the father's putting up the tent and catching fish and in the mother's preparing the family meal. But although I am fully aware of the significant wholesome effect that the emotional closeness to such parental leisure activities provides for the child's forming self, I submit that the emotional participation in the parental play and leisure activities do not supply the child's nuclear self with the same nutriment as the emotional participation in the activities of real life — particularly with regard to the limited, optimal, nontraumatic parental failures that provide the fuel for transmuting internalizations.

The psychoanalyst is not a social psychologist and even less a historian of civilization or a sociologist — he lacks the scientific equipment to undertake the specific comparative examination of the significance for the formation of the child's self of parental leisure activities, on the one hand, and of parental work activities, on the other. And he would also not be able, unaided, to do justice to a general comparative examination of the changing social factors that are correlated to the changing psychological disorders encountered by various generations of depth psychologists. This is a task for scientists from neighboring disciplines; in particular it is a task in which the sociologist and the depth psychologist should be able to cooperate to great advantage. The analyst, unaided by colleagues from neighboring disciplines, will have no way, for example, to find the answer to the important question about the length of time that tends to be interposed between the ascendancy of certain social factors (one might call them *psychotropic* social factors) — such as industrialization, or the increasing employment of women, or the vagueness of certain sectors of the father image because of the father's employment away from home (see A. Mitscherlich, 1963), or its diffuse blurring because of the father's absence during a war (see Wangh, 1964, concerning the psychological consequences of the father's absence from the family during the 1914-1918 war) — on the one hand, and the changes in the psychology of the individual —a shift of the predominant personality patterns or of the predominant forms of psychological disturbance—on the other, which they produce. But whatever the societal determinants may be, and however complex and delayed their influence upon the psychology of the individual, the analyst can have little doubt that—at least as concerns the areas about which he can make inferences on the basis of his clinical experience—a psychological change is occurring at the present time.[1]

To repeat some earlier statements and to expand on them: The environment which used to be experienced as threateningly close, is now experienced more and more as threateningly distant; where children were formerly *over*stimulated by the emotional (including the erotic) life of their parents, they are now often *under*stimulated; where formerly the child's eroticism aimed at pleasure gain and led to internal conflict because of parental prohibitions and the rivalries of the oedipal constellation, many children now seek the effect of erotic stimulation in order to relieve loneliness, in order to fill an emotional void. But it is not only through their direct influence that

[1] I would like to make the following comments here concerning the psychosocial excursion on which I have embarked. First, that, in outlining the shift of man's dominant psychological task, I am disregarding the historical phase—one might call it the prepsychological phase—in which man's energies were still almost exclusively directed toward the attempt to deal with external threats to his survival. And, second, that I am confining my reflections to the populations of the densely settled, more or less highly industrialized democracies of the Western world. I will add to my second comment, however, that it is my impression that soon—as evaluated from a broad historical perspective—the psychological problems that may now be felt only in our Western democracies will also begin to be felt by populations under totalitarian regimes and in undeveloped areas whose social organizations differ from ours.

these changes in the adult environment bring about the changed meaning that certain nuclear experiences — including in particular his sexual experiences — now have for the child: they also exert their influence indirectly by changing the significance of his relations with other children — relations, it can be added, that may establish the ultimate pattern of the future attitude vis-à-vis friends, co-workers, and family, in the life of the adult.[2] Such interactions can be healthily exciting if the child moves toward other children from the basis of an emotional security provided by a firmly sustaining relationship to his adult self-objects; they can involve him in serious conflicts that may form the nucleus of later structural disorders if the parents, even though functioning appropriately in their role as self-objects, are traumatizing the child in the object-libidinal sphere; and they can serve defensive purposes, in the object-libidinal and, especially, in the narcissistic sphere. With regard to the last-mentioned possibility, it is clear that children often undertake both solitary sexual activities and group activities of a sexual, near-sexual, or sexualized nature in the attempt to relieve the lethargy and depression resulting from the unavailability of a mirroring and of an idealizable self-object. These activities are the forerunners of the frantic sexual activities of some depressed adolescents (cf. vom Scheidt, 1976, pp. 67-70) and of adult perversions. The picture of mixed and alternating states of overstimulation and lethargy characteristic of these traumatic conditions emerges at times in the transference, particularly in the so-called "sexualizations" of the

---

[2] For a discussion of the fact that children who are deprived of idealizable parents will idealize the peer group, see Bronfenbrenner (1970, pp. 101-109).

transference — states that are, I believe, all too often erroneously looked upon as (counterphobic) resistances motivated by oedipal castration fears.

True enough, to return to the examination of the relation between the child's self and his self-objects, it can be maintained that the overstimulation that used to predominate and the understimulation prevalent today are both manifestations of personality disorders of the parents, and that structural pathology and diseases of the self are therefore due to the same cause. Broadly speaking, they are. But the pathogenic personality of parents that leads to the propensity for structural neurosis in their children differs from the pathogenic personality of parents that leads to the propensity for a disorder of the self.

The overstimulation due to parental overcloseness that is a decisive factor in the genesis of structural disturbance is a manifestation of a structural neurosis in the parent, an acting out of a neurotic conflict with the aid of the child. The pathogenic effect of parents in this realm has been widely investigated[3] and needs no discussion here.

[3] August Aichhorn expressed this view most succinctly in a letter written to and quoted by R. S. Eissler (1949, p. 292). The "intrafamilial equilibrium," he wrote, "is maintained at the expense of the child who, overburdened..., develops into a delinquent or a neurotic." As the result of the psychotherapeutically achieved cure, Aichhorn adds, the child now "defends himself against the libidinal overburdening, and the family member who misused him for his own needs will break down neurotically." This description of the needs of the latently neurotic overstimulating parent and his resulting manifest neurosis when the child "defends himself" should be compared with the analogous considerations presented earlier with regard to the needs of the parent with a latent disorder of the self who has brought about a merger with his or her child and his resulting manifest serious self pathology when the merger is broken (p. 208n., above).

The understimulation due to parental remoteness that is a pathogenic factor in disorders of the self is a manifestation of a disorder of the self in the parent. In many instances, the parents of those who suffer from disorders of the self are quite manifestly walled off from their children, and it is thus easy to see that they deprive them of empathic mirroring and of a responsive target for their idealizing need. In other instances, however, the child's deprivation from the side of the parental self-object is not as easily discerned—indeed, evaluated in terms of behavior, these parents give an appearance of overcloseness to their children. But the appearance is deceptive, for these parents are unable to respond to their children's changing narcissistic requirements, are unable to obtain narcissistic fulfillment by participating in their children's growth, because they are using their children for their own narcissistic needs.

Let us take, for example, the parent who cannot say "no" to the child's demands. This inability might be explained within the framework of drive psychology by saying that these parents cannot tolerate frustrating the child because they are unable to tolerate being frustrated themselves; or that they envy the child's drive gratification and thus become involved in a paralyzing conflict about sadistic impulses vis-à-vis the child; etc. While the inability of a certain group of parents to say "no" to their children is indeed due to structural conflicts and can be adequately explained within the framework of drive psychology, there are other parents who cannot say "no" because they are afraid of the frustrated child's anger as the manifestation of the fact that the child's self is beginning, phase-appropriately, to become separated from the self of the adult, to become an independent center of initiative. The predicament of such parents, in other words, does not concern conflicts about frustrating the child's drive-wishes; nor are they avoiding the frustrated child's anger as the feared expression of a dangerous drive—they are reluctant to give up the merger-enmeshment with the child whom they, phase-inappropriately, because of the defective condition of their own self, still need to retain as part of their own self. These conclusions are not arrived at intuitively—the changing needs of the child's growing self may be reconstructed with great clarity on the basis of the manifestations of the self-object transference during psychoanalytic treatment. And it is the empathic scrutiny of the reactivated and reconstructed relations of the childhood self with the self-objects of childhood, and not experience-distant theorizing, however attractive and plausible its results might be, that reveals to us that in certain cases the seeming overcloseness of the adult to the child obscures the child's essential loneliness, i.e., it obscures the fact that neither the child's pridefully offered exhibitionism nor enthusiastically expressed idealizing needs had been phase-appropriately responded to and that the child, therefore, becomes depressed and lonesome. Such a child's self is psychologically undernourished and its cohesion is weak.

It should be added here that the relationship between psychotropic social factors and the change in leading personality pattern and dominant psychopathology that takes place under their influence is indirect and complex—it must not be conceptualized in analogy to the direct and comparatively simple causal relationship existing between the specific personality structure and psychopathology of parents and the specific personality structure and psychopathology acquired by the children of these parents. If we compare the psychotropic influence upon their children of parents with structural disorders and parents with disturbances of the self under the social conditions of the time when Breuer and Freud made their pioneering observations—let us say close to a hundred years ago—with the analogous psychotropic dynamics of our day, we can tentatively formulate several differences. In the second half of the nineteenth century the pathogenic effect of parents suffering from structural disorders was especially great because, within the confines of the closely knit family situation, the parents' opportunity to act out their conflicts with their children was especially great. Narcissistically disturbed parents of that period, however, may have been less likely to deprive their children of the requisite narcissistic nutriment because—in view of such factors as the prevalence of large families; or the presence of servants[4] who formed part of the family, particularly in the middle-class, upper-middle-class, and

---

[4] It is probably too late now to undertake a reliable systematic study of the influence of servants upon the forming personality organization of children in Freud's time, at the turn of the century. My hypothesis that the presence of servants tended to increase the emotional burden put upon an overstimulated child, but tended to counteract the influence of narcissistic deprivation, is buttressed by the fact that, at least in the middle-class Vienna of that period, the servants were in general young, healthy unmarried country-girls who, without ties in the big city, became deeply involved with the families for whom they worked. And the fact that the children became the emotional targets of these emotionally deprived young women, tended, on the one hand, to increase the likelihood of an emotional overburdening of the children, while, on the other hand, it counteracted understimulation and emotional isolation of children with narcissistically disturbed parents. While the significance of the role of the servant with regard to the child's experiences in the European and North American middle-class society has now changed, there are parts of the world—some South American countries, for example—in which the situation may still be similar to that of the Vienna of 1900, permitting the sociopsychological investigation of the problem.

(lower-level) upper-class social layers which supplied the bulk of patients to the pioneers of depth psychology—the pathogenic personality of the parents tended to be counteracted. The opposite can be said to hold true with regard to the psychogenesis of these two major types of psychological disturbances in the world of today. The increasing frequency of self pathology, in particular, may be explained by the fact that the relevant psychotropic social factors—small families, absence of parents from the home, frequent change of servants, as well as decreasing use of servants in the home—promote either the creation of an understimulating, lonely environment for the child, and/or expose the child, without the opportunity for effective relief, to the pathogenic influence of a parent suffering from self pathology (especially when the self pathology is not gross and overt—i.e., when other members of the family do not feel compelled to take remedial action).

It is clear, therefore, that my hypothesis concerning the psychotropic influence exerted by social factors with regard to the changing personality patterns encountered in recent times must only be taken in a relative sense, i.e., I am merely proposing an explanation for the gradual decrease of structural disorders and for the simultaneously occurring gradual increase in disorders of the self. These conditions require a great deal of further examination, and my tentatively proposed formulations about the nature of the changing social factors that might account for the nature of the changing parental self-object matrix and, thus, in turn, for the changing numerical distribution of the forms of psychopathology in succeeding generations, is clearly in need of critical evaluation by social scientists and historians who are well grounded in psychoanalysis. The impression, however, that instances of oedipal pathology are seen less frequently now, whereas instances of self pathology are encountered with increasing frequency, appears to me to rest on solid clinical experience—although I do not believe it is possible at present to give a definitive answer to the question whether the change from oedipal pathology to self pathology was already beginning to take place when depth psychology made its first investigations. The reexamination of the case reports of the pioneers, in particular, is fraught with the danger of the biased interpretation of the available data. Only protracted empathic immersion into the unfolding clinical material by observers who are open to perceiving the data of oedipal pathology *and* the data of self pathology as they emerge in the object-instinctual or in the self-object transference can lead to reliable conclusions.[5]

If it is true that self pathology is now in the as-

---

[5] The changeover from the predominance of one form of psychopathology (structural neurosis) to another (self pathology) is, as I have stated before, very gradual, and we have no reliable way of estimating in quantitative terms the degree of change that has already taken place. A questionnaire approach asking analysts for the percentage of their cases of analyses dealing predominantly with self pathology rather than with the pathology of structural conflict would at this time not give us satisfactory results. Those analysts who for a variety of reasons reject the diagnostic categories of narcissistic personality disorders and of other disturbances of the self and who remain convinced that all analyzable psychopathology is ultimately and in essence due to the conflicts of the object-instinctual wishes of the oedipal period would report that they are not seeing any diseases of the self. Those, on the other hand, who live in the honeymoon of their newly acquired insights about the psychology of the self might tend to overestimate the incidence of self psychopathology. And even if their judgment is unbiased, or has become so after they have truly integrated their new insights, those who recognize the existence of both forms of analyzable psychological illness may well attract more than the average number of patients with self pathology.

cendance, then we will understand why psychoanalysis, the science that more than any other is in touch with the deepest concerns of the individual, is shifting the focus of its attention away from the already carefully investigated inner conflicts of man (in particular the conflicts about repressed oedipal and other incestuous strivings) and why it is beginning, however haltingly, to pay more attention to the investigation of the vicissitudes of the self. And we will also understand why the theories concerning the dynamics of drive and defense, the unconscious, the tripartite model of the mind, object-cathexis, identification, etc., which served as an adequate framework for the explanation of the individual's structural conflicts must now be supplemented — I emphasize once more, as the expression of the depth-psychological principle of complementarity that retains *both* explanatory approaches — by theoretical conceptualizations concerning self-fragmentation, the nuclear self, the constituents of the self, self-object relationships, transmuting internalization, etc., which serve to explain the dominant pathology of our time.

In summary, I am suggesting, then, that each change in man's social surroundings confronts him with new adaptational tasks, and that the demands made on him by changes of such magnitude that one can speak of the dawn of a new civilization are, of course, especially great. In order to ensure his survival in the new surroundings, certain psychological functions of man will not only have to work overtime, they will — I am thinking here of the task of several generations — have to achieve a position of predominance in man's psychic organization. It is man's ability or inability to create new adaptational structures (or rather to increase the strength of already existing ones) that will determine his success or failure—indeed, his psychological survival or death.

And I submit, finally, that the analyst's attitude toward the clinical and technical questions with which our time is confronting him will be shallow, that his answers to them will be erroneous, if he disregards the shift in man's psychic organization which, as I suggested, has gradually been taking place. To repeat what I said at the beginning of the present chapter: if analysis is to remain the leading force in man's attempt to understand himself, it must respond with new insights when it is confronted with new data, and, thus, with the challenge of new tasks.

Two Concepts of Psychological Cure

The foregoing considerations are by no means unrelated to the psychological problems of the individual with whom the psychoanalyst as therapist must deal. Indeed, I believe that my postulate of the existence of two major types of analyzable psychological disorders—each requiring a different analytic focus and a different yardstick with which to measure therapeutic failure or success—can be appreciated fully only if examined against the background of the psychosocial changes I have discussed. The specific endopsychic area activated by the specific broad adaptational task required by a new cultural frontier determines the form of man's most intense anxieties and the content of his deepest fears, on the one hand, and the form of his most intense desires and the content of his most central goals, on the other. And no satisfactory definition of the concept of a cure, and thus of the concept of a proper termination of an analysis, can be given if we fail to determine the patient's greatest terror—whether castration anxiety or disintegration anxiety

—and his most compelling objective—whether conflict solution or the establishment of self-cohesion—or, stated in different terms, if we disregard the question whether the analysis had enabled him to perform those central psychological tasks through which he can establish the conditions that will guarantee his psychological survival. Because psychological health was formerly established through the solution of inner conflicts, cure, whether in a narrow or in a broad sense, was then seen exclusively in terms of conflict solution through the expansion of consciousness. But because psychological health is now achieved with ever-increasing frequency through the healing of a formerly fragmented self, cure, whether in a narrow or broad sense, must now also be evaluated in terms of achieving self-cohesion, particularly in terms of the restitution of the self with the aid of a re-established empathic closeness to responsive self-objects.

Our self—or should we say: the specific condition of our self?—influences our functioning, our well-being, the course of our life, both comprehensively and in depth. As I said earlier when discussing the significance of the depressions of later middle age (cf. p. 241, above)—but this crucial point bears repetition—there are, on the one hand, many people with poorly constituted selves who, despite the absence of symptoms, inhibitions, and disabling conflicts, lead joyless and fruitless lives and curse their existence. And there are, on the other hand, those with firm, well-defined selves who, despite serious neurotic disturbance—and yes, occasionally even despite their psychotic (or borderline) personalities[6]—are leading worthwhile lives and are blessed with a sense of fulfill-

---

[6] I have in mind those whose selves oscillate between (1) serious and protracted fragmentation or enfeeblement and (2) solid cohesion and firmness during prolonged (creative) periods of their lives.

ment and joy. It is the central position of the self within the personality that accounts for its broad influence on our life; and it is this central position that explains the vast increase in well-being provided for our patients by even a comparatively small improvement of self pathology. But in the absence of such improvement—however successful an analysis may have been in eradicating symptoms and inhibitions via a causal dynamic-genetic approach—the patient will remain unfulfilled and dissatisfied.

With regard to this second group of patients, analysts have, on the basis of their theoretical conviction that their patients' psychopathology was to be understood within the framework of conflict psychology and of the structural model of the mind, tended to shrug their shoulders in modest realism, consoling themselves with the thought that they have done all they possibly could. They have said, with Freud (1923a, p. 50n.), that all they could do was to open new choices for their patients; or they have said, again with Freud (Breuer and Freud, 1893-1895, p. 305), that they changed neurotic "misery into common suffering" over which they had no control.

I believe that some of these limitations can be seen in a different light—that a patient's continuing inability to make the right choices and his continuing inability to alter the suffering inflicted on him by unfortunate circumstances are in some cases at least (probably in many) not the result of unalterable internal or external factors, but of curable self pathology. Only increasing clinical experience, particularly the data of follow-up studies of analyses of narcissistic personality disorders, will give us reliable answers to the questions raised by the foregoing statement.

My own evaluation of possible progress in this area, derived from experience with the analysis of patients with narcissistic personality disorders, is on the whole optimistic.[7] Not that I believe that anyone exists who could learn always to make realistic choices, i.e., choices in complete harmony with the innate abilities he possesses and with the external opportunities open to him, choices that serve his principles or fully support the pursuit of attainable goals; that anyone exists who could learn never to retreat from unpleasant tasks; that anyone exists who could ever become able, on the strength of a more vigorous self-experience, to dispense totally with false optimism or other illusions. Nor do I claim that anybody who has indeed acquired through analysis a strong cohesive center of his personality will therefore unfailingly be able to deal with the environment in accordance with his deepest purposes and his highest ideals. We must not expect miracles to result from our increased attention to the pathology of the self or from our increasing ability to discern its various forms and to open them up to the appropriate working-through processes. But I do know that, through a properly conducted analysis of these forms of pathology, the potential toward improvement in all the aforementioned areas is generally greatly increased.

Mental health is often defined by analysts, in har-

[7] I know that any psychotherapist who rightly or wrongly has become convinced that he has something new to offer his patients is in danger, on the basis of his enthusiasm, of producing cures by suggestion (cf. my remarks about Freud's early successes on p. 36n., above). But I believe that my awareness of this danger has protected my patients from being unduly influenced by my convictions. I think so because the improvements were always brought about through time-consuming, persevering work, and, while definable and often of very favorable impact on the patient's life, they were nevertheless always incomplete.

mony with a remark ascribed to Freud (Erikson, 1950, p. 229), rather loosely and extrascientifically as a person's ability to work and to love. Within the framework of the psychology of the self, we define mental health not only as freedom from the neurotic symptoms and inhibitions that interfere with the functions of a "mental apparatus" involved in loving and working, but also as the capacity of a firm self to avail itself of the talents and skills at an individual's disposal, enabling him to love and work successfully.

The two frames of reference—mental-apparatus psychology and self psychology—that permitted two different but complementary definitions of mental health, will also assist us now in our endeavor to formulate differentiating definitions of the concept of cure in the two classes of analyzable psychic disorders. In cases of structural conflict, the principal indicators that a cure has been established will be the disappearance or amelioration of the patient's neurotic symptoms and inhibitions, on the one hand, and his comparative freedom from neurotic anxiety and guilt, on the other. And, on the whole, the positive achievement of a good analysis in these cases will be confirmed by the fact that the patient is now able to experience the pleasures of life more keenly than before. In cases suffering from analyzable forms of self pathology, however, the principal indicators that a cure has been established will be the disappearance or the amelioration of the patient's hypochondria, lack of initiative, empty depression and lethargy, self-stimulation through sexualized activities, etc., on the one hand, and the patient's comparative freedom from excessive narcissistic vulnerability (the tendency, for example, to respond to narcissistic injuries with empty depression and lethargy, or with an increase of perverse self-soothing activities), on the other. And, on the whole, the positive achievement of a good analysis will here be confirmed by the fact that the patient is now able to experience the joy of existence more keenly, that, *even in the absence of pleasure,* he will consider his life worthwhile—creative, or at least productive.

Have I overdrawn the contrast between the two forms of psychopathology? Perhaps. But I think it better to risk being overly schematic than to risk being obscure. Clinical experience will do its part in demonstrating the compromises between different forms of psychopathology, i.e., it will demonstrate the presence of the mixed case, and it will teach the analyst to shift his attention from one realm to the other.

The Artist's Anticipation of the Psychology of the Self

There is another line of thought that supports the claim that significant changes in the human condition have been taking place since the decisive decade from 1890 to 1900 when the basic formulations that determined the direction in which analysis developed were laid down. This line of thought rests on the hypothesis—I shall call it the hypothesis of artistic anticipation (it was first sketched out in an address given in 1973 [see Kohut, 1975a, pp. 337-338])—that the artist—the great artist, at any rate—is ahead of his time in focusing on the nuclear psychological problems of his era, in responding to the crucial psychological issue man is facing at a given time, in addressing himself to man's leading psychological task. The work of the great artist, according to this hypothesis, reflects the dominant psychological issue of his era. The artist stands, as it were, in proxy for his generation: not only for the general population but even for the scientific investigators of the sociopsychological scene.

As contrasted with the central artistic challenge of our day, the art of yesterday—I am thinking especially of the great European novelists of the second half of the nineteenth and of the beginning of the twentieth century —dealt with the problems of Guilty Man—the man of the Oedipus complex, the man of structural conflict—who, strongly involved with his human environment from childhood on, is sorely tested by his wishes and desires. But the emotional problems of modern man are shifting, and the great modern artists were the first to respond in depth to man's new emotional task. Just as it is the under-stimulated child, the insufficiently responded-to child, the daughter deprived of an idealizable mother, the son deprived of an idealizable father, that has now become paradigmatic for man's central problem in our Western world, so it is the crumbling, decomposing, fragmenting, enfeebled self of this child and, later, the fragile, vulner-able, empty self of the adult that the great artists of the day describe—through tone and word, on canvas and in stone—and that they try to heal. The musician of dis-ordered sound, the poet of decomposed language, the painter and sculptor of the fragmented visual and tactile world: they all portray the breakup of the self and, through the reassemblage and rearrangement of the frag-ments, try to create new structures that possess wholeness, perfection, new meaning. The message of the greatest of them—Picasso's perhaps, or Ezra Pound's—may be ex-pressed with such visionary originality, through the em-ployment of such unconventional means, that it is still not easily accessible. But others come closer to speaking to us in intelligible terms. Gregor Samsa, the cockroach of Kafka's *Metamorphosis,* may serve here as an example. He is the child whose presence in the world had not been blessed by the empathic welcome of self-objects—he is the child of whom his parents speak impersonally, in the third-person singular; and now he is a nonhuman monstrosity, even in his own eyes. And Kafka's K., the Everyman of our time, engages in an endless search for meaning. He tries to get close to the great ones in power (the adults, the parents who reside in *The Castle*), but he cannot reach them. And in *The Trial* he perishes, still searching for a redeemable, at least for an understandable guilt—the guilt of Man of yesterday. He cannot find it; and thus he dies a meaningless death—"like a dog." Eugene O'Neill, too, the greatest playwright the New World has produced, dealt in his work (especially in his late plays *The Iceman Cometh* and *Long Day's Journey Into Night*) with man's leading psychological problem— the problem of how to cure his crumbling self. And nowhere in art have I encountered a more accurately pointed description of man's yearning to achieve the restoration of his self than that contained in three terse sentences in O'Neill's play *The Great God Brown.* These are Brown's words close to the end of his long day's journey into night, after a life torn by uncertainty about the substance of his self: "Man is born broken. He lives by mending. The grace of God is glue." Could the essence of the pathology of modern man's self be stated more impressively?[8]

[8] We can assume that Arthur and Barbara Gelb, O'Neill's biographers (1962), recognized the significance of Brown's words because they used them as the motto for their comprehensive study.

My hypothesis that the artist anticipates the dominant psychological problem of his era does not, of course, imply the absence of individual motivation. A Michelangelo, a Shakespeare, a Rembrandt, a Mozart, a Goethe, a Balzac, each was propelled toward his specific artistic goals by motivations that were deeply grounded in his personality. Yet, whatever the individual motivations, they were all also giving expression to the leading psychological problem of their specific time, just as is true for the greatest artists of our day.

The work of such creators as Henry Moore, O'Neill, Picasso, Stravinsky, Pound, Kafka,[9] would have been unintelligible even a hundred years ago—but now it is daring, profound, and beautiful for those of us who are open to their message, and we feel that they are in touch with the deepest problems of our age.[10]

We can surely still grasp, reverently and admiringly, the formal perfection of the works of the great artists of

[9] Dostoevski, to my mind, occupies a specific transitional position that is much harder to pinpoint. His works deal with structural conflict—with the Oedipus complex and with guilt. Yet they also depict the fact that it is a weak, crumbling, precariously coherent self that faces these problems. The study of some of Dostoevski's writings—*The Idiot,* for example, or *The Double*—will help us to understand the analysands, occasionally encountered, who cannot be approached—as is appropriate in the majority of instances—as suffering predominantly from structural neurosis *or* of self pathology, but who require empathic understanding for the simultaneous presence of both disturbances.

[10] It may seem ridiculous to some, it will be blasphemy to others, when, in the context of the claim that the great artist can speak to his contemporaries with a penetrating power with which he is not likely ever to speak again to later generations, I suggest that, for example, the modern reader will experience Proust's description of the Baron de Charlus' humble greeting of Mme. de Saint-Euverte (Vol. Two, pp. 986ff.) as a more intimately moving rendition of the tragic breakdown of the self in old age than the rendition contained in those unsurpassed peaks of literature, Shakespeare's *King Lear* and Sophocles' *Oedipus on Colonus,* to which Proust himself feels obliged to allude.

the past; and we are moved by them because we sense the authenticity with which they express the essence of an age in which the desires and conflicts of the cohesive self of the individual cried for expression. And furthermore, since human nature, despite the profound changes in man's psychological condition that are brought about by sociohistorical change, remains sufficiently the same to allow us to build bridges of understanding empathy into the past, we continue to respond to the artistic rendition of a psychological world whose problems are not in the center of man's world today. Still, I have no question about it: we can no longer recapture the full excitement, produced by the discovery of new artistic solutions to the then dominant emotional problems, experienced by the contemporaries of these great men.

True enough, there are occasionally great artists whose individuality takes them out of the mainstream of their time, at least temporarily. And then they create works that strangely transcend the scope of what is intelligible in their day. I have here in mind such profound evocations of the struggles of the threatened self — perhaps under the impact of old age, physical decline, imminence of death — as Leonardo's *Deluge* series, Michelangelo's *Pietà Rondanini*,[11] and Beethoven's B-flat-major string quartet (*Grosse Fuge*), opus 133. They are modern

---

[11] The fact that not only the *Pietà Rondanini* but also many other great sculptures of Michelangelo's last period remained unfinished (the *Slaves* in the *Accadèmia;* the *Pietà* in *Santa Maria del Fiore;* etc.) and that the very unfinishedness of their state is deeply moving to the modern beholder (though it was probably not to Michelangelo's contemporaries) leads me to think that the aged artist expressed his growing experience of self-fragmentation in this way. Freud (1914b, p. 213) characteristically responded most deeply to the Moses statue — the finished rendition of a strong, fully cohesive self.

art despite the fact that they were created long ago. Kleist, too, in his essay "On the Marionette Theatre" (1811) and, to a slightly lesser extent, in his *Micheal Kohlhaas* (1808) deals with the problems of the crumbling (or the deeply injured) self, and these works can therefore again be considered "modern" art. Still, great as these individual creations are, they did not psychologically belong to the time when they were created—they remained isolated flashes in the artistic life of man—and it is only now, in retrospect, that we can respond to them in depth. It is the modern beholder, listener, and reader —the eye and ear and the reflective thought of the child of the era of the endangered self—who lifts these creations out of the matrix of individual meaning from which they arose and, in so doing, transforms them into modern art.

On the Influence of Freud's Personality

The thesis that psychoanalysis must respond to the new data now confronting it by creating new conceptual tools and therapeutic techniques—that it now requires a psychology of the self—is itself in need of scrutiny. Clearly, in a strict sense, the data now confronting us are not really new. But, of course, as implied by the earlier discussion of sociopsychological change and the preceding remarks about the shifted focus of modern art, we are not posing the question in this form. We are not asking whether the disorders of the self have arisen *de novo* since Freud formulated the basic theories of analysis—even to consider such a possibility would be ludicrous. We are asking our question in a relative sense, namely, whether the disorders of the self have gained ascendancy over the conflict neuroses or, put differently, whether the disorders of the self, even if they have not increased in absolute number or relative proportion, are now more intense, cause greater suffering, are, to put it in still different terms, more significant now, in view of a shift of the leading psychological problem of Western man from the area of guilt-ridden overstimulation and conflict to that of inner emptiness, isolation, and unfulfillment. Or, putting the question in concrete terms that would, at least in theory, admit the possibility of an answer by empirically based research, we could ask whether individuals suffering from disorders of the self, although of course a great number of them existed even during the pioneering days of analysis, either did not seek out the help of the analyst of earlier times or, another possibility, whether the analyst of those times was simply too busy, mining as it were the psychological gold offered him by the transference neuroses, to devote intense research interest to other disorders.

It is impossible to provide exact answers to these questions and, although I generally dislike the use of the word "never" in such contexts, I have no hesitation in stating that definitive answers will indeed never be available.

But one task remains. In view of the fact that analysis was for a long time the work of one man, we must try to arrive at as much clarity as possible concerning the question whether we can discern any features in Freud's personality that—apart from the influence exerted on his approach by the style of thinking that dominated late-nineteenth-century science, and apart from the fact that he focused on the psychological problems that were indeed prevalent in his day—played a role

among the factors that led to analysis becoming a psy
chology of drives and large-scale cohesive structures, that
were responsible for its not also turning from the beginning to the vicissitudes of the self. We must consider the
possibility, in other words, that Freud's personality determined his preferences with regard to the empirical data
on which he focused and with regard to the kind of theory
he found congenial.

Another book needs here to be written. I will not
write it. A glance at a few aspects of Freud's personality I
consider relevant to our problem will have to suffice.

First, some remarks about Freud's narcissistic vulnerability, or, to be exact—since narcissistic vulnerability
is a ubiquitous burden of man, a part of the human condition from which no one is exempt—about the specific
psychic area that was involved and about the way in which
he dealt with this aspect of his personality. He was least
sensitive to (or most protected against) the kind of narcissistic blows that the great majority of people are most
prone to experience as serious narcissistic injuries: he was
not only able to withstand attacks (on himself and on his
work), and to tolerate belittling attitudes and ostracism,
but I believe that he became even especially self-assured
and self-assertive under such conditions. I think the explanation for this seemingly paradoxical fact is that
under such circumstances he was protected against the
kind of narcissistic injury to which he was most sensitive
and against which he had to protect himself most
strongly.

Freud did not consider himself a great man, although he undoubtedly was one (cf. Jones, 1955, p. 415).
I believe his inability to feel himself as great—in combination with other, related symptoms such as his embar-

rassment at being looked at: "I cannot put up with being stared at by people for eight hours a day (or more)" (1913b, p. 134); his oversensitivity vis-à-vis the possibility that others, his patients, might be embarrassed by being looked at: "If Freud did not want to embarrass them by looking at them, he would often focus his eyes on the figures on the intervening table" (Engelman, 1966, p. 28); his excessive reluctance to accept praise at face value and to react to congratulations with pleasure; his shunning of public celebrations; his aspiration to cut established idealized values down to life size (cf., for example, his letter to Binswanger of October 8, 1936 [Binswanger, 1957])—may well have been a manifestation of a part of his personality, the narcissistic sector, he did not analyze sufficiently in his self-analysis. He thus did not achieve full insight and control over this psychological sector, but enacted the fulfillment of its demands with Fliess, Jung, and others (see Kohut, 1976, p. 407n.). The evidence that Freud could not comfortably accept praise and celebration is plentiful, and those familiar with his biography will have no trouble finding it. Suffice it to say that Freud himself acknowledged this tendency, e.g., when he said that he disliked being the "'object' of a celebration" (Binswanger, 1957, p. 108). I would draw attention only to one very characteristic feature: When Freud felt exposed to open praise or admiration he seemed to be forced to react with an assertion of cool objectivity (e.g., Jones, 1955, pp. 182-183, p. 415) or irony —even where he ultimately accepted the praise. (For a striking example of his use of irony as a defense see his otherwise warmly accepting letter of May 7, 1916 to E. Hitschmann which begins with the words, "Only a funeral oration at the Central Cemetery is normally as

beautiful and affectionate as the speech you did not
deliver" [E. L. Freud, 1960, p. 311].) However well
rationalized these attitudes may be—and however tempting it may be to idealize them as a sign of true greatness
—I have no doubt, on the basis of broad clinical experience with similar behavior, that they betray a sharply
circumscribed vulnerability—to be exact: a fear of
overstimulation—in the narcissistic sector, in the area of
exhibitionism.

Another aspect of Freud's personality that is relevant
in the present context was his inability to open himself to
the experience of music and to the experience of modern
(twentieth-century) art. It could be claimed that these
features might be partially accounted for as being an aspect of the man of the Age of Enlightenment—but I believe that the major factor lay in Freud. It was his personality that determined his preference for the content of
thought, for the clearly defined and definable; it was his
personality that made him shun the areas of contentless
forms and intensities and unaccountable emotions.

As concerns Freud's inability to give himself over to
the experience of pure music[12] I have little to say, except
that it appears to be in conformity with the general trend
of his intellect and personality. He was aware of this defect in himself but was—and, it seems to me, rightly so—
satisfied with the conclusion that it formed the unavoidable price he had to pay for those aspects of his person-

---

[12] Opera, songs, and so-called "program music" are musical forms
which in the present context must be clearly distinguished from "pure"
music. The first have verbalizable content and may thus be mastered and
enjoyed in an essentially nonmusical way by a nonmusical listener; the
second one has not, and therefore requires from the listener the ability to
confront intense nonverbal experiences (cf. Kohut and Levarie, 1950,
pp. 72-75; Kohut, 1957, p. 392).

ality that were his greatest assets. Works of art, he said
(1914b, p. 211), exercised in general a powerful effect on
him so long as they allowed him to explain to himself
what their effect was due to. And he continued: "Wher-
ever I cannot do this, as for instance with music, I am
almost incapable of obtaining any pleasure. Some
rationalistic, or perhaps analytic, turn of mind in me
rebels against being moved by a thing without knowing
why I am thus affected and what it is that affects me."
Although it would be tempting to examine the question
to what extent the restrictedness of Freud's capacity to
respond to music was a manifestation of compensatory
structures and to what extent it was defensive, I will not
pursue this topic—particularly in view of the fact that
Freud's attitude toward music has recently become the
object of investigation by others (K. R. Eissler, 1974;
Kratz, 1976) who will, I hope, continue to examine the
relevant issues. In general, I feel that Freud's limitations
vis-à-vis the experience of music, while clearly of deep
significance, should not be evaluated as a defect, but as a
characteristic feature of his personality—a personality
defined by the need for the steadfast predominance of
rationality.

   The situation is somewhat different with regard to
Freud's attitude toward modern art. Here we are dealing
not with an inability or inhibition that he mildly re-
gretted himself but with a rejecting and fun-poking attitude, uncomfortably—and disappointingly—similar to
the attitude prevalent among the *petite bourgeoisie* of his
time—witness his letter to Abraham, written late in 1922
(H. Abraham and E. Freud, 1965, p. 332). Would one
not expect from a psychological genius such as Freud,
even if not wholehearted acceptance of modern art, at

least a respectfully reflective curiosity vis-à-vis this new and puzzling manifestation of the human spirit? Yet, on further reflection, it seems likely that Freud's rejection of modern art goes hand in hand with his reluctance to immerse himself in archaic narcissistic states (see his letter to Hollós of 1928 [Schur, 1966, pp. 21-22]) and with his failure to recognize the importance of the vicissitudes of the cohesion and disintegration of the self—topics that, as the leading psychological tasks of our times, had entered into the work of the pioneering artists of the day long before they became targets for the investigative efforts of the scientific psychologist.

I believe that the foregoing reflections support the conclusion that certain features of Freud's personality led him to emphasize one aspect of psychic life and to deemphasize another. Some of Freud's theoretical writings undoubtedly prepared the soil for the development of certain sectors of the psychology of the self. It is my impression, however, that within the area of narcissism he did not elaborate—with regard to the role of narcissism in clinical analysis, for example, or with regard to the role of narcissism in history—the themes he had discussed theoretically with the same freedom and vigor with which he advanced his investigations in the direction of structural psychology, of the psychology of conflict. Even where he made his most profound contributions to the area of archaic narcissism (1911), he shifted confusingly between the recognition of the importance of the regressive narcissistic position, on the one hand, and conflict issues on much higher developmental levels, namely, conflicts concerning homosexuality, on the other. This ambiguity of Freud's position cleared the way for contradictory arguments for generations of apologists (cf., for example, Kohut, 1960, pp. 573-574) and attackers (cf., for example, Macalpine and Hunter, 1955, pp. 374-381).

It is hard for us to accept the limitations of a revered figure. Yet, I believe that in Freud's work, as is the case with all great achievement, the intensity and profundity of insight in one area had to be paid for by a comparative flatness in another. Freud was not able or willing to devote himself in close empathic immersion to the vicissitudes of the self as he had been able to do with regard to the vicissitudes of object-instinctual experiences. I would assume that his pioneering mind could not have moved into both of these directions without interfering with the depth of his insights in the one to which he primarily devoted his creative life.

But let us be done with details. Even if everything I have said in the foregoing could be proved beyond doubt —what have I achieved? Does it not go without saying that Freud's personality had features that determined his scientific predilections? That Freud, raised scientifically by some of the greatest teachers of nineteenth-century science, approached his researches by methods, and formulated the results of his researches by the application of theoretical structures, which, however novel and daring, still showed the influence of what he had been taught?

These conclusions are surely not earthshaking, and I undertook to present them mainly to clear the way toward this ultimate, important question. If, for whatever reason—either because of the specific type of prevalent psychopathology that claimed the investigator's attention, or because of the determining focus of the science of the day, or because of Freud's personal pre-

dilections, or, which is probably the case, by the con-
fluence of all these—classical psychoanalysis did not sufficiently encompass the whole field that is open to depth-
psychological investigation, then we must ask whether the
addition of a new, more encompassing focus—such as
that provided by the psychology of the self—constitutes a
change of such magnitude, shifts our basic outlook to
such an extent, that we can no longer speak of psychoanalysis, but must, however reluctantly, admit that we
are now dealing with a new science; or whether we can
integrate the new with the old and thus maintain the
sense of continuity that allows us to see the change, however great it may be, as a move toward a new phase of a
living and growing science. It is clear that if we want to
cast an intelligent vote concerning this crucial question,
we cannot shrink from the attempt to answer this fundamental question first: what is the essence of psychoanalysis?

What Is the Essence of Psychoanalysis?

It is dangerous to rely on the qualities that defined
the simple source of a complex set of activities in order to
explain the significance of their mature and developed
functions (Langer, 1942; Hartmann, 1960). But there are
developmental sequences for which the generally valid
cautionary rule about the pitfalls of the genetic fallacy
does not apply because we can show that all later development, complex though it may be, remains in essence in a
meaningful unbroken contact with the very first move.

One may view the development of human thought,
especially of scientific thought, in analogy to biological
evolution. Most of the time the development follows in-

telligible rules, proceeds in an orderly fashion. Errors are discarded, new truths are established, and new theories are built to explain newly discovered sets of facts. Imperceptibly, gradually, as well as by perceptible steps — through the elaborating and refining contributions made by the trained minds of industrious investigators as well as through the substantial advances made by the brilliant intellect of the genius — human thought, scientific thought, moves on. Like biological development, it does not progress in ways that we can at the present time predict (at least not over long stretches of time), and we are not yet able to direct it intentionally (at least not toward distant goals). But it proceeds in a logical fashion — at any rate, it is open to retrospective scrutiny. Very rarely, however, there occurs a forward leap in the development of man's perception of the world — at first it may to all appearances seem to be a small step — that provides access to a whole new aspect of reality. A move of this type may be compared with a mutation in biological evolution. Through it, a new direction is given to human thought. It is an event that cannot be called an advance in method alone. Nor can it be defined by the fact that old and well-known data of observation are now seen in a new light — the light of a new explanatory paradigm (see Kuhn, 1962). No, the phenomenon in question, the mutation of human thought I have in mind, is neither a revolutionizing new technique nor a revolutionizing new theory. It is both — and, being both, it is more than both. It is an advance on that basic level of man's relationship to reality where we cannot yet differentiate data from theory, where external discovery and internal shift in attitude are still one and the same, where the primary unit between observer and observed is still unobstructed and unobscured by secondary abstracting reflection. On this basic level of experience, the most primitive and the most developed mental functions appear to be at work simultaneously, with the result not only that there is no clear separation between observer and observed, but also that thought and action are still one. The greatest steps made in the history of science—the pioneering experiments of the greatest scientists—are thus, as I said earlier (pp. 36-37, above) sometimes "not primarily arrangements designed to facilitate discovery or to test hypotheses" but "concretized thought"; or, put more correctly, they are "action-thought," a precursor of thinking. Although I have little empirical material on which to test this hypothesis, I can turn to the reflections of a great poet concerning a related topic, Goethe's reflections about the essence of biblical creation—the prototype of creativity for Western Man. Faust, quite early in the tragedy (Part One, 1224-1237), begins to translate the New Testament (John 1/1) from the original Greek. But how to render the very first line; how should he refer to the *fons et origo* of the world—to its "Beginning"? "In the Beginning was the *Word,*" he tries. But he discards this version. "The *Thought,*" perhaps? This term, too, fails to give the meaning. "The *Power,*" then? No; still not right! But then, inspired, he finally sees the light: "In the Beginning was the *Act,*"[13] he writes.

Whatever the psychological essence of the ideational process might be by dint of which the forward leap in the development of man's perception of the world of which I

[13] Goethe's *"die Tat"* in *"Am Anfang war die Tat,"* could be translated either as "deed" or "act," two closely related but not synonymous terms. Although both contrast with "word" and "thought," because "act" contrasts more strongly with "thought," I prefer it.

spoke earlier is carried out, the step that is taken at such moments does not seem to be logically connected with previous ones. We seem to witness the parthenogenesis of an idea of enormous power, accompanied by an act that, despite its simplicity, implies the consummation of innumerable further acts, as if a planful mind had indeed presented a blueprint for the future—the emergence of an idea, in other words, that enables numerous followers to till new soil wrested from the wilderness of the heretofore unexplored. Once the new continent has been made accessible, others will survey it—some by introducing comprehensive ordering principles (paradigmatic, yet replaceable and improvable theories) and by shaping the principal methodologies (paradigmatic, yet replaceable and improvable techniques) for the investigation of the new field, others by elaborating and refining these techniques and theories, and by adding further data. The results of the preceding basic step, however, do not seem to be ephemeral (in the sense of their being replaceable or improvable)—at least not within the confines of the recorded history of human thought.

The mutation that opened the door to the new field of introspective-empathic depth-psychology (psychoanalysis) took place in 1881, in a country house near Vienna, in the encounter between Josef Breuer and Anna O. (Breuer and Freud, 1893). The step that opened the path to a whole new aspect of reality—a step that established simultaneously both the novel mode of observation and the novel content of a revolutionary science—was made by the patient who insisted that she wanted to go on "chimney-sweeping" (p. 30). Yet it was Breuer's joining her in this venture, his permission for her to go on with it, his ability to take her move seriously (i.e., to observe its results and to commit the observations to paper) that established that unity of observer and observed which forms the basis for an advance of the first magnitude in man's exploration of the world.

In my view, then, the essence of psychoanalysis lies in the scientific observer's protracted empathic immersion into the observed, for the purpose of data-gathering and explanation. All further progress — the contributions made by Freud's ordering mind, by his courage and persistence; the contributions made by the best of the succeeding generations of analysts — is logically connected with this essence, and the activities that bring it about, directly or through trial and error, occur in intelligible sequences. The essence-creating first step, however, seems to lie outside the realm of causal sequences — we are unable to account for it with our present means of logical or psychological explanation.

We are now ready to return to the central issue of our present inquiry, the question what constitutes the essence of psychoanalysis. My answer, which seeks to highlight the features of psychoanalysis that have since its inception differentiated it from all other branches of science — an answer, I will add, for which, by referring to the origins of psychoanalysis, I have now also supplied a genetic justification — is that psychoanalysis is a psychology of complex mental states which, with the aid of the persevering empathic-introspective immersion of the observer into the inner life of man, gathers its data in order to explain them.

Among the sciences that inquire into the nature of man, psychoanalysis, I believe, is the only one that, in its essential activities, combines empathy, employed with scientific rigor in order to gather the data of human experience, with experience-near and experience-distant theorizing, employed with equal scientific rigor in order to fit the observed data into a context of broader meaning and significance. It is the only one among the sciences of man that explains what it has first understood.

Psychoanalysis is unique among the sciences, in other words, by virtue of the fact that it has consistently based itself on the data of introspection and empathy. The significance of its theories, old and new—their internal consistency and relevance—can be fully grasped only if one realizes that they are correlated to this specific data-gathering process. There is no question that the technical refinements (especially the consistent employment of free association) with which analysis implemented its basic observational stance are of the greatest importance. And there is also no question about the ingenuity and helpfulness of the various theoretical frameworks (for example, the topographic and the structural models of the mind), with the aid of which analysts have been ordering the data that they collected via empathy. Still, despite their value, these devices supplied by psychoanalytic theory and technique are not irreplaceable; they are—as I once said about free association and resistance analysis—improvable tools, "auxiliary instruments, employed in the service of the introspective and empathic method of observation" (Kohut, 1959, p. 464). Here then, to my mind—in the fact that its subject matter is that aspect of the world that is defined by the introspective stance of the observer—lies the essence of psychoanalysis; here indeed lay the essence of depth psychology at the moment it was born.

But we must pause now to consider objections that might be raised against this definition of the essence of psychoanalysis. There are those who might seize on the popular resonance evoked by the unscientific use of the term empathy—namely, on such fuzzily related meanings as kindness, compassion, and sympathy, on the one hand, and intuition, sixth-sense perception, and inspiration, on the other. And there are those who might fasten on the fact that my definition fails to limit the field by the inclusion of any specific theoretical tenets—that it does not even refer to Freud's famous dictum (1914a, p. 16) that it is the acknowledgment of the mechanisms of transference and resistance that defines the analytic approach.

I can well understand these objections. I know, in particular—to address myself first to the misgivings aroused by my emphasis on empathy—that some of my colleagues will say that by assigning a position of basic importance to empathy I am just trying to bring about what others have tried to bring about before me: the replacement of the staunch acceptance of the cold facts of reality by a regressive, sentimental flight toward illusions. And no doubt, some critics will say that my claim that the empathic stance is a necessary and defining ingredient of the analyst's attitude—as a therapist *and* as a researcher —is only the first step in an ultimately fatal direction, a cleverly disguised first move toward nonscientific forms of psychotherapy which provide cure through love and cure through suggestion, and that it is a replacement of the scientific mode of thought by a quasi-religious or mystical approach—imposters against which analysis has had to maintain itself and toward which it has had to define its borders carefully ever since it came into being.

Even the most convincing arguments in support of the respectability of the position held by empathy in psychoanalytic theory—that empathy is not only an irreplaceable tool in depth psychology, but that it also defines the field of depth psychology—cannot, of course, invalidate the fears I put into the mouth of my imaginary critic—analysis is indeed exposed to the twin dangers of sentimentalizing obfuscation in the scientific area and the covert introduction of cure via suggestion in the clinical field. We must thus be on guard about the possibility that our insights might be used as rationalizations for unscientific therapeutic activities. Such abuses must not, however, be fought by repudiating empathy and intro-spection—a move that would abolish depth psychology—but by conceptual clarity concerning their definition in the theoretical field (see Kohut, 1971, pp. 301-305) and by the insistence on the rigorous observance of scien-tific standards in their employment in research and therapy.

My definition will also be criticized, as I said, on the grounds that it lacks any specific reference to the estab-lished theories of analysis, in particular to the theoretical framework created by Freud. A science, however, and above all a basic science like psychoanalysis, cannot be defined by the tools it uses: not by its methodological tools, i.e., by the instruments it employs in its investiga-tions, and not—and I would like to lay special stress on this point—by its conceptual tools, i.e., by its theories. It can only be defined by its total approach, which deter-mines the aspect of reality to which we then refer as the subject matter of the science.

But is not empathy just a tool—a specific tool of ob-servation and does not my emphasis on it, therefore, make my own definition as arbitrary as if I had said that analysis is defined by the use of a couch in the therapeutic situation and by the use of the concept of repression in theory? My answer to these questions is "no." Empathy is not a tool in the sense in which the patient's reclining position, the use of free associations, the employment of the structural model, or of the concepts of drive and defense are tools. Empathy does indeed in essence define *the field* of our observations. Empathy is not just a useful way by which we have access to the inner life of man — the idea itself of an inner life of man, and thus of a psychology of complex mental states, is unthinkable without our ability to know via vicarious introspection — my definition of empathy (cf. Kohut, 1959, pp. 459-465) — what the inner life of man is, what we ourselves and what others think and feel.[14]

By defining psychoanalysis as being, in essence, a psychology of complex mental states which, with the aid of the persevering empathic-introspective immersion of the observer into the inner life of man, gather its data in order to explain them, we have gone as far as I believe we must go in loosening the shackles of an all too narrow definition of analysis that would prevent us — and the succeeding generations of analysts — from adapting our

---

[14] My view is in harmony with the following statements by Freud and Ferenczi. Despite the fact that they are no more than *obiter dicta,* they are of great significance and deserve careful attention.

"A path leads from identification by way of imitation to empathy, that is, to the comprehension of the mechanism by means of which we are enabled to take up *any attitude at all* towards another mental life" (Freud, 1921, p. 110, n.2, italics are mine).

"[Freud] discovered that it is just as possible to obtain new knowledge through the scientific ordering of the data of introspection as through the utilization of the data of external perception gathered with the aid of observation and experiment." And later: "Thanks to psychoanalysis we are now able to undertake a systematic approach to a new group of data — a group of data that has been disregarded by the natural sciences. Psychoanalysis demonstrates the activity of inner forces that can only be perceived through introspection" (Ferenczi, 1927, my translation).

theories and explanations in accordance with the new data which we will continue to collect.

On the basis of my broad, yet, I believe, clearly delimiting definition, I am now also able to solve a problem that has puzzled me for a long time. I had in the past often wondered why it was possible for me to consider as analysts members of certain groups with whose theoretical tenets I strongly disagreed, while I could not accept the members of certain other groups as analysts despite the fact that, on the whole, I myself subscribed to many of their theoretical views. I never questioned, for example, that the followers of Melanie Klein were analysts, although, in my opinion, they were basing themselves on erroneous premises in their theoretical formulations and although I disagreed with certain aspects of their psychoanalytic practice which were the outgrowth of their theoretical errors. On the other hand, I could not, for example, accept as analysts the followers of Franz Alexander's suggestion (Alexander et al., 1946) that traditional long analyses were resistance phenomena (i.e., that they dealt with evasive maneuvers from the side of the patient or, at any rate, with the patient's nonproductive regression) and that they should be replaced by brief, actively steered forms of treatment—I could not accept them as analysts even though they continued to adhere strictly to the basic formulations of classical analysis, i.e., they continued to uphold the primacy of the Oedipus complex and ordered their data in accordance with the structural model of the mind.

It has now become clear to me that these (formerly not clearly thought out) differentiations did not rest on the criterion that a scientific or therapeutic undertaking is defined as analytic if it is established that the observer

has espoused a certain philosophy (such as the psychobiological standpoint) or that he bases himself on certain
ordering principles (such as the genetic, dynamic,
economic, or structural points of view) or holds certain
theories (such as the theories of transference and resistance, as Freud had specified), but that they rested on the
criterion that such an undertaking is defined as analytic if
it involves persevering immersion into a set of psychological data, with the instrument of empathy and introspection, for the purpose of the scientific explanation of
the observed field. While, for example, I have not the
slightest doubt that crucially important activities of the
analysand exist (and that they can be observed in the
analytic situation) that are explainable as amalgamations
of repressed desires from childhood with wishes directed
toward the analyst; and, similarly, that crucially important activities of the analysand exist that are explainable as impulse-inhibiting endopsychic forces turned
against the analyst when his interpretations begin to
threaten the neurotic equilibrium of forces; and while,
furthermore, I am not able to imagine how analysis
could at this time do away with the two concepts—
transference and resistance—that are the experience-
distant distillate of these two activities, I would still insist
that some future generation of psychoanalysts might discover psychological areas that require a novel conceptual
approach—areas where even in the therapeutic realm
these two now universally applicable concepts have become irrelevant. Modern physics—Einstein's, and in
particular, Planck's and Bohr's—is still physics, even
though these investigators focused on heretofore unexplored aspects of physical reality and had to construct
formulations that differ from those of the classical physics

of Newton. Should the attitude of psychoanalysts toward their science be different from that of the physicists toward theirs?

With the preceding reflections about the definition of depth psychology—a definition that considers psychoanalysis as basic a science as physics or mathematics or biology—I have, starting from a new direction, returned to the very conclusion that I presented in 1959. Although my views concerning many areas of psychoanalytic theory and practice have changed since I first formulated my thoughts on the basic significance of our empathic-introspective observational stance, my opinion concerning this fundamental question has not.

True enough, the acceptance of my views concerning the essence of psychoanalysis does not in itself lend support to the claim that this or that specific new explanatory hypothesis is correct, that it constitutes a relevant expansion of psychoanalytic theory, or that it contributes an effective new leverage to psychoanalytic practice—even if the new hypothesis is derived from empirical data obtained by the investigator via prolonged empathic immersion into the inner life of his analysands. But their acceptance would do away with the *ex cathedra* rejection of findings and thoughts that are at variance with established doctrine—making it possible for psychoanalysts to set aside habitual modes of ordering the empathically perceived data, and, while temporarily but for sufficiently long stretches of time adopting the attitude that Coleridge (1817) referred to as the "willing suspension of disbelief," give themselves over to the task of recognizing the newly described configurations and processes. And the broad definition of psychoanalysis will ultimately permit, if the genuineness of new findings and the relevance of new formulations have been established, the inclusion of the new data and of the new theories, and their subsequent gradual modification through the on-going work of the analytic profession.

Having in the foregoing expressed my conviction that neither loyalty to established modes of thought nor fear of defining too broadly the subject matter with which analysis deals must prevent the psychoanalyst from testing new concepts, theories, and techniques that are presented by investigators who feel that new data, or the newly discovered meaning of known data, demand their adoption, I have gone as far as I should in my plea for an open-minded attitude toward the psychology of the self. Only one more statement on behalf of this step in psychoanalysis that I support: Even if the open-minded psychoanalyst should give an adequate hearing to the psychology of the self; even if he should concede that its tenets are relevant and that they explain certain phenomena inside and outside the clinical situation that the classical outlook could not explain—will he not still object to it because of the incompleteness and lack of finished elegance of some of its theories and because of the haziness of some of its concepts?

Let me in this context refer in particular to a feature of the present work that might appear to some as a serious defect. My investigation contains hundreds of pages dealing with the psychology of the self—yet it never assigns an inflexible meaning to the term self, it never explains how the essence of the self should be defined. But I admit this fact without contrition or shame. The self, whether conceived within the framework of the psychology of the self in the narrow sense of the term, as a specific structure in the mental apparatus, or, within the framework of the psychology of the self in the broad sense of the term, as the center of the individual's psychological universe, is, like all reality — physical reality (the data about the world perceived by our senses) or psychological reality (the data about the world perceived via introspection and empathy) — not knowable in its essence. We cannot, by introspection and empathy, penetrate to the self per se; only its introspectively or empathically perceived psychological manifestations are open to us. Demands for an exact definition of the nature of the self disregard the fact that "the self" is not a concept of an abstract science, but a generalization derived from empirical data. Demands for a differentiation of "self" and "self representation" (or, similarly, of "self" and a "sense of self") are, therefore, based on a misunderstanding. We can collect data concerning the way in which the set of introspectively or empathically perceived inner experiences to which we later refer as "I" is gradually established, and we can observe certain characteristic vicissitudes of this experience. We can describe the various cohesive forms in which the self appears, can demonstrate the several constituents that make up the self — its two poles (ambitions and ideals) and the area of talents and skills that is interposed between the two poles — and explain their genesis and functions. And we can, finally, distinguish between various self types and can explain their distinguishing features on the basis of the predominance of one or the other of their constituents. We can do all that, but we will still not know the essence of the self as differentiated from its manifestations.

These statements strike me as a fitting end to my efforts on behalf of the new psychology of the self because they express my belief that the true scientist — the playful scientist as I put it before—is able to tolerate the short-comings of his achievements—the tentativeness of his formulations, the incompleteness of his concepts. Indeed, he treasures them as the spur for further joyful exertions. I believe that the deepest meaning of science is revealed when it is seen as an aspect of transient yet continuing life. The sense of continuity despite change—even despite deeply significant change—supports the scientist in his ever-repeated return from theory to observation, in his ever-repeated attempt to devise new, more deeply or more comprehensively explanatory models, to construct new, more deeply or more comprehensively explanatory theories. A worshipful attitude toward established explanatory systems—toward the polished accuracy of their definitions and the flawless consistency of their theories—becomes confining in the history of science—as do, indeed, man's analogous commitments in all of human history. Ideals are guides, not gods. If they become gods, they stifle man's playful creativeness; they impede the activities of the sector of the human spirit that points most meaningfully into the future.

I hope, of course, that many results of the investigation of the psychology of the self presented here will prove to be valid. My deepest wish, however, is that my work—in amplification or emendation, in acceptance and even in rejection—will contribute to motivate the rising generation of psychoanalysts to pursue the path opened by the pioneers of yesterday, a path that will lead us further into the immense territory of that aspect of reality that can be investigated through scientifically disciplined introspection and empathy.

Bibliography

Aarons, Z. A. (1965), On Analytic Goals and Criteria for Termination. *Bull. Phila. Assn. Psychoanal.*, 15:97-109.

Abend, S. M. (1974), Problems of Identity: Theoretical and Clinical Applications. *Psychoanal. Quart.*, 43:606-637.

Abraham, H. C. & Freud, E. L. (1965), *A Psycho-Analytic Dialogue (The Letters of Sigmund Freud and Karl Abraham)*. New York: Basic Books.

Abraham, K. (1921), Contributions to the Theory of the Anal Character. In: *Selected Papers of Karl Abraham*. New York: Basic Books, 1953, pp. 370-392.

Aichhorn, A. (1936), The Narcissistic Transference of the "Juvenile Impostor." In: *Delinquency and Child Guidance: Selected Papers by August Aichhorn*, ed. O. Fleischmann, P. Kramer, & H. Ross. New York: International Universities Press, 1964, pp. 174-191.

Alexander, F. (1935), The Logic of Emotions and its Dynamic Background. *Internat. J. Psycho-Anal.*, 16:399-413.

——————— (1956), Two Forms of Regression and their Therapeutic Implications. *Psychoanal. Quart.*, 25:178-196.

———————, French, T. M., et al. (1946), *Psychoanalytic Therapy: Principles and Applications*. New York: Ronald Press.

Altman, L. L. (1975), A Case of Narcissistic Personality Disorder: The Problem of Treatment. *Internat. J. Psycho-Anal.*, 56:187-195.

Apfelbaum, B. (1972), Psychoanalysis without Guilt. *Contemporary Psychol.*, 17:600-602.

Argelander, H. (1972), *Der Flieger*. Frankfurt: Suhrkamp.

313

Arlow, J. A. (1966), Depersonalization and Derealization. In: *Psychoanalysis—A General Psychology*, ed. R. M. Loewenstein, L. M. Newman M. Schur, & A. J. Solnit. New York: International Universities Press, pp. 456-478.

Bach, S. (1975), Narcissism, Continuity and the Uncanny. *Internat. J. Psycho-Anal.*, 56:77-86.

──────── & Schwartz, L. (1972), A Dream of the Marquis de Sade: Psychoanalytic Reflections on Narcissistic Trauma, Decompensation, and the Reconstitution of a Delusional Self. *J. Amer. Psychoanal. Assn.*, 20:451-475.

Balint, M. (1950), On the Termination of Analysis. *Internat. J. Psycho-Anal.*, 31:196-199. (Also in: *Primary Love and Psychoanalytic Technique*. London: Hogarth Press, 1952, pp. 236-243.)

──────── (1968), *The Basic Fault: Therapeutic Aspects of Regression*. London: Tavistock Publications.

Barande, R., Barande, I. & Dalibard, Y. (1965), Remarques sur le narcissisme dans le mouvement de la cure. *Rev. Franç. Psychoanal.*, 29: 601-611.

Basch, M. F. (1973), Psychoanalysis and Theory Formation. *The Annual of Psychoanalysis*, 1:39-52. New York: Quadrangle.

──────── (1974), Interference with Perceptual Transformation in the Service of Defense. *The Annual of Psychoanalysis*, 2:87-97. New York: International Universities Press.

──────── (1975), Toward a Theory that Encompasses Depression: A Revision of Existing Causal Hypotheses in Psychoanalysis. In: *Depression and Human Existence*, ed. E. J. Anthony & T. Benedek. Boston: Little Brown, pp. 485-534.

Beigler, J. (1975), A Commentary on Freud's Treatment of the Rat Man. *The Annual of Psychoanalysis*, 3:271-285. New York: International Universities Press.

Benedek, T. (1938), Adaptation to Reality in Early Infancy. *Psychoanal. Quart.*, 7:200-214.

Beres, D. (1956), Ego Deviation and the Concept of Schizophrenia. *The Psychoanalytic Study of the Child*, 11:164-235. New York: International Universities Press.

Bing, J., McLaughlin, F., & Marburg, R. (1959), The Metapsychology of Narcissism. *The Psychoanalytic Study of the Child*, 14:9-28. New York: International Universities Press.

Binswanger, L. (1957), *Sigmund Freud. Reminiscence of a Friendship*. New York/London: Grune & Stratton.

Bleuler, E. (1911), *Dementia Praecox or the Group of Schizophrenias*. New York: International Universities Press, 1950.

Blum, H. P. (1974), The Borderline Childhood of the Wolf Man. *J. Amer. Psychoanal. Assn.*, 22:721-742.

Boyer, B. & Giovacchini, P. (1967), *Psychoanalytic Treatment of Characterological and Schizophrenic Disorders.* New York: Science House.

Braunschweig, D. R. (1965), Le narcissisme: aspects cliniques. *Rev. Franç. Psychoanal.*, 29:589-600.

Brenner, C. (1968), Archaic Features of Ego Functioning. *Internat. J. Psycho-Anal.*, 49:426-429.

Breuer, J. & Freud, S. (1893-1895), Studies on Hysteria. *Standard Edition*, 2:255-305. London: Hogarth Press, 1955.

Bridger, H. (1950), Criteria for Termination of an Analysis. *Internat. J. Psycho-Anal.*, 31:202-203.

Bronfenbrenner, U. (1970), *Two Worlds of Childhood: U.S. and U.S.S.R.* New York: Russell Sage Foundation.

Buxbaum, E. (1950), Technique of Terminating Analysis. *Internat. J. Psycho-Anal.*, 31:184-190.

Chasseguet-Smirgel, J. (1974), Perversion, Idealization and Sublimation. *Internat. J. Psycho-Anal.*, 55:349-357.

Coleridge, S. T. (1817), *Biographia Literaria,* Chap. 14. London: Oxford University Press, 1907.

Cooper, A. et al. (1968), The Fate of Transference Upon Termination of the Analysis. *Bull. Assn. Psychoanal. Med.*, 8:22-28.

Dewald, P. (1964), *Psychotherapy: A Dynamic Approach.* New York: Basic Books.

———— (1965), Reactions to the Forced Termination of Therapy. *Psychiat. Quart.*, 39:102-126.

Edelheit, H. (1976), Complementarity as a Rule in Psychological Research. *Internat. J. Psycho-Anal.*, 57:23-29.

Eidelberg, L. (1959), The Concept of Narcissistic Mortification. *Internat. J. Psycho-Anal.*, 40:163-168.

Eisnitz, A. J. (1969), Narcissistic Object Choice, Self Representation. *Internat. J. Psycho-Anal.*, 50:15-25.

———— (1974), On the Metapsychology of Narcissistic Pathology. *J. Amer. Psychoanal. Assn.*, 22:279-291.

Eissler, K. R. (1974), Über Freuds Freundschaft mit Wilhelm Fliess nebst einem Anhang über Freuds Adoleszenz und einer historischen Bemerkung über Freuds Jugendstil. *Jahrbuch der Psychoanalyse*, 7:39-100.

———— (1975), A Critical Assessment of the Future of Psychoanalysis: A View from Within. Panel reported by I. Miller. *J. Amer. Psychoanal. Assn.*, 23:151.

Eissler, R. S. (1949), Scapegoats of Society. In: *Searchlights on Delinquency,* ed. K. R. Eissler. New York: International Universities Press.

Ekstein, R. (1965), Working Through and Termination of Analysis. *J. Amer. Psychoanal. Assn.*, 13:57-78.

Engelmann, E. (1966), Freudian Memorabilia. Freud's Office as His Patients Saw It. *Roche Medical Image*, 8/3:28-30.

Erikson, E. H. (1950), *Childhood and Society.* New York: Norton.

—————— (1956), The Problem of Ego Identity. In: *Identity: Youth and Crisis.* New York: Norton, 1968, pp. 142-207; 208-231.

Federn, P. (1947), Principles of Psychotherapy in Latent Schizophrenia. In: *Ego Psychology and the Psychoses,* ed. E. Weiss. New York: Basic Books, 1952, pp. 166-183.

Fenichel, O. (1953), From the Terminal Phase of an Analysis. In: *Collected Papers, First Series.* New York: Norton, 1953, pp. 27-31.

Ferenczi, S. (1927), Die Anpassung der Familie an das Kind [The Adaptation of the Family to the Child]. *Zeitschrift f. psychoanalytische Pädagogik,* 2:239-251. (Also in: *Final Contributions.* New York: Basic Books, 1955, pp. 61-76.)

—————— (1928), The Problem of the Termination of the Analysis. In: *Final Contributions.* New York: Basic Books, 1955, pp. 77-86.

—————— (1930), Autoplastic and Alloplastic Adaptation. In: *Final Contributions.* New York: Basic Books, 1955, p. 221.

Firestein, S. K. (1974), Termination of Psychoanalysis of Adults: A Review `of the Literature. *J. Amer. Psychoanal. Assn.*, 22:873-894.

—————— , reporter (1969), Panel on: Problems of Termination in the Analysis of Adults. *J. Amer. Psychoanal. Assn.*, 17:222-237.

Fleming, J. & Benedek, T. (1966), *Psychoanalytic Supervision.* New York: Grune & Stratton.

Forman, M. (1976), Narcissistic Personality Disorders and the Oedipal Fixations. *The Annual of Psychoanalysis,* 4:65-92. New York: International Universities Press.

Freeman, T. (1963), The Concept of Narcissism in Schizophrenia States. *Internat. J. Psycho-Anal.*, 44:293-303.

Freud, A. (1936), *The Ego and the Mechanisms of Defense. The Writings of Anna Freud,* 2. New York: International Universities Press, 1966.

—————— (1965), *Normality and Pathology in Childhood. The Writings of Anna Freud,* 6. New York: International Universities Press.

Freud, E. L., ed. (1960), *Letters of Sigmund Freud.* New York: Basic Books.

—————— & Meng, H., ed. (1963), *Psychoanalysis and Faith. The Letters of Sigmund Freud and Oskar Pfister.* New York: Basic Books.

Freud, S. (1900), The Interpretation of Dreams. *Standard Edition,* 4 & 5. London: Hogarth Press, 1953.

—————— (1908), Character and Anal Erotism. *Standard Edition,* 9:167-175. London: Hogarth Press, 1959.

_____ (1909), Notes Upon a Case of Obsessional Neurosis. *Standard Edition*, 10:151-249. London: Hogarth Press, 1955.

_____ (1911), Psycho-Analytic Notes on an Autobiographical Account of a Case of Paranoia (Dementia Paranoides). *Standard Edition*, 12: 9-82. London: Hogarth Press, 1958.

_____ (1912), Recommendations to Physicians Practising Psycho-Analysis. *Standard Edition*, 12:109-120. London: Hogarth Press, 1958.

_____ (1913a), On Beginning the Treatment. *Standard Edition*, 12:123-144. London: Hogarth Press, 1958.

_____ (1913b), The Disposition to Obsessional Neurosis. *Standard Edition*, 12:311-326. London: Hogarth Press, 1958.

_____ (1914a), On the History of the Psycho-Analytic Movement. *Standard Edition*, 14:7-66. London: Hogarth Press, 1957.

_____ (1914b), The Moses of Michelangelo. *Standard Edition*, 13:211-238. London: Hogarth Press, 1955.

_____ (1914c), On Narcissism: An Introduction. *Standard Edition*, 14: 67-102. London: Hogarth Press, 1957.

_____ (1914d), Remembering, Repeating and Working Through. *Standard Edition*, 12:145-156.

_____ (1915), The Unconscious. *Standard Edition*, 14:159-215. London: Hogarth Press, 1957.

_____ (1917a), A Difficulty in the Path of Psycho-Analysis. *Standard Edition*, 17:135-144. London: Hogarth Press, 1955.

_____ (1917b), Introductory Lectures on Psycho-Analysis. Part III. General Theory of the Neuroses. *Standard Edition*, 16. London: Hogarth Press, 1963.

_____ (1918), From the History of an Infantile Neurosis. *Standard Edition*, 17:1-122. London: Hogarth Press, 1955.

_____ (1920), Beyond the Pleasure Principle. *Standard Edition*, 18:3-64. London: Hogarth Press, 1955.

_____ (1921), Group Psychology and the Analysis of the Ego. *Standard Edition*, 18:65-144. London: Hogarth Press, 1955.

_____ (1922), Some Neurotic Mechanisms in Jealousy, Paranoia, and Homosexuality. *Standard Edition*, 18:221-232. London: Hogarth Press, 1955.

_____ (1923a), The Ego and the Id. *Standard Edition*, 19:3-66. London: Hogarth Press, 1961.

_____ (1923b), Two Encyclopaedia Articles. *Standard Edition*, 18:233-259. London: Hogarth Press, 1955.

_____ (1925), Negation. *Standard Edition*, 19:235-239. London: Hogarth Press, 1961.

_____ (1926), Inhibitions, Symptoms and Anxiety. *Standard Edition,* 20:75-174. London: Hogarth Press, 1959.

_____ (1927a), Fetishism. *Standard Edition,* 21:147-157. London: Hogarth Press, 1961.

_____ (1927b), The Future of an Illusion. *Standard Edition,* 21:1-56. London: Hogarth Press, 1961.

_____ (1933), New Introductory Lectures on Psycho-Analysis. *Standard Edition,* 22:1-182. London: Hogarth Press, 1964.

_____ (1937), Analysis Terminable and Interminable. *Standard Edition,* 23:209-253. London: Hogarth Press, 1964.

_____ (1940), The Splitting of the Ego in the Process of Defence. *Standard Edition,* 23:271-278. London: Hogarth Press, 1964.

Frosch, J. (1970), Psychoanalytic Considerations of the Psychotic Character. *J. Amer. Psychoanal. Assn.,* 18:24-50.

Gedo, J. E. (1972), On the Psychology of Genius. *Internat. J. Psycho-Anal.,* 53:199-203.

_____ (1975), Forms of Idealization in the Analytic Transference. *J. Amer. Psychoanal. Assn.,* 23:485-505.

_____ & Goldberg, A. (1973), *Models of the Mind: A Psychoanalytic Theory.* Chicago: University of Chicago Press.

Gelb, A. & Gelb, B. (1962), *O'Neill.* New York: Harper & Row.

Gill, M. M. (1963), *Topography and Systems in Psychoanalytic Theory* [*Psychological Issues,* Monograph 10]. New York: International Universities Press.

Giovacchini, P. (1975), *Psychoanalysis of Character Disorders.* New York: Jason Aronson.

Gitelson, M. (1952), Re-evaluation of the Role of the Oedipus Complex. In: *Psychoanalysis: Science and Profession.* New York: International Universities Press, 1973, pp. 201-210.

Glover, E. (1931), The Therapeutic Effect of Inexact Interpretation; A Contribution to the Theory of Suggestion. *Internat. J. Psycho-Anal.,* 12:397-411.

_____ (1956), The Terminal Phase. In: *The Technique of Psychoanalysis.* New York: International Universities Press, pp. 150-164.

Goethe, J. W. von (1808-1832), *Faust.* Leipzig: Hesse & Becker, 1929.

Goldberg, A. (1974), On the Prognosis and Treatment of Narcissism. *J. Amer Psychoanal. Assn.,* 22:243-254.

_____ (1975a), The Evolution of Psychoanalytic Concepts Regarding Depression. In: *Depression and Human Existence,* ed. E. J. Anthony & T. Benedek. Boston: Little Brown, pp. 125-142.

_____ (1975b), A Fresh Look at Perverse Behavior. *Internat. J. Psycho-Anal.,* 56:335-342.

_____ (1975c), Narcissism and the Readiness for Psychotherapy Termination. *Arch. Gen. Psychiat.*, 32:695-704.

_____ (1976), A Discussion of the Paper by C. Hanly and J. Masson. *Internat. J. Psycho-Anal.*, 57:67-70.

Green, A. (1972), Aggression, Femininity, Paranoia and Reality. *Internat. J. Psycho-Anal.*, 53:205-211.

_____ (1976), Un, autre, neutre: valeurs narcissiques du Même. *Nouvelle Revue de Psychanalyse*, 13:37-79.

Greenacre, P. (1956), Re-evaluation of the Process of Working Through. In: *Emotional Growth.* New York: International Universities Press, pp. 641-650

Greenson, R. (1965), The Problem of Working Through. In: *Drives, Affects, and Behavior,* Vol. 2, ed. M. Schur. New York: International Universities Press, pp. 277-314.

_____ (1967), *The Technique and Practice of Psychoanalysis.* New York: International Universities Press.

Grinker, R. R. (1968), *The Borderline Syndrome: A Behavioral Study of Ego Functions.* New York: Basic Books.

Grunberger, B. (1971), *Le Narcissisme.* Paris: Payot.

Gunther, M. S. (1976), The Endangered Self—a Contribution to the Understanding of Narcissistic Determinants of Countertransference. *The Annual of Psychoanalysis,* 4:201-224. New York: International Universities Press.

Habermas, J. (1971), *Knowledge and Human Interest.* Boston: Beacon Press.

Hanly, C. & Masson, J. (1976), A Critical Examination of the New Narcissism. *Internat. J. Psycho-Anal.*, 57:49-66.

Hartmann, H. (1939), Psychoanalysis and the Concept of Health. In: *Essays on Ego Psychology.* New York: International Universities Press, 1964, pp. 3-18.

_____ (1950), Comments on the Psychoanalytic Theory of the Ego. In: *Essays on Ego Psychology.* New York: International Universities Press, 1964, pp. 113-141.

_____ (1960), *Psychoanalysis and Moral Values.* New York: International Universities Press.

_____ & Kris, E. (1945), The Genetic Approach in Psychoanalysis. *The Psychoanalytic Study of the Child,* 1:11-30. New York: International Universities Press.

Heinz, R. (1976), J. P. Sartre's existentielle Psychoanalyse. *Archiv für Rechtsund Sozialphilosophie,* 62:61-88.

Henseler, H. (1975), Die Suizidhandlung unter dem Aspekt der psychoanalytischen Narzissmustheorie. *Psyche,* 29:191-207.

Hitschmann, E. (1932), Psychoanalytic Comments About the Personality of Goethe. In: *Great Men—Psychoanalytic Studies*. New York: International Universities Press, 1956, pp. 126-151.

Holzman, P. S. (1976), The Future of Psychoanalysis and Its Institutes. *Psychoanal. Quart.*, 45:250-273.

Hurn, H. (1971), Toward a Paradigm for the Terminal Phase: Current Status of the Terminal Phase. *J. Amer. Psychoanal. Assn.*, 19:332-348.

Jacobson, E. (1964), *The Self and the Object World*. New York: International Universities Press.

James, M. (1973), Review of *The Analysis of the Self* by Heinz Kohut. *Internat. J. Psycho-Anal.*, 54:363-368.

Jones, E. (1936), The Criteria of Success in Treatment. In: *Papers on Psycho-Analysis*. Boston: Beacon Press, 1961, pp. 379-383.

————— (1955), *The Life and Work of Sigmund Freud*, Vol. II. New York: Basic Books.

————— (1957), *The Life and Work of Sigmund Freud*, Vol. III. New York: Basic Books.

Kavka, J. (1975), Oscar Wilde's Narcissism. *The Annual of Psychoanalysis*, 3:397-408. New York: International Universities Press.

Kepecs, J. (1975), The Re-integration of a Disavowed Portion of Psychoanalysis (unpublished manuscript).

Kernberg, O. F. (1974a), Contrasting Viewpoints Regarding the Nature and Psychoanalytic Treatment of Narcissistic Personalities: A Preliminary Communication. *J. Amer. Psychoanal. Assn.*, 22:255-267.

————— (1974b), Further Contributions to the Treatment of Narcissistic Personalities. *Internat. J. Psycho-Anal.*, 55:215-240.

————— (1975), *Borderline Conditions and Pathological Narcissism*. New York: Jason Aronson.

Kestemberg, E. (1964), Problems Regarding the Termination of Analysis in Character Neurosis. *Internat. J. Psycho-Anal.*, 45:350-357.

Khan, M. M. R. (1974), *The Privacy of the Self*. New York: International Universities Press.

Klein, G. (1970), *Perception, Motives, and Personality*. New York: Knopf.

Klein, M. (1950), On the Criteria for the Termination of an Analysis. *Internat. J. Psycho-Anal.*, 31:8-80.

Kleist, H. von (1808), *Michael Kohlhaas*. New York: Oxford University Press, 1967.

————— (1811), On the Marionette Theatre, transl. T. G. Neumiller. *Drama Rev.*, 16:22-226, 1972.

Kligerman, C. (1975), Notes on Benvenuto Cellini. *The Annual of Psychoanalysis*, 3:409-421. New York: International Universities Press.

Kohut, H. (1957), Observations on the Psychological Functions of Music. *J. Amer. Psychoanal. Assn.*, 5:389-407. Also in: Kohut (in press).

———— (1959), Introspection, Empathy, and Psychoanalysis. *J. Amer. Psychoanal. Assn.*, 7:459-483. Also in: Kohut (in press).

———— (1960), Beyond the Bounds of the Basic Rule. *J. Amer. Psychoanal. Assn.*, 8:567-586. Also in: Kohut (in press).

———— (1961), Discussion of D. Beres's paper: "The Unconscious Fantasy." Presented at Meeting, Chicago Psychoanalytic Society. Abstr. in: *Phila. Bull. Psychoanal.*, 11:194-195, 1961. Also in: Kohut (in press).

———— (1966), Forms and Transformations of Narcissism. *J. Amer. Psychoanal. Assn.*, 14:243-272. Also in: Kohut (in press).

———— (1971), *The Analysis of the Self.* New York: International Universities Press.

———— (1972), Thoughts on Narcissism and Narcissistic Rage. *The Psychoanalytic Study of the Child*, 27:360-400. New York: Quadrangle. Also in: Kohut (in press).

———— (1975a), The Future of Psychoanalysis. *The Annual of Psychoanalysis*, 3:325-340. New York: International Universities Press. Also in: Kohut (in press).

———— (1975b), Remarks About the Formation of the Self. Presented at Meeting, Chicago Institute for Psychoanalysis. Also in: Kohut (in press).

———— (1976), Creativeness, Charisma, Group-Psychology. Reflections on Freud's Self Analysis. In: *Freud: Fusion of Science and Humanism*, ed. J. Gedo & G. H. Pollock [*Psychological Issues*, Monograph 34/35]. New York: International Universities Press, pp. 379-425. Also in: Kohut (in press).

———— (in press), *Scientific Empathy and Empathic Science: Selected Essays*, ed. P. Ornstein. New York: International Universities Press.

———— & Levarie, S. (1950), On the Enjoyment of Listening to Music. *Psychoanal. Quart.*, 19:64-87. Also in: Kohut (in press).

———— & Seitz, P. F. D. (1963), Concepts and Theories of Psychoanalysis. In: *Concepts of Personality*, ed. J. M. Wepman & R. Heine. Chicago: Aldine, pp. 113-141. Also in: Kohut (in press).

Koyré, A. (1968), *Metaphysics and Measurement: Essays in Scientific Resolution.* Cambridge: Harvard University Press.

Kramer, M. K. (1959), On the Continuation of the Analytic Process After Psychoanalysis. *Internat. J. Psycho-Anal.*, 40:17-25.

Kratz, B. (1976), Sigmund Freud und die Musik (unpublished).

Kris, E. (1956), On Some Vicissitudes of Insight in Psycho-Analysis. In:

Selected Papers. New Haven: Yale University Press, 1975, pp. 252-271.

Kuhn, T. S. (1962), *The Structure of Scientific Revolutions.* Chicago: University of Chicago Press.

Lacan, J. (1937), Le stade de miroir comme formateur de la fonction de Je. In: *Ecrits.* Editions du Seuil, Paris, 1966, pp. 93-100.

——— (1953), Some Reflections on the Ego. *Internat. J. Psycho-Anal.,* 34:11-17.

Laforgue, R. (1934), Resistance at the Conclusion of Psychoanalytic Treatment. *Internat. J. Psycho-Anal.,* 15:419-434.

Lampl-de Groot, J. (1965), *The Development of the Mind.* New York: International Universities Press.

——— (1975), Vicissitudes of Narcissism and Problems of Civilization. *The Psychoanalytic Study of the Child,* 30:663-681. New Haven: Yale University Press.

Langer, S. (1942), *Philosophy in a New Key.* Cambridge: Harvard University Press, third edition, 1957.

Lebovici, S. & Diatkine, R. (1973), Discussion on Aggression: Is it a Question of a Metapsychological Concept. *Internat. J. Psycho-Anal.,* 53: 231-236.

Leboyer, F. (1975), *Birth Without Violence.* New York: Knopf.

Levin, D. C. (1969), The Self: A Contribution to Its Place in Theory and Technique. *Internat. J. Psycho-Anal.,* 50:41-51.

Lichtenberg, J. (1975), The Development of the Sense of Self. *J. Amer. Psychoanal. Assn.,* 23:453-484.

Lichtenstein, H. (1961), Identity and Sexuality: A Study of Their Interrelationships in Man. *J. Amer. Psychoanal. Assn.,* 9:179-260.

——— (1964), The Role of Narcissism in the Emergence and Maintenance of a Primary Identity. *Internat. J. Psycho-Anal.,* 45:49-56.

——— (1971), The Malignant No: A Hypothesis Concerning the Interdependence of the Sense of Self and the Instinctual Drives. In: *The Unconscious Today.* New York: International Universities Press, pp. 147-176.

Lipton, S. D. (1961), The Last Hour. *J. Amer. Psychoanal. Assn.,* 9:325-330.

Loewald, H. (1960), On the Therapeutic Action of Psycho-Analysis. *Internat. J. Psycho-Anal.,* 41:16-33.

——— (1962), Internalization, Separation, Mourning and the Superego. *Psychoanal. Quart.,* 31:483-504.

Macalpine, I. & Hunter, R. (1955), *Daniel Paul Schreber, Memoirs of My Nervous Illness.* Cambridge, Mass.: Robert Bentley.

McDougall, J. (1972), Primal Scene and Sexual Perversion. *Internat. J.*

Psycho-Anal., 53:371-384.

Mahler, M. (1965), On the Significance of the Normal Separation-Individuation Phase. In: *Drives, Affects, Behavior,* Vol. 2, ed. M. Schur. New York: International Universities Press, pp. 161-169.

_____ (1968), *On Human Symbiosis and the Vicissitudes of Individuation.* New York: International Universities Press.

_____, Pine, F. & Bergman, A. (1975), *The Psycholgoical Birth of the Human Infant.* New York: Basic Books.

Miller, I. (1965), On the Return of Symptoms in the Terminal Phase of Psychoanalysis. *Internat. J. Psycho-Anal.,* 46:487-501.

Miller, S. C. (1962), Ego-Autonomy in Sensory Deprivation. *Internat. J. Psycho-Anal.,* 43:1-20.

Mitscherlich, A. (1963), *Society Without the Father: A Contribution to Social Psychology.* New York: Harcourt, Brace & World, 1969.

Moberly, R. B. (1967), *Three Mozart Operas.* New York: Dodd, Mead & Company, 1968.

Modell, A. H. (1975), A Narcissistic Defence Against Affects and the Illusion of Self-Sufficiency. *Internat. J. Psycho-Anal.,* 56:275-282.

_____ (1976), "The Holding Environment" and the Therapeutic Action of Psychoanalysis. *J. Amer. Psychoanal. Assn.,* 24:285-307.

Moore, B. E. (1975), Toward a Clarification of the Concept of Narcissism. *The Psychoanalytic Study of the Child,* 30:243-276. New Haven: Yale University Press.

Morgenthaler, F. (1974), Die Stellung der Perversionen in Metapsychologie und Technik. *Psyche,* 28:1077-1098.

Moser, T. (1974), *Years of Apprenticeship on the Couch.* New York: Urizen Books, 1977.

M'Uzan, M. de (1970), Le même et l'identique. *Rev. Franç. Psychoanal.,* 34:441-451.

_____ (1973), A Case of Masochistic Perversion and an Outline of a Theory. *Internat. J. Psycho-Anal.,* 54:455-467.

Nunberg, H. (1931), The Synthetic Function of the Ego. In: *Practice and Theory of Psychoanalysis.* New York: Nervous and Mental Disease Publishing Co., 1948, pp. 120-136.

Oremland, J. D. (1973), A Specific Dream During the Terminal Phase of Successful Psychoanalysis. *J. Amer. Psychoanal. Assn.,* 21:285-302.

Ornstein, A. (1974), The Dread to Repeat and the New Beginning: A Contribution to the Psychoanalysis of the Narcissistic Personality Disorders. *The Annual of Psychoanalysis,* 2:231-248. New York: International Universities Press.

_____ & Ornstein, P. H. (1975), On the Interpretive Process in Psychoanalysis. *Internat. J. Psychoanal. Psychotherapy,* 4:219-271.

Ornstein, P. H. (1974a), A Discussion of Otto F. Kernberg's "Further Con tributions to the Treatment of Narcissistic Personalities." *Internat. J. Psycho-Anal.*, 55:241-247.

_____ (1974b), On Narcissism: Beyond the Introduction, Highlights of Heinz Kohut's Contributions to the Psychoanalytic Treatment of Narcissistic Personality Disorders. *The Annual of Psycho-Analysis*, 2:127-149. New York: International Universities Press.

_____ (1975), Vitality and Relevance of Psychoanalytic Psychotherapy. *Comprehensive Psychiat.*, 16:503-516.

Painter, G. (1959), *Proust. The Early Years*. Boston: Little, Brown.

_____ (1965), *Proust. The Later Years*. Boston: Little, Brown.

Palaci, J. (1975), Reflexions sur le transfert et la theorie du narcissisme de Heinz Kohut. In: *Rev. Franç. de Psychoanal.*, 39:279-294.

Pasche, F. (1965), L'antinarcissisme. In: *Rev. Franç. de Psychoanal.*, 29:503-518.

Pfeffer, A. Z. (1961), Follow-up Study of a Satisfactory Analysis. *J. Amer. Psychoanal. Assn.*, 9:698-718.

_____ (1963), The Meaning of the Analyst After Analysis. *J. Amer. Psychoanal. Assn.*, 11:229-244.

Pollock, G. H. (1964), On Symbiosis and Symbiotic Neurosis. *Internat. J. Psycho-Anal.*, 45:1-30.

_____ (1971), Glückel von Hameln: Bertha Pappenheim's Idealized Ancestor. *Amer. Imago*, 28:216-227.

_____ (1972), Bertha Pappenheim's Pathological Mourning: Possible Effects of Childhood Sibling Loss. *J. Amer. Psychoanal. Assn.*, 20:476-493.

Pontalis, J. B. (1975), Naissance et reconnaissance du self. In: *Psychologie de la connaissance de Soi*. Paris, Presses Universitaires de France, pp. 271-298.

Proust, M. (1913-1928), *Remembrance of Things Past*. New York: Random House, 1934.

Rangell, L., reporter (1955), Panel on: The Borderline Case. *J. Amer. Psychoanal. Assn.*, 3:285-298.

Rank, O. (1929), *The Trauma of Birth*. New York: Harcourt Brace.

Reich, A. (1950), On the Termination of Analysis. In: *Psychoanalytic Contributions*. New York: International Universities Press, 1973, pp. 121-135.

_____ (1960), Pathologic Forms of Self-Esteem Regulation. In: *Psychoanalytic Contributions*. New York: International Universities Press, 1973, pp. 288-311.

Robbins, W. S., reporter (1975), Panel on: Termination: Problems and Techniques. *J. Amer. Psychoanal. Assn.*, 23:166-176.

Rosenfeld, H. (1964), On the Psychopathology of Narcissism. *Internat. J. Psycho-Anal.*, 45:332-337.

Rosolato, G. (1976), Le narcissisme. *Nouvelle Revue de Psychoanalyse*, 13: 7-36.

Sandler, J., Holder, A., & Meers, D. (1963), The Ego Ideal and the Ideal Self. *The Psychoanalytic Study of the Child,* 18:139-158. New York: International Universities Press.

Schafer, R. (1968), *Aspects of Internalization.* New York: International Universities Press.

———— (1973a), Action: Its Place in Psychoanalytic Interpretation and Theory. *The Annual of Psychoanalysis,* 1:159-196. New York: Quadrangle.

———— (1973b), Concepts of Self and Identity and the Experience of Separation-Individuation in Adolescence. *Psychoanal. Quart.,* 42: 42-59.

Scharfenberg, J. (1973), Narzissmus, Identität und Religion. *Psyche,* 27: 949-966.

Scheidt, J. vom (1976), *Der falsche Weg zum Selbst.* Munich: Kindler.

Schlessinger, N., Gedo, J. E. et al. (1967), The Scientific Style of Breuer and Freud in the Origins of Psychoanalysis. *J. Amer. Psychoanal. Assn.,* 15:404-422.

———— & Robbins, F. (1974), Assessment and Follow-up in Psychoanalysis. *J. Amer. Psychoanal. Assn.,* 22:542-567.

Schur, M. (1966), *The Id and the Regulatory Principles of Mental Functioning.* New York: International Universities Press.

Schwartz, L. (1974), Narcissistic Personality Disorders—A Clinical Discussion. *J. Amer. Psychoanal. Assn.,* 22:292-306.

Spruiell, V. (1974), Theories of the Treatment of Narcissistic Personalities. *J. Amer. Psychoanal. Assn.,* 22:268-278.

———— (1975), Three Strands of Narcissism. *Psychoanal. Quart.,* 44: 577-595.

Stewart, W. (1963), An Inquiry into the Concept of Working Through. *J. Amer. Psychoanal. Assn.,* 11:474-999.

Stolorow, R. D. (1975), Addendum to a Partial Analysis of a Perversion Involving Bugs: An Illustration of the Narcissistic Function of Perverse Activity. *Internat. J. Psycho-Anal.,* 56:361-364.

———— (1976), Psychoanalytic Reflections on Client-Centered Therapy in the Light of Modern Conceptions of Narcissism. *Psychotherapy: Theory, Research and Practice,* 13:26-29.

——— ———— & Atwood, G. E. (1976), An Ego-Psychological Analysis of the Work and Life of Otto Rank in the Light of Modern Conceptions of Narcissism. *Internat. Rev. Psycho-Anal.,* 3:441-459.

_____ & Grand, H. T. (1973), A Partial Analysis of a Perversion Involving Bugs. *Internat. J. Psycho-Anal.*, 54:349-350.
Stone, L. (1961), *The Psychoanalytic Situation*. New York: International Universities Press.
Straus, E. W. (1952), The Upright Posture. *Psychiat. Quart.*, 26:529-561.
Terman, D. M. (1975), Aggression and Narcissistic Rage: A Clinical Elaboration. *The Annual of Psychoanalysis*, 3:239-255. New York: International Universities Press.
Thomä, H. & Kächele, H. (1973), Problems of Metascience and Methodology in Clinical Psychoanalytic Research. *The Annual of Psychoanalysis*, 3:49-118. New York: International Universities Press, 1975.
Ticho, G. (1967), On Self Analysis. *Internat. J. Psycho-Anal.*, 48:308-318.
Tolpin, M. (1970), The Infantile Neurosis: A Metapsychological Concept and a Paradigmatic Case History. *The Psychoanalytic Study of the Child*, 25:273-305. New Haven: Yale University Press.
_____ (1971), On the Beginnings of a Cohesive Self. *The Psychoanalytic Study of the Child*, 26:316-354. New Haven: Yale University Press.
_____ (1974), The Daedalus Experience: A Developmental Vicissitude of the Grandiose Fantasy. *The Annual of Psychoanalysis*, 2:213-228. New York: International Universities Press.
Tolpin, P. H. (1971), Some Psychic Determinants of Orgastic Dysfunction. *Adol. Psych.*, 1:388-413.
_____ (1974), On the Regulation of Anxiety: Its Relation to "The Timelessness of the Unconscious and its Capacity for Hallucination." *The Annual of Psychoanalysis*, 2:150-177. New York: International Universities Press.
Volkan, V. D. (1973), Transitional Fantasies in the Analysis of a Narcissistic Personality. *J. Amer. Psychoanal. Assn.*, 21:351-376.
Waelder, R. (1936), The Principle of Multiple Function: Observations on Overdetermination. In: *Psychoanalysis: Observation, Theory, and Application*. New York: International Universities Press, 1976, pp. 68-83.
Wangh, M. (1964), National Socialism and the Genocide of the Jews: A Psychoanalytic Study of a Historical Event. *Internat. J. Psycho-Anal.*, 45:386-395.
_____ (1974), Concluding Remarks on Technique and Prognosis in the Treatment of Narcissism. *J. Amer. Psychoanal. Assn.*, 22:307-309.
Weigert, E. (1952), Contribution to the Problem of Terminating Psychoanalysis. *Psychoanal. Quart.*, 21:465-480.
Whitman, R. M. & Kaplan, S. M. (1968), Clinical, Cultural and Literary Elaborations of the Negative Ego-Ideal. *Comprehensive Psychiat.*, 9:358-371.

Winnicott, D. W. (1953), Transitional Objects and Transitional Phenomena. *Internat. J. Psycho-Anal.,* 34:89-97.

———— (1960a), Ego Distortion in Terms of True and False Self. In: *The Maturational Processes and the Facilitating Environment.* New York: International Universities Press, 1965, pp. 140-152.

———— (1960b), The Theory of the Parent-Infant Relationship. In: *The Maturational Processes and the Facilitating Environment.* New York: International Universities Press, 1965, pp. 37-55.

———— (1963), From Dependence Towards Independence in the Development of the Individual. In: *The Maturational Processes and the Facilitating Environment.* New York: International Universities Press, 1965, pp. 83-92.

Wolf, E. S. (1971), Saxa Loquunter: Artistic Aspects of Freud's The Aetiology of Hysteria. *The Psychoanalytic Study of the Child,* 26:535-554. New Haven: Yale University Press.

———— (1976), Ambience and Abstinence. *The Annual of Psychoanalysis,* 4:101-115. New York: International Universities Press.

———— & Gedo, J. E. (1975), The Last Introspective Psychologist Before Freud: Michel de Montaigne. *The Annual of Psychoanalysis,* 3:297-310. New York: International Universities Press.

———— ————, & Terman, D. M. (1972), On the Adolescent Process as a Transformation of the Self. *J. Youth & Adol.,* 1:257-272.

———— & Trosman, H. (1974), Freud and Popper-Lynkeus. *J. Amer. Psychoanal. Assn.,* 22:123-141.

Wurmser, L. (1974), Psychoanalytic Considerations of the Etiology of Compulsive Drug Use. *J. Amer. Psychoanal. Assn.,* 22:820-843.

Wylie, A. W., Jr. (1974), Threads in the Fabric of a Narcissistic Disorder. *J. Amer. Psychoanal. Assn.,* 22:310-328.

Zeigarnick, B. (1927), Über das Behalten von erledigten und unerledigten Handlungen. *Psychol. Forsch.,* 9:1-85.

Concordance of Cases*

---

* The designation by letters of cases in this book conforms to the designation of cases in *The Analysis of the Self* and in other published articles of Heinz Kohut, as well as to the designation of cases in the forthcoming *The Psychology of the Self—A Clinical Casebook.*

Index

Sartre, J-P., xix
Schafer, R., xx, 85n.
Scheidt, J. v., 272
Schizoid personalities
  classified, 192
Schreber case, 190
Schur, M., 296
Science
  classical nineteenth century and
    metapsychology, 67
  deepest meaning of, 312
  definition of, 305
  evidence in psychoanalysis, 140-
    170
  playfulness of research, 311-312
  religion and, 207
Science of man
  in vitro psychoanalysis and natur-
    al habitat, 116n.
Secondary disturbance of self, 191
Seitz, P. F. D., 22, 31n., 251
Self
  beginning of independence, 171
  bipolar nature, 3, 49, 133, 171-
    219, 243
  as center of initiative, 94, 99, 134-
    135
  central position in personality,
    282-283
  cohesive, 76-77, 93-94, 102, 127-
    128, 134, 137, 195, 235
  constituents of, 177-178
  defensive structures of, 49-50
  defined, 99, 133, 310-312
  depleted, 243
  development of, *see* Development
    of self
  fragmented, 243
  function, defined, 63
  functional rehabilitation of, 3, 48-
    54
  genetic matrix of, 7, 8
  grandiose, *see* Grandiose self,
    Grandiosity
  intermediate area of, 49
  life curve of, 241

and Oedipus complex, 227
origins of, 93-111
primary defect, 3
rudimentary, *See* Rudimentary
  self
sectorial unit, 218-219
self-representation and, 311
sense of continuity and, 182-183
sense of initiative and, 245
sense of self and, 311
in statu nascendi, 100
subordinated content of, 97
as supraordinated configuration,
  97
tension gradient of, 180
transient and beyond, 182
types, 311
untreated part as stimulus, 176n.
virtual, defined, 101
see also Nuclear self
Self development, *see* Development
  of self
Self-expression, 224
Self-object, xiii
  analyst as, 32
  childhood relations reconstructed,
    275
  empathic failure, 89, 118, 125-
    126
  empathic response, optimal, 116
  empathic responses to child, 85
  failures, optimal, 87
  functional absence of, 155n.
  functions of, reconcretized, 16
  healthy admiration for, 172
  idealized, 10, 12, 23, 40, 42, 61,
    100, 125-126, 185, 211, 265
  identification with, 16
  mirroring, 50, 185-186, 235, 275
  need for, adult and child, 188n.
  needed in healthy maturity, 187n.
  parental failure and neuroso-
    genesis, 190, 195-196
  and rudimentary self, 99-100
  see also Parental attitudes
Self-object transference, xiii-xiv